Henry Pratt

New aspects of life and religion

Henry Pratt

New aspects of life and religion

ISBN/EAN: 9783743351899

Manufactured in Europe, USA, Canada, Australia, Japa

Cover: Foto ©Thomas Meinert / pixelio.de

Manufactured and distributed by brebook publishing software (www.brebook.com)

Henry Pratt

New aspects of life and religion

NEW ASPECTS

OF

LIFE AND RELIGION.

In preparation by the Author.

KABBALA,

PRIMITIVA, ADUMBRATA, OCCULTATA AC REGUSTATA:

THE PRIMITIVE, SPIRITUAL, OCCULT AND NATURAL KABBALAH.

NEW ASPECTS

OF

LIFE AND RELIGION.

BY

HENRY PRATT, M.D.

AUTHOR OF "ASTRONOMICAL INVESTIGATIONS."

"Man's uses of life should be such as neither to animalize, nor to spiritualize, but to humanize self."

WILLIAMS AND NORGATE,

14, HENRIETTA STREET, COVENT GARDEN, LONDON;

AND

20, SOUTH FREDERICK STREET, EDINBURGH.

1886.

LONDON:

PRINTED BY C. GREEN AND SON,

178, STRAND

TO ONE

WHO HAS STOOD BY ME IN GOOD REPORT AND IN EVIL REPORT,

WHO HAS ENCOURAGED ME UNDER VARYING FORTUNES
AND IN FAILING HEALTH,

WHOSE UNPARALLELED FORGETFULNESS OF SELF HAS BEEN
TO ME AN EXEMPLAR OF THE DIVINE IN THE HUMAN,

AND WHO IS MY ONLY EARTHLY CONSOLATION,

This Volume

IS AFFECTIONATELY AND GRATEFULLY INSCRIBED.

" If thou art base and earthly, then despair.
    Thou art but mortal as the brute that falls.
Birds weave their nests, the lion finds a lair,
        Man builds his halls,—

These are but coverts from earth's war and storm,
    Homes where our lesser lives take shape and breath;
But, if no heavenly man has grown, what form
        Clothes thee at death?

And when thy meed of penalty is o'er,
    And fire has burnt the dross, where gold is none,
Shall separate life, but wasted heretofore,
        Still linger on?

God fills all space; whatever doth offend
    From His unbounded Presence shall be spurned;
Or deem'st thou He should garner tares, whose end
        Is to be burned?

If thou wouldst see the Power that round thee sways,
    In whom all motion, thought, and life are cast,
Know, that the pure, who travel heavenward ways,
        See God at last."

(From *Echoes of the Night*, by the Rev. Francis Henry
Wood, M.A.)

" L'esprit des *miroirs divins*, ou la raison pour laquelle Dieu a produit des millions d'êtres-esprits où il se mire et apprend à se connaître. Car il ne se connaît que dans son produit : son centre est éternellement enveloppé dans son ineffable magisme."

(Saint-Martin, *l'Esprit des Choses.*)

" En fait de signes il s'agit moins de la formation des idées, mot peu juste, que du développement de ces idées. Car, si nous ne trouvions pas dans nos semblables des germes propres à recevoir la fécondation, une chose analogue à l'idée que nous voulons leur faire entendre, jamais nous ne pourrions en former en eux la moindre trace."

(Saint-Martin sur les *Signes de la Pensée.*)

CONTENTS.

PROLOGUE.

PROLOGUE.

THE BIBLE THEORY OF THE ORIGIN OF SPEECH.

THE earlier chapters of the Book of Genesis epitomize man's knowledge, when they were written, of the subjects of which they treat.

In doing this, they even state the divergent ways in which these subjects were viewed. But this is due to the labours of successive editors, who have blended the writings and teachings of opposing leaders of thought into a single whole, without acknowledgment of their respective sources ; just as in the Talmud, at a later period, the diverging interpretations of the rabbinical schools of Shammai and Hillel were brought together. And it is to this blending that such contradictions are due as are found on the juxtaposition of its first and second chapters.

Of these, the first contains the doctrine of those who held that man was the last of the created beings, and that he was only placed upon the

b

earth after it had been fully organized and animated—in which the earliest conception of evolution is indicated; while the second sets forth the view of their opponents, that man was the first created terrestrial being, and that his creation even preceded the production of vegetable as well as that of animal life.

Such a combination can only have been brought about after an imagined reconciliation of the opposing teachings, when the equally venerated Scriptures of either party were brought together, and their contradictory statements passed over or explained away.

Perhaps the most interesting of the accounts given in these earlier chapters—certainly the most interesting as regards some of the views set forth in the following pages—is that which suggests the theory then held of the origin of speech.

It is found in the second chapter.

Adam is supposed to be alone; alone in the garden of Eden; alone in a garden void of animal life, itself planted in a world otherwise void of vegetation.

His Creator, Jehovah, contemplating this solitude, says, "It is not good that Adam should be alone. I will make for him a helper—helpmate or companion—conformable to his showing."

Now Jehovah is said, in this narrative, to have formed man—*Adam*—out of the dust of the ground —*Adamah;* and the derivation of his name is thus assumed to have been drawn from the name of that from which he was himself derived ; though who named the ground, and Adam from the ground or the ground from Adam, is passed over in silence.

But was Adam named after the ground ? Was he so named because created therefrom ?

Hardly, according to the teaching of the first account of his creation ; for it is expressly stated there that God called the dry land *Erets*, and that he created Adam in his own image.

Whoever reads these statements in the original, and reflects upon the meanings of the Hebrew word-sign *Ad'm*, " I am like," " I am blood," will realize that this name was given to the first man because he was held to have been a living image or flesh-and-blood likeness of his Creator ; and that the difference between the teachings of these opposing schools was far-reaching in character. And since the first man was called *Adam* by those who termed the dry land *Erets;* and since these, so far from associating his name with *Adamah*, contrasted his creation, through this word, with that of the things creeping on the *Adamah*, in order to obviate such an association ; it is evident not only that theirs was the more ancient

teaching of the two, but that the word *Adam*
—purposely dissociated **by them from** the word
Adamah—was, subsequently, as purposely held to
have been derived therefrom by those seeking to
transmute the earlier doctrine on this subject and
mould it in accordance with their own views, for
which **they thus** sought a constructive foundation.
Indeed, such an association, without comparison of
the roots from which either sprang and of the relations in which each was first used, savours strongly
of a doctrinal growth.

Now to **those** who held that Jehovah had formed
man—*Adam*—out of the ground—*Adamah*—it was
evident that his proposed companion and helpmate,
to be conformed **to** his nature as well as to his
desire, must be, like him, formed out of the ground,
or of that which had been so formed. And so,
according to them, Jehovah formed the beast of the
field and the fowl of the air—each of the typical
animals which might enter into companionship
with man—out of the ground ; and, as he formed
them, caused them to pass before or brought them
under the notice of Adam, to see what he would
say of each ; and, through this showing, learn whether
either of these would satisfy his desires.

As yet, according **to this view,** Adam had not
spoken ; for he had no one to speak **to.** He was

companionless. Hence he had no speech. But he had the power of exclaiming, of giving voice to the impressions which the objects he observed produced on him. And each impression evoked its appropriate exclamation; to which he was prompted by a natural impulse urging him to give expression to his feelings.

These impressions were, so to say, copies or reflections of the objects viewed ; and the exclamations they called forth were what might well be termed reproductions in sound of these copies or reflections.

Under this aspect of his organism, man, as created, was potentially a speaking being ; but his powers of speech, like his intellectual, his reasoning and other faculties, were dormant—ready to be called into action, but waiting for the natural impulses to which they would respond. That is to say, man's nature was true—attuned to the truth set forth in the natural ; and, as of a truthful nature, in whatever way he reflected it, he gave a truthful reflection of the natural. In other words, man was, for the purposes of speech, likened to a spontaneously acting musical instrument—an instrument so acting responsively to every impression made thereon ; or was regarded as a being ready for vocalization, and as in such perfect tune that discord was impossible to him, which is more than can be said of his descendants.

Now the animals, as created, were brought **under** the observation of the solitary man, endowed with this truthfully responsive nature and potential faculty of speech, to see, from his awakening sympathies, whether the companionship of either of them would satisfy him ; which again **was** to be learnt by observing what he exclaimed at and of each, as it attracted his attention.

And as Adam observed each animal and gazed **at** it inquiringly, he—as **was** expected of him, and as **he** had already done in regarding the other natural objects of his surroundings—uttered an exclamation, an exclamation of wonder, of admiration, of delight ; an exclamation which was a vocal reflection of the image **it** had produced on his perceptive faculties, and was therefore what might be very properly called a vocal picture. And, owing **to** this truthfulness and truthful responsiveness of his nature, each time that he viewed the same object, the same animal, the same effect was produced on his mind, the same exclamation passed **from** his lips, and thus became its name.

But the exclamations thus called forth on this occasion **and in this** regard were simply exclamations of admiration. They were in no wise exclamations of appropriation, for they were void of sympathetic desire ; so that, according to this showing, Adam failed to find a suitable companionship in the animal kingdom.

Not so when the woman came under his notice. Until he saw his female counterpart, though he expressed his emotions by ejaculation at every object that attracted his attention, he remained speechless, having no one to converse with. But now, under the stimulus of a wholly new order of sensations, of emotions, his pent-up speech burst forth, as, looking lovingly and longingly at the woman, "'Bone of my bone and flesh of my flesh'— of this he exclaimed—'I take her'" (Gen. ii. 23). For this exclamation is prefaced by the statement, "And Adam spoke this time," to show that this was his first speech ; that the desire for companionship, for sympathy, for affection, had called it forth; and that this desire, with its vocal expression, could only be aroused and evoked by one of his own kind, by a kindred human being.

This theory of the natural origin of language must have been suggested to the mind of a keen observer, a deep thinker and a close and acute reasoner, who justly regarded speech as a reflection of nature and a portraiture of thought, and shows that the science which produced it was of no mean order.

It assumes that man's knowledge is derived from impressions which reach him through the avenues of sense, and lead him through perception, by comparison of experiences, to judgment and understanding. But it also assumes that the intellectual operation thus initiated is instantaneously and insensibly or spontaneously performed, as an instinctive and intuitive process of unconscious reasoning ; and leaves it to be inferred that its framers held this to be the source of the process from which the faculty of conscious reasoning is gradually evolved ; for it claims that the individual man, whether objectively or subjectively viewed, as wholly natural, is one and indivisible ; that he is a unity, in every sense of the word, for the purposes of his natural life—an embodied unity in which spirit and body are combined in one, and not merely a temporary vesture, habitat or instrument for an occupying spirit, whose prison-house the objective man has been by some held to be, the contaminator and degrader of the subjective self.

Under this theory, the root of thought, of speech, of reason — his consciousness — was regarded as innate in man. But it was so regarded as a faculty of his being, and not as an endowment ; nor even as the suggester of reminiscences of an experience and knowledge gathered up in a past existence, unless indeed of such reminiscences as a knife might be supposed to have of the stone on which it had been ground to a fine edge. And it was so regarded as the outcome of the uses of antecedent life, which had prepared for and produced in him an organism perfectly fitted for the purposes to which it was to be applied.

Hence it was claimed by its advocates that the subjects through the contemplation of which the operations of this potential faculty were to be called forth, were the natural objects of his surroundings. For the profound thinkers who had devised it did not look upon primitive man as a complex being endowed with a will, a memory, an understanding ; with an intellect and reason, imparted to him in some mysterious way by his Maker, and not acquired by use. On the contrary, they regarded him as an organically constituted unity, whose intelligence, derived like himself by natural process through nature, was intimately associated with his organiza-tion, that it might be naturally called into play, and grow with his organic growth, or be evolved and developed by the natural uses of a natural life. And they believed that he was constituted to this intent, and was, on coming into existence, a poten-tially intellectual being, who was to gather up knowledge by observation and experience, and thus gradually develop a power of reasoning from the known to the unknown, that he might in this way prepare and fit himself for the life **uses** of a future state.

They did not teach that Adam deliberately gave names to the animals, when these first came under **his** observation. They must have been too well informed to have made any such statement; for when they taught and wrote, the earth was already peopled by races speaking divers tongues, each of which had its own name for the several objects of nature; so that to have claimed that Adam had been endowed with a wisdom which enabled him suitably to name the animals in succession, would have been to have failed to perceive of that wisdom that it lacked the essential quality of realizing that such a nomination would be futile as to its assumed intent, since the names so given would, under the wear and tear of dialectic change, gradually melt away and disappear.

But they have been long held to have so taught, and this belief carries therewith its own lesson.

The primitive, the natural language of man, as they conceived it, must have been, in a measure, a pictorial tongue, such as music continues to be to some in the present day. That is to say, each nominating or denominative word must by its meaning or meanings, by its various significances, have suggested and depicted, or portrayed in a more or less definite way, the qualities and properties of that which it named.

Even in modern languages the same words have several meanings, as reference to any dictionary will show, some of which are by no means akin each to the others.

In the Semitic languages, and especially in the Hebrew dialects of the Jewish sacred Scriptures, this portraying quality is very marked, a slight variation in the vocalization or accentuation of any such word at once giving it a varied meaning and causing it to express a different sense, and thus to attribute another, an added quality or property, to that which it named.

Hence, in the written Hebrew of the Bible, each word can be variously vocalized and accentuated, and thus can be and is variously interpreted, according to the idea its varied vocalization and accentuation suggests, and the meaning it thus carries to the mind of the hearer ; and it is owing to this fluctuating character of the suggestiveness of the word-signs, according to their vocalization and accentuation, that they have come to be recognized as representing more words than one in their unpointed state ; and this fluctuating character, which is partly

due to and has been in great part the cause of dialectic change, has caused the sacred writings of the Hebrew and other branches of the **Semitic** family to be vocalized by vowel-points **and accents** affixed to the text, in order by these to limit each word-sign to the meaning **thus** attributed to and grafted on it in the passage in which it is found, which is only **too** often other than was in the mind of the writer.

Not that this arbitrary vocalization has checked the change it was intended to obviate ; for dialectic change has its root in the instability of the human organism, physically, physiologically and psychologically viewed, and is constantly operating in all spoken tongues, and re-acting through these on the written speech, whose significance is consequently apt to be transformed under its action. And the cumulative character of the outcome of this transforming influence, associated with the cumulative changes which take place in successive generations of human minds and schools of thought when spread over long periods of time, has produced and is producing surprising results.

That the effects of dialectic change were well known to the originators of the Biblical theory of the origin of language, is very plainly to be learnt from the parable of the attempt to build the tower of Babel, where the effort to reach heaven by a scientifically designed method and organization is made to fail through a dialectic confusion of tongues.

But this arbitrary vocalization is due to man's desire for certain knowledge and sure guidance on all that concerns himself in his relations to the finite and the infinite, the undue indulgence of which often leads him astray in his search for the un-attainable ; for absolute certainty has been with-held from him, in the results of his researches after knowledge, on all those subjects in which he is most deeply interested—just as an absolutely reliable way of transmitting the results of experimental science, when dissociated from the observations and demon-strations through which they have been acquired, is still wanting—perhaps because knowledge so transmitted is liable to be misunderstood.

The precise and exact way in which the mind of Adam, thus viewed, received and reflected impres-sions from without, is well illustrated by his first speech—" Bone of my bone, and flesh of my flesh, I take her."

Setting aside its fabulous character, it cannot be admitted that Adam said this with reference to the attributed process of the creation of Eve, as tradi-tionally understood, for it is expressly stated, as an intrinsic part of that process, that he was in a deep

sleep at the time.   **Hence, necessarily** having no
knowledge of what had happened in the interval—
as is meant to be understood—his language is a
figurative representation of the recognized likeness
of the woman to himself, and is therefore a precise
and formal example of the way in which his perceptions acted by producing impressions on, and
re-acted responsively through, his sense organs—
thus causing him to reproduce in speech a concise
but exact portraiture of what was passing **in his**
mind.

Neither can it be questioned that Adam, instead
of naming his just recognized wife, or calling her
Woman, simply said, in the word *Ish-shah*, with
which he concluded his speech, " I take her ;" for
the sentence immediately following this first re-
corded connected utterance of Adam—" For this
was taken of man "—which could not have been
spoken by one ignorant of her imputed origin, is
an explanatory note or commentary added by the
narrator of the parable or some subsequent scribe,
and therefore, by re-affirming, endorses and **deter-**
mines the meaning of what he then said in a direct
and most positive manner.

Moreover, the first man was not called *Ish*, " I
take "—not **even** by those who sought to impute
this designation generically to him—but *Adam*,

"I am like ;" and it is obvious that the word *Ish,* in its sense "man," was derived from *Ish-shah,* after that word had acquired the meaning "woman." Indeed, had Adam been endowed with the science attributed to him in the imputation that he gave formal names to the animals, and, in virtue of this science, named his thus welcomed wife on this occasion, he would undoubtedly have done so after himself ; for she was to him the female Adam, and is, conjointly with himself, called Adam in the preceding chapter of Genesis, as well as subsequently.

But Adam did not then name his wife, not even generically, for she was of course of the genus Adam ; and, since the older narrative says, "Male and female made he them"—to show that their origin was identical—constructively no more of kin to himself than is the bride to her just wedded husband, who is to become one flesh with him, and whose name she takes. Indeed, that Adam did not then name his wife is evident from the statement at the close of the parable of the fall of man, when, with *reference to what is, in this parable, held to have just happened,* he is said to have called his wife Eve—one who defaces or smudges, as well as gives, life—not merely because she was to be the mother of his offspring, that is, of the human race, of all living, but *because she was the stainer of life.*

The Hebrew word-sign *Chav-vah*, rendered " Eve," as thus depicting the imputed relations of the assumed mother of all to the human race, is a good example of the portraying character of originally denominative words naturally derived, when varyingly vocalized and accentuated. This characteristic is present, in a more or less marked degree, in the analogous or analogously derived words of all languages. Thus even in the English the word *woman* might be pronounced *woo-man, womb-man*, and *woe-man*, and thus be brought into association with the several ideas these vocalizations and accentuations respectively constructively express. Indeed, either of these has been at different times suggested as a possible source of the word as used.

Those who accepted and adopted the still received teaching of the fall of man believed in his God-like origin, but sought to harmonize it with their own views. Hence they taught that Adam was God-like in his solitary grandeur ; that he was created for non-sexual relations, and, as a uni-sexual being, was to become unsexed, in order more closely to resemble his heavenly Maker, and so more perfectly represent him upon earth. That he might do this without let or hindrance, he was not to have a companion of his own kind, but to find happiness in the surveillance and companionship of the lower orders of being, and in becoming to these a representative providence, who devoted himself to promoting their welfare and advance in the order of nature. And they looked upon his desire for further companionship as a tendency to a spiritual fall, which prepared the way for and finally entailed the moral fall which followed the condescension of his Creator in yielding to his impetuous longings.

The character of the fall of Adam, as they understood and wished it to be interpreted, is transparently veiled in the parable to which the preservation of their doctrine was committed. Its consequence was the production of the human race, which modified the primary scheme of creation and gained for its objective cause the designation Eve, the defacer and stainer of life—a designation whose significance in the course of time melted into and disappeared in its secondary sense, the mother of all living.

In reading the earlier chapters of the Book of Genesis, it is necessary to remember that in those days, and up to a period long subsequent to the lifetime of Jesus of Nazareth—witness the method of the Talmudic and rabbinical writers—teaching by parable was the usual and habitual way of imparting knowledge, as it is in the East to the present day; and that from the commencement of the traditional period, **all** knowledge, however acquired, was so handed down.

It is also necessary to remember **that, in the para-** bles of the Hebrew sacred Scriptures, the teacher, while veiling his doctrine from the vulgar **under** the diction and interpretation attributable thereto through the form given to its fabular vehicle, kept its doctrinal sense for those initiated in the vocalization and accentuation proper to the doctrinal readings of the recorded words. And the sole justification of preaching **from texts of** Scripture, and interpreting the **same, is the view that** a meaning purposely veiled by the writer is to **be** thus brought to light by his interpreter. But *these veiled meanings are only to be found, in the Old Testament, in the vowel-less word-signs of the original* **text.**

The parable **of** the twin children struggling in the womb of Rebekah, of which the younger by **fraud and cunning** supplants the elder—a fraud and cunning endorsed by the Roman Church **in** the representative character it gives to the gauntlets **worn by** its officiating bishops—points to the struggle between **two sets of teachers as** going on in the then schools, and foreshadows its results, in which the younger **always supplants** the elder ; and the consequences of this struggle can be very clearly traced in the Hebrew sacred Scriptures.

These two contending schools taught contrary
and opposing doctrines, based upon antagonistic
theories as to the nature of man and his relations
to the natural order.

These differences permeated and moulded the
details of their respective systems.

The one termed God *Elohim*, "forces," to identify his action with that of the forces of nature.

The other called him *Jehovah*, and viewed him
as something more than the first cause, as the personal and direct fashioner of all things.

The one called the first or typical man *Adam*,
the "God-like"—the incarnate divine image.

The other saw in him *Ish*, the "I take"—the
opulent man of the Hebrews: their typical man
of substance, as contrasted with the more humble
Adam, their typical husbandman.

The one held that man was the last created
being, the crowning glory of terrestrial fruitful-
ness.

The other maintained that he was the first, and
that he was fashioned in a void and arid world.

The one drew the distinction between the things
produced by and moving on the earth, or made of
God through its instrumentality, and man, made of
and created by God in his own image and likeness,
to use his delegated powers and have dominion

over all, and so be only a little lower than his
Maker.

The other depicted him as of the earth, earthy ;
and, by his imputed fall, made him even lower than
the animals.

The one made man one—one being in two
persons, male and female.

The other held that the human—at first one—
had a double constitution, and divided it into man
and woman ; each of which was, in its regard, a
distinct individual being, with its own spiritual aims
and spirit resources.

The one made the sex relations the basis of life,
and the object of the Divine blessing.

The other associated them in man with his degradation and fall, and made them the object of the
Divine curse.

The opposing views of these contending schools
permeated their respective ways of regarding the
order of creation.   But the younger derived many
of its doctrines from a misapprehension of those of
the elder, unless indeed it wilfully misread and misinterpreted the teachings of the earlier school.   In
either case the misreadings it adopted are singular
and instructive.

The one taught that, " To create a vesture, God
created the heavens and the earth."

The other accepted this dictum in the sense, " In the beginning God created the heavens and the earth."

The one taught that the earth in its first state was a watery globe, whose constituents were acting and re-acting on each other, and whose surface was agitated by a mighty wind.

The other accepted this dictum in the sense that the primary watery globe was without form and void, and that the Spirit of God was brooding on the surface of the waters.

The one taught that the first action produced on the watery globe was that of fire, of fire acting from within in the form of *aor*, volcanic action ; and that the phase of activity thus initiated was characterized by the successive *ereb*, mingling, and *boker*, cleaving —the decomposition and recomposition of its elementary constituents—as the first *yom* or functional evolution of nature.

The other accepted this dictum as the creation of *aor*, light ; and in the sense that this was the work of the first *yom*, day of creation, which was likened to the natural day as having its *boker*, morning or dawn, and its *ereb*, evening or decline—although the rendering, " And there was evening and there was morning, one day," by assuming that the work was done in the interval between the evening and the morning, or in the night, actually excludes the day it is supposed to designate.

The one taught that the internal fire, by its continuous action, produced an expansion of certain of the elements of the earth, and of these constituted the beginnings of the atmosphere ; completing this action by upheaving the dry land, and so dividing the original watery globe into its three physiological elements, water, air **and earth,** crowning the whole by the introduction of vegetation. These it regarded **as the second and** third *yoms,* phases of evolutional activity.

The other accepted this dictum in the sense that the expansion was an expanse, a transparent and solid firmament fixed above the earth to separate it from the heavens, and **so divide** the waters of the one from those **of** the other ; **and** that this separation of waters from waters on the one hand, and of **the** land from the water on the other, was the work of the second and third *yoms,* days of creation.

The one taught that the action of the heavenly **bodies, and** especially of the **sun, was** then brought to bear upon the earth, to develop its vegetative, and quicken it with animal, life, and to progressively advance these, each in its order and after its kind ; and that this was the function of, and constituted the fourth, fifth and sixth *yoms,* phases of evolution, crowning the whole with the creation of man.

The other accepted the first part of this dictum in the sense that the sun, moon and stars were then created, as the work of the fourth *yom*, day of creation—tacitly accepting the work of the fifth and sixth phases or days, while absorbing them into and supplanting them by its own doctrinal kosmogony.

And, finally, the one taught that God gave unto man the fruits of the earth and the vegetable-feeding animals, to be his food.

Whereupon the other accepted this dictum in the sense that God gave the fruits of the earth to man, and to the animals the green herbage, to be their food ; forgetting that under this view the animal kingdom must have violated the divine commandment, and fallen from its assumed first condition irrespective of the imputed fall of man, since whole classes of animals prey upon each other. Though how this could be, seeing that they were constructed by their Maker so to live, so to prey, does not appear.

These schools were succeeded by a third, which sought through compromise to reconcile the opposing teachings and blend them in a single whole ; and the qualified success of this compromise, under which the teachings of the first for the most part disappeared in that of the second, which was again modified by that of the third, has been the cause of a confusion of ideas whose effects have made themselves felt even to the present day.

This school, gradually developed from the other two, found certain points of contact in the sacred Scriptures of each, certain verbal bases on which to bring them together.

These sacred Scriptures were already in part misunderstood and misinterpreted; and it was from this misunderstanding and misinterpreting that a tendency to a coalescing party and a common teaching had arisen, and through it that the bases for a common doctrine were found.

The first of these points of contact was discovered in the use by the elder school of the word-sign *Ihvh*, of the verb "caused to be"—now come to be read Jehovah—in conjunction with the word-sign *Alhim* —now read Elohim—in the sentence, "God caused heavens and earth to be," at the close of its kosmogony in Gen. ii. 4, which was then supposed to stand for Jehovah Elohim. For they could thus show that the two Divine names, which had become symbols of division, had been originally used together by the earlier teachers, and signified one and the same Being; so that all that was necessary was to use these names in juxtaposition on suitable occasions, and combine them in suitable places, to effect a very important reconciliation.

Then finding the word-sign *Ha-Adamah* in Gen. i. 25, where it was used to mark the distinction between that which is of the ground and the to-God-likened Adam, they claimed that Adam's name was derived from *Adamah*, to prove that he was held in the first instance, by the elder, to have sprung from the earth, and thus show that both schools had attributed to him a common origin.

While in the word *Ish-shah*, "I take her," used by Adam in his first speech, associated with *Ish*, "I take," by an early commentator, in the sentence, "For this was taken of man," they found the means of identifying the typical *Adam* with his anti-typical supplanters *Ish* and *Ish-shah*, after the derivation of these words had been lost sight of, and their original meanings merged in the arbitrary designations man and woman, when they became mere generic terms.

Thus while the second school originated in opposing views which induced different doctrines, through which it sought to supplant the teachings of the first, the third school found in the re-interpretation of these already misapprehended teachings a basis on which to bring the differing systems together, and blend them in a not very congruous whole.

Man seems from the dawn of history to have had the same eager desire to know from whence he comes, and whither he is bound when he quits this life.

This desire has led him to devise theories as to the origin of the world on which he dwells; of the verdure which clothes it; of the animated life spread over its surface; and finally of himself, the dominator of all.

Two of these theories have been handed down in the Book of Genesis, one of which makes his origin divine and himself God-like; while the other, making him God-like in his first solitary grandeur, says that he is of the earth, earthy, and by his fall degraded.

The authors or transmitters of each of these theories attributed them to a superhuman source, so that if they were revealed—and there is no desire through these pages to contest their inspired origin and revealed character—then, unless their structural form has been misunderstood and their verbal sense misinterpreted—that is, unless their character and method have been completely misconceived—they show that the inspired teachings of revelation can be contradictory to each other on fundamental points and first principles, and that, upon occasion, they are mutually destructive each of the other's doctrine.

Whether Adam was the first man, and Eve the first woman; whether Ish was the first husband, and Ish-shah the first wife; whether these designations represent one and the same couple, or merely shadow the two types of mankind, the God-like and the grasping, and, with their fabled offspring are the formal veils of a doctrinal history,—has but little practical bearing from a scientific point of view. The teachings from which they spring, and the form in which they have been preserved, stamp the narratives relating to them as doctrinal parables pointing to the knowledge they were framed to clothe and even to conceal.

The real question which suggests itself to the thoughtful inquirer from such a standpoint is, Can that knowledge be recovered, at least in so far as to show its probable character and tendencies, and possible bearing on the intellectual and moral development of the present day? And how far will a re-examination of the veiled theories which the Biblical parables enfold, and their careful comparison with the hypotheses of modern science, lead to this recovery?

One of the most instructive of these parables is that which suggests the Bible theory of the origin of speech.

A careful consideration of this theory makes it

hardly possible to avoid the conclusion that its devisers held that the dawning intellect of primitive, of infant man, was potential and not positive; a power, and not a possession; an acquisition, and not an endowment. They evidently viewed it as a simple outcome of applied consciousness; a capacity of knowing—that is, of receiving and interpreting impressions, and storing up the fruits of their interpretation as knowledge, to be applied to the promotion of further advance in the intellectual uses of life; and as evidently held that this intuitive capacity was prepared for by, derived from and due to, the developing influence, on the advancing organization of the being under creation in man, of the life uses of antecedent existence.

Whether the authors of the older Bible kosmogony believed in the gradual evolution of the human through the several intermediate orders of being, starting from the simple germ to attain to a finished and perfected humanity, as the earlier Kabbalists taught, is a question deserving of study. To this question the author desires to draw the attention of the reader.

SELECTIVE EVOLUTION.

B

FROM UNITY TO INFINITY:

THE MEANING AND METHOD OF SELECTIVE EVOLUTION.

Space, a substantial Unity.

SPACE, the all-containing uncontained, is the primary embodiment of simple unity.

Without intelligible limits, it can be defined as boundless extension. Hence it has no dimensions: so that to speak of the dimensions of space is to give expression to a confusion of ideas.

But if space is boundless extension, the question necessarily arises, Boundless extension of what? For a boundless extension of emptiness, that is of nothing, is a contradiction of terms which, while formulating an unintelligible proposition, assumes a possibility contrary to all experience and to any intellectual conception.

The abstract idea of space, as a limitless void, is comparatively modern.

This view is due to the abstraction of the idea from its source, as the point of departure of a vicious

process of reasoning ; and is, moreover, unphiloso-
phical, and opposed to the teaching enforced by the
aphorism, " Nature abhors a vacuum."

Turning, therefore, from the abstract idea to that
from the misunderstanding of which it was derived,
the inquirer finds himself obliged to admit that
he is absolutely ignorant of the real nature of this
source ; and that actual space, the *something*, which
ideal space, the *nothing*, has been made to supplant
and misrepresent, can only be accurately defined as
the unknown container of all.

Space, *the unknown first Cause.*

This unknown something, thus recognized as and
identified with the primary embodiment of simple
unity, is invisible and impalpable ; and, because
invisible and impalpable, therefore incognizable.
And this incognizability has led to the error of
supposing it to be a simple void, a mere receptive
capacity.

But, even viewed as an absolute void, space must
be admitted to be *either* self-existent, infinite and
eternal ; *or* to have had a first cause outside, behind
and beyond itself.

And yet, could such a cause be found and defined,
this would only lead to the transferring thereto of
the attributes otherwise accruing to space, and thus

merely throw the difficulty of origination a step further back, without gaining additional light as to primary causation.

Hence, in the present state of knowledge on this subject, space—the unknown something from which, owing to its being unknown, the idea of nothingness has been derived—must be regarded as self-existent, infinite and eternal, as well as everywhere present ; for it is impossible to conceive of anything outside space. So that, until the causation thereof is demonstrated, it is necessary to regard space as the primary cause of everything contained therein.

Space, the living Source of Life.

In this self-existent, infinite and eternal, in this ever-abiding space, the heavenly bodies are ceaselessly circulating.

Now the circulation of globes, globules or corpuscles is, in the organized kingdoms of nature, the distinguishing mark of life. So much so, that such a circulation is absolutely necessary thereto in the higher orders of being ; and, where it cannot be shown to exist, there organized life is known not to be.

But the ever-abiding space possesses such a circulation.

Is not, then, this ever-abiding space, this inscrutable upholder of all that exists therein, a living, life-giving entity—the living, life-giving source of life ?

Force and Matter, Potencies of Space.

In the original simple unity termed space, force and matter are primarily latent.

Force and matter are latent in space as potencies therein, as constituents and agencies thereof.

Force and matter pass from the latent state, and become known phenomenally as force and matter, in consequence of some unperceived action in space.

Hence force and **matter** originate in changes in **the** substance **of space, and are the** expression and outcome of the activities which produce the changes implicated.

What, then, are force and matter, so viewed ?

The terms force and matter, like the term space, with which they **are** associated, are misleading. They are intended **to** distinguish the *something* underlying and acting through the observed phenomena of nature from the assumed *nothingness* of **space.**

This something is a unity, an acting and reacting, **an** interacting unity ; **and,** as the condensed substance of the primary unity—space—from which it proceeds, is a potentially active material, of which the terms force and matter represent the potencies.

Hence force and matter are the conjoint constituents of the material whose potencies they indicate.

And hence, just as the term space has veiled and taken the place of the first cause of all and primary source of life, so have the terms force and matter taken the place of the active material whose potencies, whatever those potencies (which they represent) may be, carry on the workings of nature.

"Space," "Force," "Matter," their symbolical Character.

Force, as force, and matter, as matter, are as absolutely unknowable as is the assumed empty space in which they are held to interact.

The terms space, and force, and matter, are, to the physicist, what signs in algebra are to the mathematician, merely conventional symbols.

As symbols, they represent abstract ideas—ideas drawn from and resting on the assumptions on which the physicist bases reasoned hypotheses of the origin of things.

Judging from the necessities of his own works, he thinks he sees three needs in what he terms creation :

A place wherein to create.

A medium by which to create.

A material from which to create.

And in giving a logical expression to this hypothesis through the terms space, force, matter, he believes he has proved the existence of that which each of these represents, *as he conceives it to be.*

Force and Matter, unknown Revealers of the Unknown.

But if space be a substantial though unknowable living entity :

And if the circulating heavenly bodies are the functioning organs of this living entity, and the instruments through which—otherwise unknown—it passes into knowable relations :

Then the phenomena of nature manifested through these organs, instruments and agencies, will simply be the functional expression of the action of the potencies through, and the processes by, which the unknown becomes knowable—of the action of potencies proceeding, and of processes resulting from, and promoting, changes in the condition and relations of the substance of the primary unknown living entity.

While, if so, the terms force and matter only represent the unknown potencies of the active material, through the functional action of which these changes, these manifestations, are produced.

Force and Matter, inseparable.

The physicist has never been able to separate force from matter.

Why?

Because to do so would be to send both back to the latent, that is to the incognizable state.

Hence in talking of the interactions of force and matter, he is discussing *the actions and reactions of different qualities of the original active material on each other, in conformity with the progressively varying conditions and relations through which it successively passes.*

The ultimate Atom, indiscoverable.

The physicist has never been able to demonstrate the existence of the ultimate atom.

Why?

Because, since force and matter, as potencies of an active material, are the outcome and expression of a changed condition in the unknown substance of the primary simple unity—a changed condition, whose aim is the passage from latent to cognizable relations; and since this changed condition is produced by a form of condensation, not of atoms but of substance, the search for an unknown, an assumed ultimate atom, cannot succeed, owing to the susceptibility of this condensed substance, under any process of investigation, to re-pass into the latent state by infinite expansion.

Force and Matter, an interacting Unity.

The terms force and matter, as has been already indicated, represent the potencies of an interacting unity—of a unity proceeding from the primary unity ; and, in the successive interactions of the divergent qualities of this interacting unity in the complex relations by which the phenomena of nature are produced, it alternately passes and re-passes from the latent to the phenomenal, and from the phenomenal to the latent states.

The Interactions of Force and Matter, a combined Function.

The whole of the changes produced by the interactions of force and matter, as potencies of the active material, are functional in character, and the expression of functional processes whose point of departure is an initial activity in the unknown substance of space ; whose method is the production of change in that unknown substance—of change through which it passes to the cognizable state ; whose aim is the maintenance of life—by the production, multiplication and use thereof.

The triune Character of Space.

Space, as the all-containing uncontained, is the primary unity.

In this primary unity force and matter are latent. Of this primary unity they are constituents. From this primary unity they proceed, that therein they may act and re-act, and so enter into cognizable phenomenal relations.

Thus this primary unity might be said to have a triune character; the ideal space and force and matter then representing the three potencies of the living entity. But, even so, this character could only be imputed thereto in the sense that force and matter proceed therefrom, depend thereon, and take the place of the energies thereof.

Force and Matter, the Outcome of the unknown Life of Space.

Force and matter proceed from space, as the condensed substance thereof and outcome of its hidden life, to become the energizing agencies through whose instrumentality that hidden life is maintained.

But though force and matter proceed from space, they cannot pass out thereof. All that accrues to them by this procession is the power of manifesting their presence therein by the phenomena they produce ; for they are inseparable therefrom, just as, in their several interactions therein, they are insepa- rable from each other, until they re-pass into the latent state.

Thus the relations of force and matter, as ener- gizing agencies, to the hidden life of space, are these, that coming out therefrom as potencies, they, by evolutional interaction, change the potential into the actual, that it may be fitted to re-enter that hidden life.

Evolution, a Function in regard to Space.

The phenomenal or interacting and phenomena- producing state of force and matter, as potencies of the active material or condensed substance of space, is a functioning state ; a state whose activities are primarily directed to maintaining the existence, the hidden life from which they have proceeded, on which they depend, and to a return to which they tend.

The Heavenly Bodies, functioning Organs.

The functioning activity of force and matter, as potencies of the condensed substance of space, expresses itself through the agency of the heavenly bodies.

These, as they pass through space, gather up

and re-distribute the nascent force and matter continuously passing therefrom, as a potentially active
material ; and pass these through processes, and
submit them to uses, which gradually prepare and
fit the material, whose potencies they are, for a
return thereto as renewed and recruited energies of
space. For this material passes from the substance
of space in a crude and exhausted, a potential condition, that it may have its energies renewed by
evolutional interaction. And it is by the functioning
action of the heavenly bodies that this interaction
is stimulated, fostered and promoted ; that these
energies are renewed ; and that it is ultimately
restored, duly refreshed, to the activities of the
hidden life of space.

The Heavenly Bodies, vitalizing Organs.

The functions of the heavenly bodies are directed
to the due maintenance of the vital relations of
space.

This is manifestly the case : for, to cite a single
but signal instance, the rays of the sun pass from
that body in every direction, or are, so to say,
universally distributed in space, as far as its range
of action reaches ; so that the giving of light, and
heat, and electricity, to the planets and their satellites can but be a mere incident of its action. But,

since upon this incidental action their vital relations, and with these their power of fulfilling their **several** special functions depend, the at least as great importance of its general action on space is self-evident.

The Heavenly Bodies, vital Organs.

The heavenly bodies are the circulating organs of the living entity termed space.

As the circulating organs of a living entity, they partake of the life **of that** entity, which is equivalent to and produces in each one of them an independent and proper life of its own.

They are constituted of the potentially active **material which** proceeds from the **substance of space ; and therefore each of** them has an indefinable commencement, and a definite individual existence of an indefinite duration, and terminates its **career** by ultimate **dissolution.** For—as in the circulation of the globules, corpuscles or cells of organic life—**there is a regular** reproduction and constant succession of circulating organs in the substance of space, that the functions they discharge may be continuous ; **and** each system, on its exhaustion, passes away **to make room** for a more vigorous successor — *because renovation is as necessary to enduring as to limited life in the order of existence.*

The Functions of the Heavenly Bodies.

The heavenly bodies, in their collective capacity as circulating organs, have a common function in regard to that wherein they circulate—space.

The heavenly bodies, in their individual capacity as circulating organs, have each a proper function of its own.

They have, moreover, a specific function as stimulators and promoters of the electrical action in space; besides which, their own circulation is regulated by this action : but further guides to the study of these relations are yet needed.

The common Function of the Heavenly Bodies.

The common function of the heavenly bodies is the collection, renovation and redistribution of the exhausted but potentially active material proceeding from space, and its ultimate restoration to the substance thereof in a renewed, a recruited and re-invigorated—a developed state.

That this is the common function of the heavenly bodies is learnt from the study of the observed phenomena of gravitation through their results in solar action : for the sun draws to itself such particles or masses of material floating in space as come within the range of its attraction ; and these,

on reaching its zone of incandescence, are kindled
and consumed, or volatilized—*that they may re-pass
to the latent state.*

The proper Function of the Heavenly Bodies.

The proper function of the heavenly bodies consists in the several individual processes by which
each accomplishes its own special share of the
common action.

The general characteristics of these are learnt
from the study of the observed phenomena of terrestrial action.   For the earth submits the material
subjected to its operation to the uses of life, that,
by passing through life-renewing processes, it may
be energized and developed, and so fitted once more
for the uses of the unknown life to which it is to be
restored.

Thus the proper function of the earth is the reproduction, the advancement and maturation, that
is the evolution, of life, *that the material thus subordinated to the uses of the lower may be refitted for
those of the higher life.*

The selective Character of functional Action.

Condensed substance proceeds from space as an
exhausted material, *as regards the uses of space,* but
in a crude state as a potentially active material,

whose potencies are termed force and matter, *as regards the uses of the heavenly bodies.*

This material, exhausted under one aspect and for one use, but potentially active under and for another, is passed by the earth, as a functioning organ, through a succession of physical, chemical and organizing processes, *that by each of these a selection may be made of that which is proved by each successive process to be capable of further advance in the evolutional order through which it is being developed;* and, after each such successive probation, that which is found to be incapable of advance, in its then condition, is remitted to other processes of conversion ; while that which is ultimately rejected by all the processes is left for final submission to solar combustion.

The selective Methods of functional Action.

The advancing active material is passed in succession through the physical and chemical into the organizing and vitalizing processes of nature, and is by these submitted, through physiological and vital action, to the uses of life.

Each of these actions results in a redistribution of the diverse constituents and diverging qualities of the active material submitted to the influences producing it.

The physical action results in disintegration ; **to be followed** by re-integration.

The chemical action results in decomposition ; to be followed by re-composition.

The organizing or physiological and vital **action** results in death ; to be followed by renewed **life in** an advancing order.

The result of each of these actions marks the termination of **the** stage of the function implicated, in regard to the material passed through it.

The resultant is the outcome of the particular function.

The results here are, consecutively—disintegration, following the physical ; decomposition, **following** the chemical ; and death, following **the** vital action.

The resultants are of two classes : *the material selected* during and fitted by the given functional action (or use) for further advance, to which in due time it is submitted ; and *the material rejected* during and by the same functional action (or use), which is left for further conversion.

The disintegration after physical, the decomposition after chemical, and the death after vital action, are the several successive crises produced by the separation of the functionally selected from the functionally rejected material.

After each of these crises, the selected, and by selection individualized, material passes into the latent state, ready for submission to further action in an advanced order; while the rejected material is subjected, as in the dead body, to dissolution and decay, that it may be used in subsequent conversions.

The selective Order of functional Action.

In terrestrial function the lower always precedes the higher; acts or can act without the higher; completes or can complete its action without the higher: but the higher cannot dispense with the lower. Thus the physical can act without the chemical, and the chemical without the vital; but the chemical cannot dispense with the physical, nor the vital with the chemical and the physical.

All these agencies act together in life, and are indispensable thereto.

So, again, in incipient and advancing life, the lower always precedes the higher; the lower, the higher function; the lower, the higher type; all combining in the production of the highest type, in which all find their completeness.

The primary Aim of functional Evolution.

The to be evolved material proceeds from space as the condensed substance thereof.

Hence the to be evolved material is, like space, a unity ; and, as a unity, is a condensed reflection of the primary unity from which it proceeds.

This condensed substance, **secreted or excreted by space,** comes **forth** in a crude and exhausted state as regards the uses of space, but as a raw **material endowed with great** capabilities and capacities as regards the functions of evolution.

This material is submitted to functional evolution, that **these capabilities and** capacities **may be developed by** the **uses to which it** is subjected.

These uses progressively **draw forth from this one material certain** qualities, properties, **powers and faculties, in order that,** re-endowed **with these, it may be returned to the** substance **of space** fitted for **the uses to which it will then be once more** applied.

But this material is a unity—is **one.** Hence, **though in the process of evolution it** develops **divergent** qualities, it will ultimately, whether in **the personal or** formless **state, be** returned to space **as a unity.**

The selective Principle in functional Evolution.

In the process of functional evolution certain differences show themselves in the quality of the condensed substance of space subjected to its action.

Owing to these differences, **a distinction in the**

individualization thereof takes place, under which the individual rates of progression vary.

Under this differentiation a proportion of the condensed substance proved to be incapable of due advance is rejected, and remitted to other processes of conversion ; while the selected and progressing portions advance, each in its own ratio.

The successive Stages of functional Evolution.

In the advancing order of functional evolution the several successive changes of the selected condensed substance of space represent so many consecutive stages—first of individualizing progression, and then of individualized life, which culminate in the individualized and personalized human being.

Hence the condensed substance under selection, which successfully passes through the successive stages of the preparatory state, and finally enters the human form, is thus gradually raised, by the uses to which it is subjected, from its primary crude or exhausted condition to the fulness of energy and capacity.

Having been duly prepared by physical and chemical action, and primarily individualized, it passes from the germ state through successive stages of individual life—each through its own series.

Of these, each stage represents a single life, and terminates in death ; and it enters these successive stages or lives that, by the use of each in succession, it may acquire and mature the powers of **sensation** and perception, of intelligence and reason, and gradually bring these to their highest point of **development.**

Terrestrial Life a functional **Use.**

Life is a use ; a use preparing for a further use ; a use by which the condensed substance of space gains certain qualities and properties, faculties and powers, which fit it to re-enter the unknown life of space.

The passage thus is from the unknown (by primary condensation), through evolution—physical, chemical and physiological—in the known (that is, the observed and recognized order of nature), back again to the unknown.

But whereas that which proceeds from space is void of the powers of sensation and perception, of **the faculties of** intelligence and **reason, that** which returns thereto has acquired **these powers and faculties, and** carries them back with it ready for the uses for which they may be required.

Thus terrestrial life is merely one of the processes by which the proper function of the earth is carried on.

The Method of functional Evolution.

The method of this process of the proper function of the earth is very simple.

A quickening impulse having been imparted to the interacting material, probably by solar action, it enters the germ state in cellular form, and then, by the instrumentality of cells, passes through a series of successive lives, with their vegetative, organizing and animating processes—each germ through its own series—until the culminating point of advance is reached.

In this progressive evolution, in which the individualized interacting material passes through a succession of advancing lives, of which the human culminates and completes the series (and which, functionally considered, are but so many separate stages of a single existence), as the special function of each stage or life is completed, it is terminated by death—by the withdrawing of the stimulus on which the thus terminated phase of the proper function depended, and consequent dissolution of the tie which had bound the evolved material or being to its evolving matrix.

What, then, under this view, is death?

Death is the crisis by which the individualized, interacting, evolving material, functionally selected for further advance by the uses of the thus ended life, is separated from the material which, under the same uses, has shown itself to be incapable of such advance, and is therefore and thus rejected.

At death, the rejected material remains as the dead body, subject to dissolution and decay, while the material or being which has been thus functionally selected for further advance passes into the latent state, to await its re-entrance by generation into another body in a higher order.

Thus each intermediate death, which breaks up the actually continuous existence into a progressively advancing series of successive lives, is merely the process by which, as the necessity arises in the natural order, the selected material or being is separated from the now encumbering and therefore rejected material operated upon.

The Incentive to functional Evolution.

The advancing, individualized, interacting material whose potencies are force and matter, and which can therefore be conveniently termed a materialized and materializing force, is the operating agent in functional evolution.

This materialized force—in which force and matter are inseparable co-agents, the one as medium of the other—carried away by impulse, by appetite, seeks, while in the body, all that promotes its enjoyment of life.

This materialized force, this spirit, as it has been named by those who look upon it as a supernatural, a mediatized agent, this advancing being improves the bodily form it is using, and increases its capacity for promoting the enjoyment of life, and consequently causes and enables it to produce offspring capable of contributing to yet further enjoyment.

Hence in each preparatory life a double advance is going on—an advance of being, and an advance of form and capacity. For the advancing being, while increasing its own capabilities, produces in its off-spring advancing bodily forms—bodily forms with increased capabilities and tendencies—for advancing beings lower down in the scale of advance, but pre-pared and ready for the use of such advanced and advancing bodies.

The advancing being enters the germ at the moment of conception, and then, fashioning for itself the generating body, advances its advancing form yet further, specially preparing and fitting it for the uses to which it means during life to apply it.

Thus appetite is the impulse, self-seeking the means, self-indulgence the channel through which the progressive evolution of bodily forms and the advance of life is sought and secured in the order of nature.

The needed Change in the Incentive to functional Evolution.

In the human form the advancing being takes an important step in its upward course.

Hitherto everything has been sacrificed to the attainment of the most perfect form.

In man this form is gained. But it has been gained as the outcome of a selfish struggle for existence, in which each step in advance has been characterized by the survival of the fittest.

But the survivors in each instance have only acquired their fitness and secured their survival—in the order of forms, that is to say—by recklessly sacrificing all to a self-seeking appetite.

Now, that the fittest might survive and secure a progressive advance in the evolution of form, the less fit were sacrificed for the good of the survivors.

They were not merely sacrificed. They were sub-jected to suffering and made the victims of cruelty— of a cruelty which, by depriving them of what they needed, on the one hand, and consuming them as food on the other, caused them to be the victims of that self-indulgence by which further advance is secured.

But counterbalancing compensation was provided for the victims in the effect of the training to which they were thus subjected, and their more rapid passage through the successive evolutionary stages.

Hence cruelty and suffering, so far from being evil in the evolutional order, are, when not the instruments, the necessary outcome of evolution— seeing that without them progressive advance would be impossible.

And hence, that cruelty and suffering may be eliminated from the human, a change must take place in the incentive to functional evolution in man.

The Step in advance of functional Evolution in Man.

In man the evolution of form culminates.

With him the necessity for inflicting cruelty and suffering ceases.

But having been developed by self-indulgence, and trained in the habit of sacrificing others to self, reckless of the cruelty thus practised and of the suffering which ensues, the advancing being brings with it into the human form a tendency to reckless self-seeking, and an indifference to the cruelty and suffering consequent on the indulgence of appetite.

Now the step in advance which the advancing

being has made in man is this—that it recognizes the cruelty and **suffering** it inflicts **by the** reckless indulgence of appetite ; instinctively feels that it ought not to act cruelly and inflict suffering ; and thus learns **to** distinguish between " good " and " evil :" and then, realizing that self-seeking and self-assertion are the causes of evil, sees that they must be met, and overcome, and cast out by self-forgetfulness and self-suppression ; and thus learns that it has entered the human *that it may humanize self and subordinate the appetites of its nature—appetites which it has derived through its processes* **of** *evolution—to the duties of its* **life.**

Now **the** one characteristic **of the living** entity known as space is self-suppression. **Is it** strange, therefore, that those ultimately to become its terrestrial offspring should at length feel called to the **practice of this virtue ?**

The Consequences of this Step in advance.

The step in advance taken by the advancing being, on entering the human, carries with it certain consequences.

The human life, **like its predecessors in the** evolutional series, is a selective functional process.

But it is a functional process in which the conditions of selection have undergone a change.

In it the highest form of terrestrial evolution has been gained.

And that the human is the highest evolutional type in the present order is learnt from the results of the researches of the geologist; for, though he has succeeded in showing that man has peopled the earth during a geological period of vast extent, in doing this he demonstrates that through all variations of race the type remains unchanged, evolution in him being an evolution of skill, intelligence, intellect and reason, with the organs on which these depend.

The inference therefore is, that in him the selection in progress involves retention of form and organization after death, which is the same as saying that *the attainment of beings in a personal form has been the end sought through evolution.*

The two Processes of functional selective Evolution in the Human.

Hence in man two processes of selection are simultaneously going on, under which each individual tends either to a personal or an impersonal future state.

Of these, the one process separates the selected from the rejected material. Under it at death the selected material passes, as at the close of each preceding stage of evolution, in the formless condition to the latent state, leaving the rejected material and form in the dead body.

Of these, the other deals with the beings under probation, when those which, by their uses of life, have become self-forgetting and self-suppressing will pass, at death, to the unknown, in human form — these also leaving the rejected material in the dead body, or matrix, by the use of which the persisting personal form has been gained.

Under this simultaneously working double process of functional selection the being under evolution passes from the body at death *either* as a persistent personal being, fitted for the personal uses of a higher life, *or* as a shapeless substance, re-energized by the evolutional processes, that it may re-pass into the substance of the unknown living entity—space.

The functional Option between two States in Man.

Reasoning from this conclusion, it would appear that man on coming into the world has the practical option between two states functionally set before him.

That he unconsciously makes his selection between these two states by the uses to which he puts his passing life.

That the self-forgetter and self-suppressor at death enters the latent state—which is to him the commencement of a renewed life—in the human form.

While the self-seeker and self-asserter passes to that state without form—simply as selected material in a particular condition.

The Incentive to functional Selection in Man.

Man is by nature self-seeking and self-asserting.

These tendencies of his nature are due to the evolutional process by which he has been created, which has developed in him the habit of sacrificing all to self.

These tendencies, this natural habit, can only be overcome by the substitution, for the habit of sacrificing all to self, of the habit of overlooking, of forgetting, of suppressing self, for the sake of that which is not self.

To enable him to do this a strong incentive must be given to man.

This incentive must cause him to prefer that which is not self to self.

Such an incentive is LOVE.

Now the functional aim sought in the human is the transforming of appetite into affection.

While the functional means are the habitual and

at length unconscious forgetting and suppressing **of** self for the sake of that which is not self.

So that the conversion of appetite into affection is the ultimate aim of functional evolution, that in the human the evolving being may acquire a **persistent** personality.

Now the only adequate natural incentive to **such a** conversion is **love.**

Hence love **is** the incentive to functional selection **in man.**

The Incentive to functional **Evolution in Man** *itself functionally evolved.*

In physical or molecular and magnetic attraction, and the attraction of gravitation, the rudimentary germ of that which is to become affection is seen.

In chemical affinity, **this germ acquires** a more effectual expression.

Through the organizing processes of nature it gradually takes on the form of appetite.

In animated nature, while developing as appetite, it branches off into instinct, and through this into **instinctive** affections.

In animal life, these instinctive affections culminate in parental attachment.

In man, these several attractions, appetites and affections combine, to find their complement in love.

Hence love, as the crown of affection, like reason, as the crown of intelligence, is the outcome and product of evolution.

The two States functionally set before Man.

The two evolutional states of which man thus has the functional option have been termed respectively the soul state and the spirit state. And by his life, by the use he makes of, the uses to which he puts that life, man, each individual human being, determines whether he shall leave his body at death as a soul or a spirit—as qualified or unqualified for a continued personal existence in a new sphere of action.

Owing to this option, thus functionally placed before him, a confusion of ideas has been fallen into as to the physical, spiritual and psychical nature of man, and it has been supposed that he is constituted of a body, a soul and a spirit, in a state of physiological combination or union ; and various theories have been devised to explain the several relations of each and either of these to the others. But this view is seen to have been a mistake as soon as the meaning of evolution is recognized and its method understood.

Man is a unity : a being in process of evolution : a living matrix submitted to regenerating processes during life, from which either a soul or a spirit will proceed at death—either a personal being or an impersonal product.

The Relations of these two States to Space.

The relations of these two states to the living entity known as space, whose terrestrial offspring man on entering the soul state becomes, are very intelligible.

This living entity is an impersonal unity.

This impersonal unity desires an infinite personality, that its boundless love may have countless objects of affection.

These objects it seeks through functional evolution.

It has made functional evolution the channel through which they are to be produced, that each may be free to make its own choice *by following its own inclinations.*

But to become objects of its love, all must prove themselves worthy of its affection by conforming themselves to its desire.

They can only do this, and thus make themselves worthy, by embodying the attributes of the Impersonal in their own personality, and so assimilating their developed nature to its aspirations. That is to say, the desire of the unknown or self-suppressed impersonal, which is changed into appetite—of which desire is the root—in the evolving, self-asserting personal, must be transformed into affection in the evolved, the self-suppressing personal, that the thus generated persistent personal may be worthy of the affection of its generator.

This is why all who fail to transform appetite into affection, by the uses to which they put their human lives, fail to become persistent personal beings. And the failure of these to attain to a persistent personality is necessary, to prevent the introduction of the self-seeking of the life of evolution into the state for which persistent personality is preparing—with the consequences which would flow therefrom.

Moreover, it is necessary that this transformation of appetite into affection should be accomplished by a functional process in the human, that there may be no room for a partial and favouring influence or extraneous selective action, but that all may be on an equal footing and have an equal chance of attaining to the persistent personality thus offered to all. For the real aim of evolution by natural selection is, *that each by following his own inclination may ultimately reach the state for which he has fitted himself*—which alone could satisfy his developed and matured desires.

Thus the working of functional, that is of natural selective evolution, excludes the idea of supernatural **intervention.**

The Working of the Relations of these two States.

The force and matter proceeding from space, as the potencies of the exhausted substance of the **living entity,** to be transformed into an active material and re-energized by **the** circulating organs thereof—the heavenly bodies—are re-energized by passing through the several processes of nature now technically known as evolution by natural selection and the survival of the fittest, **that** they may **be** restored once more to space—that is, **to the** substance **from which** they originally proceeded—in **a** condition fitted to re-enter its **unknown life.**

But they are not returned in the same state. They re-pass thereto in one of two conditions—either as **formless cellular** substance **or** persistent personal being.

The Rationale of these Relations.

The rationale of these relations is not far to seek.

The circulation in space has very significant analogies with that of organic life carried on by the intervention and circulation of cells, whose source it is.

These **analogies at** once suggest that the life of

space is associated with and expresses itself through the equivalents or antitypes of the organs and cells of organic life.

Under this view, the selected material passes to space as a cellular aliment, so to say; while the selected individuals enter it as personal organs.

Beyond this the circulating organs of space must, by their friction, develop electrical action in its substance, and draw electricity therefrom into their own substance—this friction being one of the sources of their own proper electricity, and therefore of the proper electricity of the earth.

This would seem to show that electricity is a vital principle in the life of space.

It certainly is a vital principle in the evolutional life proceeding therefrom.

The Relations of the Life of Space to evolutional Life.

All come primarily from space, and all return ultimately thereto.

But though all come therefrom in the same state —in a state of exhaustion, as an excretion thereof; with an exhaustless capacity, as a secretion therefrom—all do not return thereto in the same state; each, by its own evolutional course, deciding its final condition.

For each stage of the order of evolution influences its successor, and all are determining factors in the ultimate result ; **until in the human** the advancing beings gradually resolve themselves **into the two** classes of self-assertors, for the sake of **self, and** self-suppressors, for the sake of that which is not self—of which the latter were, **in the antecedent** stages, the victims of the former.

And here the balance is struck and compensation found for the apparent evils of evolution—which **are** only evils to those who merely recognize the last stage in the process, the last link in the chain ; for the victims of the earlier stages, owing to having been **habitually** victimized, **can** the more easily **for-** get and suppress themselves ; whereas those by whom they have been constantly victimized, having **no such facility, continue** self-assertors to the end, when, the relations being completely changed, the **one class finds itself** in the personal, the other **in** the impersonal state.

Of those which pass away in the impersonal state nothing further need be said. They enter the sub- **stance of** space as a cellular aliment thereof.

Not so those **who** enter the personal state ; for these do so **as the** offspring and organs of self- suppressing space—of the original, incomprehen- sible primary unity.

Hence these are they in whom the one Impersonal has gained a multiple personality, or passed
from unity to infinity while still maintaining its
primary unity.

This one Impersonal is absolutely incomprehen-
sible.

The manifestations of its life in the natural order
suggest the processes by which that life is carried
on in its invisible or hidden state, but fail to indicate in what the active phases of that unknown life
consist.

These processes culminate in the production of
the human.

Man is but an animal in human form, with human
faculties.

He is not the offspring of the one Impersonal;
for, even in the personal, it only produces that
which is like unto itself.

He is simply the product and outcome of functional evolution in the natural order.

But, though not the offspring of the one Impersonal, he is the matrix from which that offspring is
produced.

Functional evolution has produced, developed and
matured this matrix, whose life depends upon duly
sustained electrical relations.

These relations, when perfect, result in a complete harmony.

Now where electrical harmony exists, there the electricity of the one Impersonal is present and acting.

But this harmony is only found in the human which overlooks, forgets and suppresses self for the sake of that which is not self.

Hence in all the workings of nature, as seen in the successive stages of functional evolution, the electricity of the one Impersonal is only present in the self-forgetting, self-suppressing human.

Now this electricity by its action assimilates that on which it acts to its source.

Hence, working in the self-forgetting, self-suppressing man as a matrix, it generates of him the human soul, which is the true offspring of the one Impersonal.

The only external sign of this generation is found in the uses the human makes of its human life.

These, while conforming the personal offspring to its Impersonal progenitor, produce a harmony which reflects itself in the whole life.

But this was to be expected. For without harmony there can be no true happiness.

Now the basis of happiness consists in the absence of evil.

In this world, good and evil are inextricably interblended.

Hence the function of the life of man, who is becoming the offspring of the Impersonal, is the elimination of evil from his nature. For evil cannot enter the state for which he is preparing—which state is the kingdom of the Impersonal, personified in, through and by its offspring.

The successive evolutional phases, through which that from which the offspring of the Impersonal is to be ultimately produced passes, can now be very clearly defined.

Proceeding from the one Impersonal as a crude material—the condensed substance of space—it is subjected to processes by which, considered as matter, it is individualized and transformed into personal beings ; considered as force, it becomes sentient, perceptive, intelligent and reasoning ; considered as a moral agent, it gradually eliminates the evil which has grown up with and seems to suffocate the good ; and considered as the outcome of desire, it passes through the successive stages of attraction, affinity, appetite and affection, to love, whose fruit is perfect harmony.

But all of these are natural processes.

Nature is here found equal to the entire work— inclination being its all-sufficient instigator—that in the end each may attain to that which, through successive stages of evolution, it has sought, and the one Impersonal be revealed in an infinite personality.

A suggestive Question.

The view of progressive origination set forth in the Book of Genesis is very suggestive, and the analogies between the principle which underlies its method and that assumed by the hypothesis of selective evolution, point to the existence of such a harmony and even affinity between them as almost inevitably to raise the question, Was not the natural process of development the basis of the Mosaic kosmogony?

Such a question might be thought out of place here, and the time to discuss it has perhaps not yet arrived ; but when that time comes—and it may not be long deferred—the materials from which the answer thereto will be ultimately drawn are not far to seek, and indications are not wanting as to the direction it will take.

The Hebrew designation of the Creator, *Elohim*, in the first chapter of Genesis, is very significant in this regard ; for, literally translated, it means "forces."

Still more significant is the Jewish view set forth in the rabbinical name of God, *Ham-makom*, "space."

And this natural relation of the Increate to the created seems to have been present to the mind of the Apostle "brought up at the feet of Gamaliel and instructed according to the strict manner of the Law," and therefore in the science of creation of the Hebrews, when, preaching concerning the unknown God to the Athenians, he said, "In Him we live, and move, and have our being."

PROBLEMS IN BIBLE READING.

JOSHUA, THE SON OF NUN.

A PROBLEM IN BIBLE ASTRONOMY.

———————

JOSHUA, the leader of Israel to the fulfilment of
its territorial expectations and national aspirations,
like Cyrus, the restorer and promoter of its Mosaic
position and Messianic claims, has been regarded as
a type of the Messiah ; and the identity in name of
Joshua with Jesus, in the one case, with the affinity
between *Kyrus* and *Kurios* (Lord), in the other,
have certainly not discouraged this view.

The history of Joshua is a very remarkable one.

The book inscribed with his name, in which the
narrative of his life and deeds has been preserved
and handed down, and whose authorship has been
attributed to him, is in reality composed of dis-
jointed fragments of divers chronicles, which have
been brought together and ingeniously wrought into
a consecutive whole. But the composite character
of this whole, which is admitted in part, is, in the
original, unmistakable throughout ; and the text of

which it is constituted and composed has been, in sundry important passages, misconceived and misrepresented by its Masoretic interpreters, and then misunderstood and mistranslated by their successors.

The account of the interview between Joshua and the captain or prince of the host of Jehovah is such a fragment. And it has been so misrepresented and misinterpreted by the Masoretes and their translators as to seem to have no practical bearing on the course of the narrated events, and has in this way been deprived of its real significance.

The account given of this interview is as follows. It commences abruptly: "And it came to pass, when Joshua was by Jericho, that he lifted up his eyes and looked; and, behold, there stood a man over against him with his sword drawn in his hand : and Joshua went unto him, and said unto him, Art thou for us, or for our adversaries? And he said, Nay; but as captain of the host of Jehovah am I now come. And Joshua fell on his face to the earth and did worship, and said unto him, What saith my lord unto his servant? And the captain of Jehovah's host said unto Joshua, Put off thy shoe from off thy foot ; for the place whereon thou standest is holy. And Joshua did so." (Josh. v. 13—15.)

The Revisers of the Old Testament, recognizing the abruptness of this intercalated fragment and its

want of congruity with the context, have very ingeniously but somewhat disingenuously sought to overcome this difficulty by bracketing the first verse of
the following chapter—" Now Jericho was straightly
shut up because of the children of Israel : none went
out and none came in"—to make it appear as an
interjected explanation, and so lead the reader to
infer that the following verses—"And the Lord said
unto Joshua, See, I have given into thine hand
Jericho," &c.—are in continuation of the interview,
and relate what the captain of the host of Jehovah
said in response to Joshua's question. But it is
Jehovah who speaks now ; and if this had been
directly stated in the version, there would have been
no room for misleading here. Indeed, it is a great
pity that the so called ineffable name is not given
as Jehovah or Jahveh wherever it occurs in the
Revised Version, instead of, as in the Authorized
Version rendered, the LORD, in a blind sequence of
the superstition of the Jews in this regard. Did the
Revisers fear the effect such a change would produce
in the mind of the reader ?

This account stands by itself in the Hebrew as
an abrupt interpolation.

According to it, when Joshua asked the man with
the drawn sword whether he was for or against him,
he received the reply commencing, " Nay, but," as

though its subject were neither for nor against; and the sole object of the apparition is thus made out to have been to demand the worship of the **leader of** Israel.

This misconception has arisen from a very simple mistake.

A single Hebrew **word,** *laci,* has been divided into **two** words, and given the vowel points *lo ci,* and so rendered "nay, but."

Now this word, *laci,* is an inflection of the root *lac,* of the words *malac,* "angel," and *m'lacah,* "work."

Viewed as a verb, it means "be active," "move forward;" **and** through this significance **a flood of** light is thrown on the subject, and a meaning given to the apparition which at once explains why it took place.

The Jews **had** crossed the Jordan, had been circumcised, and had kept the Passover, and were now eating of the fruit of the land of Canaan, or pausing **in** their onward march. Was it singular, then, that the man with the naked sword, who announced himself as the leader of the host of Jehovah, should have commenced his speech to Joshua with the command, "**Move forward. I, chief of** the host of Jehovah, am now come"—thus intimating that he would be with him in his advance?

In this example we find direct evidence that the

Masoretes were not familiar with the text they were interpreting.

Turning now to the last chapter of Joshua, we read that the Jewish leader, shortly before his death, gathered all the tribes of Israel to Shechem on purpose to remind them of all that Jehovah, the God of Israel, had done for them, and urge the children of Israel always to serve Jehovah, and never to forsake him.

But then, after the people have solemnly pledged themselves so to do, he is made (v. 19) to give the remarkable rejoinder, "Ye cannot serve Jehovah," and thus deliberately to announce that they cannot do that which he so urgently invites and commands them to devote themselves to, and in which they have promised to obey him.

This singular position arises from a very simple mistake—a mistake fallen into by the Masoretes in this wise.

The unpointed Hebrew word-signs rendered by them "ye cannot," also represent words which mean "cease not," and the vowel sounds by which they are uttered express which, of these words, and thus determine which of these senses, they should bear. Under an inexplicable misapprehension, the Masoretes, by the points they attached to them, attributed to these word-signs the sounds, and with this the significance of the words, affirming *ye can-not*, **thus** actually changing **one** word into another. And the misreading thus originated has been per-petuated to this day.

And yet the context clearly shows that what Joshua really said must have been, "Cease not to serve Jehovah, for he is an holy God; he is a jealous God; he will not forgive your transgression nor your sins. If ye forsake Jehovah and serve strange gods, then he will turn and do you evil, and con-sume you, after that he hath done you good."

When such misapprehensions have arisen con-cerning important and deeply significant events at the commencement and close of Joshua's career, it is evident that other occurrences similarly recorded may have been similarly misrepresented.

Amongst the remarkable incidents connected with his conquest of the land of Canaan, none is so calculated to impress the mind as his defeat of the Amorites before Gibeon; for on this occasion he is held to have commanded the sun to stand still that the day might be prolonged; and the sun is supposed to have obeyed his behest, to give him the opportunity of completing the slaughter of his fleeing enemies.

The account of what happened on this occasion is found in the tenth chapter of the Book of Joshua.

But this account is in reality three-fold ; for a second narrative has been interpolated in the first, and this second narrative contains a quotation from a third. Hence there has been much room for misunderstanding what actually took place ; but hardly sufficient to explain such a gross misunderstanding as has arisen and been so long maintained.

The first narrative is contained in vv. 6—11, as follows—" And the men of Gibeon sent unto Joshua to the camp, to Gilgal, saying, Slack not thy hand from thy servants ; come up to us quickly, and save us, and help us : for all the kings of the Amorites that dwell in the hill-country are gathered together against us. So Joshua went up from Gilgal, he, and all the people of war with him, and all the mighty men of valour. And the Lord said unto Joshua, Fear them not : for I have delivered them into thine hands ; there shall not a man of them stand before thee. Joshua therefore came upon them suddenly ; for he went up from Gilgal all the night. And the Lord discomfited them before Israel, and he slew them with a great slaughter at Gibeon, and chased them by the way of the ascent of Beth-horon, and smote them to Azekah, and unto Makkedah. And it came to pass as they fled from before Israel, while they were in the going down of Beth-horon, that the Lord cast down great stones

from heaven upon them unto Azekah, and they died :
they were more which died with the hail-stones
than they whom the children of Israel slew with
the sword."

Here we have a full account of what occurred—
an account complete in itself and hardly needing
further comment. But a second narrative had been
written ; and this was interpolated as an extension
of the first, and is included in vv. 12—14 : " Then
spake Joshua to the LORD in the day when the
LORD delivered up the Amorites before the children
of Israel ; and he said in the sight of Israel,

> Sun, stand thou still upon Gibeon ;
> And thou, moon, in the valley of Aijalon.
> And the sun stood still, and the moon stayed,
> Until the **nation** had avenged **themselves of their** enemies.

Is not this written in the book of Jashar ? And the
sun stayed in the midst of heaven, and hasted not
to go down about **a** whole day. And there was no
day like that before it or after it, that the LORD
hearkened unto the voice of a man : for the LORD
fought for Israel."

To this narrative verse **15**—" And Joshua returned, and all Israel with him, unto the camp, to
Gilgal"—was added, to complete the history.

But the addition of this verse testifies to the in-
tercalation, for **it** infers that the whole campaign

was already completed; whereas Joshua is presently (v. 21) found at Makkedah, and does not return to the camp at Gilgal till he has destroyed the five hostile kings, overrun and conquered their territory, and completely vanquished the enemies of Gibeon and of Israel, as stated in vv. 16—43; the last of which is a repetition of v. 15, and closes the narrative and the chapter.

In order rightly to understand these accounts, it is necessary to remember that the second history covers the same ground as the first; deals with the same period of time and the same series of events; and seeks only to heighten the colour and strengthen the miraculous import of that narrative by giving it a dramatic point of departure, and setting forth its subject from a fresh point of view.

Its commencement shows this; for it begins, *Then*—that is, *on this occasion*, and not when and after all this had happened; and had it been intercalated between vv. 8 and 9, instead of between vv. 11 and 15, much of the confusion would have been avoided, as then it would have been evident that it was after receiving the assurance of Jehovah that his enemies should be delivered into his hands, that his prayer was made to Jehovah; and that this prayer was intimately related with the suddenness of his attack.

The first indication to the aim of Joshua's prayer is found in the statement (v. 9), "Joshua therefore came upon them suddenly; for he went up from Gilgal all the night"—which shows that it was his intention to attack the Amorites unexpectedly, under **cover of the** darkness that precedes the **dawn, that,** taking them by surprise, **he** might **create a panic** and **throw** them into confusion. And with this view he made a forced march in the night in order to reach Gibeon before the break of day. In this expectation, however, he was disappointed, **as the** dawn was already commencing before he was prepared to deliver his attack.

The second indication is **seen in** the way in which **that prayer** was answered, as shown by the destructive hail-storm **which** followed on the **rout** of the Amorites, **and** pursued them as they fled, taking the course of their flight.

The third indication appears in **the** relative positions **of the** sun and moon at the time of the prayer: for the sun was in the direction of Gibeon, that is, in the east; and the moon in the valley of Aijalon, **or** westward.

From these indications we learn:

1. That the sun was in the act of rising, the moon declining, in the heavens at the time of the prayer.

2. **That** Joshua, notwithstanding his forced march

through the night, which the light of the moon had facilitated, only reached Gibeon at the dawn, when the rising sun would betray his position to his enemies, and thus deprive him of the fruits of his haste.

3. That his prayer was answered by such a storm as must have completely darkened the heavens, and so enabled the Israelites to deliver their attack under the most awe-inspiring circumstances.

It thus becomes evident that Joshua did not, could not, have commanded the sun to stand still, or prayed for a prolongation of the day; and that he must, therefore, have entreated that the sun should be obscured in arising, or prayed for a continuation of the darkness of night; and that his prayer was answered by the quickly gathering storm, which burst upon his panic stricken and routed enemies, and followed the course of their flight.

From this point of view the correct reading of the Hebrew is easily recoverable, and is simple and straightforward enough to satisfy the most critical scholar. According to it—" Then spake Joshua to Jehovah, on the day when Jehovah delivered up the Amorites before the children of Israel; and he said in the sight of Israel,

Let the sun be silent **on Gibeon;**
And the moon in **the valley of Aijalon.**
And the sun was silent, **and the** moon stayed,
Until the nation had avenged themselves of their enemies.

Is not this written in the book of Jashar? And the sun **stayed in the midst of the heavens, and** hasted **not to** appear about a whole day. And **there was no day** like **that before it** or after it, that Jehovah hearkened **unto the voice** of a man : **for** Jehovah **fought for** Israel."

NOTE.

The verb *dum* signifies **to be silent, to cease from a func-**tion, as of the sun, here, **to** cease from **shining. It has been** used **once (1** Sam. xiv. 9) in the sense to tarry, and this **may** have helped to mislead translators **and revisers. Inflections** of its biliteral root *dm* are used **in the sense to cease, as** of tears **from flowing. Jer. xiv. 17,** "Let them not cease." Lam. iii. 49, **"And ceaseth not."**

The **verb** *hamad* means, not merely **to stand or abide,** but also **to stay or cease—from a function, as** of the moon, here, from reflecting light. **See Gen. xxix. 35,** "She ceased from **bearing." Gen. xxx. 9, "Leah saw that** she had ceased from bearing." 2 Kings iv. 6, **"And** the oil stayed," i.e. ceased from flowing. 2 Kings xiii. **18,** "He smote thrice and stayed," i.e. **ceased.**

The verb *bua* signifies **to** come, **to appear, as well** as to go—**that is, to go** in as well as to **go out, to go up** as well as to go down, to rise as well as to set. **See Eccles. i. 4,** "Another generation cometh." **Ps. lxxi. 18,** "**To every one** that is to come."

MELCHIZEDEK.

A PROBLEM IN BIBLE TRANSLATION.

Who was Melchizedek? Mentioned incidentally
in the Book of Genesis ; referred to typically in a
psalm ; dealt with mystically in the Epistle to the
Hebrews ; and not otherwise alluded to in the Scriptures,—it has been assumed that there is something
surprising and mysterious in the first appearance of,
and the subsequent references to, this personage.
But since the patriarch Abraham only encountered
him once, and he is not mentioned again until the
time of David—indeed some Jewish writers have
held the opinion that Melchizedek was the author
and Abraham the subject of Psalm cx., in which
case the value of the allusion therein is greatly
diminished—it is evident that the immediate descendants of Abraham did not attach importance to
this incident, and that the patriarch did not regard
it as having any peculiar significance.

That Melchizedek should have no genealogy,

therefore—that **there** should **be no record of the** beginning of his days and the **end of his** life—simply **shows** that he did **not count for much in** the eyes of Jewish historians and genealogists. **While that** David, **if the** author of the Psalm in question, should have **seen in** him a typical personage is not strange, **since the royal Psalmist was** the **first** sacred writer **who adopted the** designation *Helion,* "Most High," as applied **to God.**

The personality of Melchizedek does not seem **to** have been invested with superstitious awe till after the Babylonian captivity, when the Jews, having imbibed the **view of a recurrent** Angel-Messiah, attributed this character to him.

The Jewish tradition, recorded in **the T**argums of pseudo-Jonathan and Jerusalem—that he was the patriarch Shem—since **it** does **not** appear in the Targum of Onkelos, serves to show when these speculations commenced.

So little is known of, so indistinct is the record concerning him, with all its seeming precision, that it is **by no** means certain Melchizedek was king of Jerusalem ; for, although Josephus and the Targums assert the identity of Salem **with the** holy city, Jerome, after careful inquiry on the spot, denies that **Salem is** Jerusalem, and asserts that it is identical with a town near Scythopolis, or Bethshan, which in his time retained the name of Salem, and in which some extensive ruins were shown as the remains of Melchizedek's palace.

Is it more certain that he was priest of the Most High God?

The names of God, as recorded in the Scriptures, are generally not used in the first instance as divine appellations, but assume that character by having it imputed to them, in the course of time, through the fitness of things.

This was the case with the name Jehovah, first seen in Genesis ii. 4: "By a succession (*yom*) of formations (*hasoth*) God caused earth and heavens to be"—in which it bears the verbal force, "caused to be."

The changes through which such names subsequently pass are also instructive.

When out of a mistaken reverence the name Jehovah came to be ineffable or unutterable—hence the loss of its due pronunciation—it was abridged to Yah, from which it passed through Yod Yod (the initial letter reduplicated), to Yod, Iod, or Jod—whence, possibly, God.

The word *Helion*, "Most High," by which Melchizedek designates his God, is only used once again in the Book of Genesis (here with the article), of "the uppermost" basket in Pharaoh's chief baker's dream.

It re-appears in the Book of Numbers in the mouth of Balaam ; and again three times in the Book of Deuteronomy—twice certainly not as a divine name, and in the third place doubtfully so, or rather as certainly not so, since the writer has already made use of this expression twice, in a similar idiomatic association, to designate the children of Israel.

In the historical books it is used in ten instances, generally with the article, but adjectively.

In the Prophets it only appears five times, and of these only once as a designation, whose significance is evidently solar ; while in Lamentations it is found twice, and designates God.

In the Psalms, however, to make up for the previous (and subsequent) infrequent use, it appears on twenty-two occasions, often alternating or in association with the name Jehovah.

To interpret these several uses, it is necessary to consider the relations of early Christianity to its pagan surroundings.

Here, as nations were converted, their public festivals were retained, probably because the uneducated masses were incorrigibly wedded to the same. But they were retained as Christian feasts under a modified or new designation, and with a changed, a Christianized name.

Indeed, even between Christian sectaries this system of compromise was carried on at first — witness the reconciliation of the for a time separated followers of S.S. Peter and Paul, commemorated in the festival common to both of these apostles, while each retained his separate feast.

From the time of Abraham to the time of David, the word *Helion* only appears on two occasions in the Hebrew Scriptures as a name of God.

It is so used by Melchizedek and Balaam, and that is all.

By the prophetic and historical writers it is not even once (significant fact!) so applied. But in Lamentations it appears in this relation twice.

So that in the Pentateuch, the Psalms and Lamentations alone is the word *Helion* found as a divine appellation.

But amongst these, its relatively frequent recurrence in the Psalms is suggestive; while the fact that it is never so used with the definite article, though otherwise employed therewith, is very instructive.

In reading the Pentateuch, it is noticeable that God is first called Elohim, then Jehovah Elohim, and then Jehovah.

Of these, Elohim is in the plural, and really signifies gods. So that, philologically viewed, the

action of a plurality of gods seems to be first indicated, one of which gradually assumes prominence
amongst these, and finally supersedes the others—
which was, perhaps, the view of the writer, since
angels are called Elohim (Ps. viii. 5), as also are
spirits (1 Sam. xxviii. 13); for he may have held
that angelic beings were employed by God to carry
out his will, under whom the subordinated spiritual,
and material or natural physical forces acted; indeed he seems directly to affirm this when he places
in the mouth of Elohim the words, " Let us make
man ;" while, historically viewed, these several designations seem to have been subsequently so combined and interchanged by successive editors as to
make them appear to have always been attributive
designations of a single Deity—the one God of the
Jews, or God ; and the recorded names of other subordinate gods (angels or spirits), as the god *Shaddai,*
" God Almighty," have been similarly treated.

Here a compromise is clearly indicated as having
been effected, by which the worshippers of many
gods were brought to the worship of the one God—
worshipping him under the names of the many now
attributed to and disappearing in the one, as Jupiter
melted into Jove.

From the time of Abraham downwards, this spirit
of compromise has been at work.

In his time many gods were worshipped—each family, tribe or region having its ancestral, tribal or territorial god.

Amongst these was the god *Helion*, clearly associated by Isaiah (xiv. 14) with the sun, whom David in a spirit of conciliation sought, and successfully sought, to identify with Jehovah, that the followers of Helion, with the worshippers of the sun, might be thus gradually weaned from their idolatry and brought to the worship of the one God.

Until his time there had been a struggle between the worshippers of Helion, whose worship was associated with that of the sun, and those of Jehovah, whose worship was closely allied with the phases of the moon. And the first trace of this struggle is seen in the account of the interview between Abraham and Melchizedek.

Abram was so called because "he exalted the Father"—the fatherhood of God. His name was changed to Abraham, not merely because he was to be the "father of many nations," nor even because that name could bear other apposite significances, but to withdraw attention from the central teaching of his life—the exaltation of the Father—to which the Nazarene sought to recall his hearers. "Your father, Abraham, rejoiced to see my day," said Jesus, playing, in Jewish fashion, upon the name

Abraham—*Ab*, father, *rah*, saw, *yomi*, my day—
with which he moreover associated the name Isaac,
"rejoiced."

When this inverview took place, the victorious
patriarch was returning with the released captives
and the captured and re-captured spoil. He was a
conqueror—a conqueror who had, as it were by
magic, overcome a greatly superior force; and
magical was divine action in those days amongst
such as were ignorant of the true God—was the
channel through which the gods were held to exercise their power.

Was it strange, then, that the priest of the god
through whose territory he was passing, whose
honour he had vindicated and whose wrongs he
had avenged, should come out to meet and render
him homage in the name of his god, by presenting
bread and wine, and offering tribute?

Such at any rate was what happened, if written
words, rightly—that is, idiomatically—read, are to
be believed; for the narrative says, "And Melchizedek, king of Salem, brought forth bread and wine.
And he was priest of the god Helion. And he
knelt to him, and said, Homaged is Abram of the
god Helion, Ransomer of heaven and earth (which
the sun is daily, redeeming both from the darkness
of night). And homaged is the god Helion, who

hath charmed (i.e. by enchantment delivered) thine enemies into thy hands. And he gave him tribute of all."

Here Melchizedek assumes that his god, Helion, had given Abram the victory.

The patriarch is not said to have rejected the proffered tribute. He may have accepted it as marking emphatically to all the subjection of Helion to Jehovah; which he openly declares presently, in saying to the king of Sodom, "I lift my hand to Jehovah, the God of Helion, the Ransomer of heaven and earth," in which words he transfers the attributes claimed for Helion to Jehovah, and thus shows that the victory was really due to the latter.

CORPUS EUCHARISTICUM—THE PASCHAL "BODY."

A PROBLEM IN BIBLE INTERPRETATION.

Definitions.

The Passover, a feast of the Jews ; and the lamb, so called, of God, killed, before the destruction of the temple, for, and eaten by, every Jewish household in Jerusalem on the first day of the feast.

The Paschal Body, the body of the Passover or Paschal lamb, duly slaughtered and sacrificed.

The Eucharistic Body, the *Mazza* or unleavened bread reserved and set apart for the purpose before the celebration, and, at the appointed time, eaten as and in place of the Paschal Body.

The Paschal Body could only be eaten by those keeping the feast at Jerusalem.

The Eucharistic Body could only be eaten by those celebrating the feast away from Jerusalem.

To eat the Eucharistic Body at Jerusalem, or the

Paschal Body away from Jerusalem, was equally to break the law.

Constitution, by Dedication or Consecration.

The Passover or Paschal lamb was constituted by selection and dedication or consecration for the purpose; when it became, and was known as and called, the " Passover" of him by or for whom it had been so set apart.

The prescriptions of the Mishnah are very strict in this regard.

The Paschal Body was constituted by the due slaughtering and sacrificing of the duly constituted Passover; after which it became, and was known as and upon occasion called, the " Body" of him by or for whom it had been duly dedicated, slaughtered and sacrificed.

The prescriptions of the Mishnah are equally clear in this regard.

The Eucharistic Body was constituted by the due reserving and setting apart of the *Mazza*, or un-leavened bread, duly selected to take the place of and represent the Paschal Body at the celebration of the feast.

Now a half mazza is used for the purpose, to remind the celebrants that they are partaking of a maimed and mutilated rite.

The Celebration of the Feast *obligatory.*

The Paschal feast was a feast of obligation. The due keeping thereof was enjoined on all.

It could only be celebrated as a Passover at Jerusalem.

Hence the children of Israel were obliged to go up to the holy city to keep the Passover.

But many Jews were unable to go up to Jerusalem for that purpose.

These also were required to celebrate the feast ; but could not sacrifice the Paschal lamb and keep it as a Passover.

The alternative Fulfilment of the Obligation.

Hence the Paschal obligation came to be, could be, fulfilled in either of two ways.

At Jerusalem, by partaking of the Paschal Body of the celebrant at the close of the Paschal supper, when the giver of the feast shared his " Body " with those keeping it with him, who all then and there ate thereof in common. After which partaking, the eating of anything else was forbidden at that meal.

This celebration was known as and called the keeping of the Passover. And all zealous Jews made a point of so keeping the feast.

Away from Jerusalem, by partaking of the representative Paschal "Body" of the celebrant at the close of the Paschal supper, when the giver of the feast brought the reserved *Mazza,* previously selected for and so dedicated to the purpose, from the place where it had been carefully deposited and concealed, and taking it out of the white linen cloth in which it had been folded, broke and shared it, as his representative "Body," with those celebrating the feast with him, who all then and there ate thereof in common. After which partaking it was equally unlawful to eat anything else at that meal.

This celebration was known as and called the celebration of the *Mazza,* and was, so to say, *the Jewish Mass.* It was the familiar celebration of many, probably of most, as it now is of all Jews; certainly of the non-zealous, who would easily find excuses not to go up to Jerusalem to keep the feast.

The alternative Celebration of the Feast.

Owing to this two-fold celebration, the feast took its name according to the place and method of celebration; and hence was known in Jerusalem, and by those who went up to Jerusalem to keep it, as the feast of the Passover; while away from Jerusalem, and to those who celebrated it out of the holy city, it became and was the feast of the Mazza, the Jewish Mass.

But at either celebration the "Body" of the celebrant had to be shared with, and partaken of, and
eaten by all—at the one his actual, at the other his
representative Paschal Body.

The Attention concentrated on the Mazza.

Now **as** unleavened bread was eaten, could only
be eaten at each of these celebrations, as well as
throughout the subsequent week ; and as the searching for and destroying of leaven and leavened bread
was a formal ceremonial act, strictly prescribed and
rigorously carried out in every household, the attention of the observer was concentrated on the Mazza;
so that at length, even in Jerusalem, the feast came
to be indiscriminately called the feast of the Passover and the feast of the **Mazza ; just** as either
celebration had come to be known as the celebra-
tion of the **Passover or of** the Mazza respectively.
And at length, after the destruction of the temple
and final dispersion of the Jews, when the keeping
of the Passover ceased, the celebration of the Mazza
necessarily took its place and became universal.

The Cause of the two Methods of Celebration.

The two-fold character of the Paschal celebration
was due primarily to the double obligation of eating
the Passover with **mazzas** instead of leavened bread

at the appointed time, and of eating mazzas instead
of leavened bread during the whole of the ensuing
week ; and, in the second place, to the restriction
of only eating the Passover at Jerusalem, which
necessarily led to a celebration of the feast through
a representative Paschal Body by those away from
the holy city.

The representative Mazza.

This representative celebration of the Passover
led to a distinction between the Pascho-mazzal
supper and all the subsequent mazzal meals of the
Paschal season, analogous to the distinction between
the Paschal supper and the subsequent mazzal meals
at Jerusalem.

Under this distinction the Pascho-mazzal supper,
at which the reserved mazza was broken and distributed, and taken and eaten as the Paschal Body of
the celebrant, was known as and called the feast or
celebration of the Mazza, and was, so to say, the
Jewish Mass. Whereas at the subsequent mazzal
meals, *the* Mazza, the representative "Mazza," like
the "Passover" it had represented, ceased to be the
central object of attention, and was lost sight of in
the ordinary mazzas of the continued feast.

The representative Mazza not blessed.

This distinction was realized and expressed in a very marked way ; for *the* Mazza, the representative Paschal Body, was not blessed before it was broken ; was not blessed because it represented the " Body of the Passover," and was no longer considered bread.

And that it might not be blessed, might be excluded from the blessing pronounced on breaking the mazzas at the beginning of the supper, it was removed from the table before the ceremonial meal commenced.

In this way *the* Mazza, the representative Mazza, was distinguished from all other mazzas, both at the celebration and throughout the week ; for these were blessed at the commencement of each meal.

The blessing of Bread and Wine at Meals obligatory on the Jew.

The Jewish custom is obligatory here ; for the blessing and breaking of bread is the religious act by which the principal meal of the day is commenced in all Hebrew households.

The blessing and passing round of the cup always follows the blessing and breaking of bread, and is of equal obligation.

These acts were done by the head of the family, or, at his invitation, by the guest of highest rank present.

The representative Wine not blessed.

As regards the wine, also, there was a wide distinction between the usage at the Paschal supper and at every other meal throughout the year ; for whereas at the ordinary meal the cup was blessed, and passed round to each in succession, at the Paschal supper each had his own cup, and the representative cup was not blessed.

The representative cup was the second of the four ceremonial cups of wine which were prescribed for each person at the Paschal supper. And the usage in its regard was peculiar.

All at table, having previously reclined like royal personages, rose on filling the representative cup, and, each with uplifted cup, chanted the customary ritual, and at the commemoration of the plagues of Egypt—from the last of which their ancestors were spared by the sprinkling of the blood of the Passover—dipping a finger in the uplifted cup, each in his own cup, sprinkled some of the wine, of the representative blood, in the prescribed way.

Of the remaining ceremonial cups, the third, which was blessed, was called "the cup of blessings," as commemorating the many favours conferred by God on his chosen people ; and the **fourth, "the** cup of cursings," because **with it they** invoked his anger on **their enemies.**

The peculiar Characteristics of the Jewish Mass.

Thus **the** peculiar characteristic of the celebration of the Mazza was this, that the bread and wine which represented the body and blood of the Passover were not blessed, because they were no longer looked upon as bread and wine, but were the representative body and blood ; and that the representative blood was sprinkled at **the** beginning **of the** supper, indeed before its commencement as a meal, **and** then drank to remind the celebrants, who could not otherwise **have** partaken thereof, that it was not actual but representative blood used as a commemorative ceremonial act—though the cup was immediately carefully cleansed, because its contents had represented blood, and the following cup blessed ; while the representative body was eaten at the close **of the** supper, in fulfilment of the obligation.

*The Distinctions between **the** Paschal Supper and **an** ordinary Meal.*

As a meal, the celebration, whether by the " Passover" or the " Mazza," partook of the characteristics and shared the ceremonial of an ordinary Jewish meal.

As a feast, it modified this ceremonial usage, and grafted on to it a ceremonial and usage of its own.

Now every Jewish meal commenced, as has been already stated, with the blessing and breaking of bread and the blessing of wine.

But there were two distinguishing features here. For, as regards the bread, it was the custom of the Jews at their ordinary meals to reserve some of that which had been blessed, and leave it on the table for the sick, the poor, and those who might come later, which was not done at the Paschal supper. While, as regards the wine, whereas at the ordinary meal each partook of the one cup, which was passed round after having been blessed, as has been already noticed, at the Paschal supper each drank from his own cup, as just mentioned.

The Paschal Feast the Commemoration of a Passover.

The all-important point to remember, in considering this festive celebration of the Jews, is that the feast is of the Passover ; and that its intent is to remind its observers not merely of the first-born having been passed over and spared in Egypt, but of their ancestors passing over, immediately afterwards, from bondage to freedom. For the Passover was to the Israelites the great festival of national emancipation.

In this regard it is useful to remember that the Hebrew verb *pasach*, "to pass over," is kindred in meaning with the Hebrew verb *habar*—as a proper name read *Eber*—from which the children of Israel, through the patriarch's remote ancestor of that name, derived their designation as Hebrews; and that the Hebrews are thus distinguished by their name as unsettled people, pilgrims or wanderers.

A Passover to spiritual Bondage.

As though presaging the physical bondage into which the children of Israel passed later, the descendants of Eber passed over into spiritual bondage —a bondage in which trustful dependence on the Father of all was transformed into and supplanted by a deprecatory worship of territorial and other deities.

A Passover to spiritual Freedom.

In Abram, a descendant of Eber, who, with his immediate relatives, migrated from Ur of the Chaldees, and so passed over from spiritual bondage to the freedom of those who trust solely in God, we find the first emancipated Hebrew.

His name, indeed, expresses in what his emanci-

pation consisted ; for *Ab-ram* says, not merely
" Exalted Father," but " He exalted the Father."
And it would appear that it was to this fact in the
life, and to this sense of the name, that Jesus of
Nazareth pointed when he said, " Your father Abraham rejoiced to see (or show forth) my day ;" for
the exaltation of the Father was the teaching and
the practice of his life.

A Succession of Scriptural Passovers.

A succession of passings over is recorded in the
Old Testament history.

Cain was passed over and Abel accepted, in their
respective offerings—because Cain, as the first-born,
claimed spiritual and sacerdotal prerogatives.

Ishmael was passed over and Isaac made the
child of promise—Isaac, the " Mocker" or " shower
forth," who acted the part of the model or representative child of God and typical man, by his
absolute surrender of self, even unto death, and
complete submission to his father, even in the
acceptance of the wife that father chose for him ;
and by preferring the naturally endowed to the
spiritually aspiring of his children.

Esau was passed over and Jacob preferred—
Jacob, " the Crooked," who by fraudulent devices
took advantage of his father, his brother and his

father-in-law, that he might acquire spiritual privileges and material possessions; and, succeeding in his aspirations, left his descendants an easy prey to physical and spiritual bondage.

The Hebrew first-born were passed over, and those of the Egyptians slain, that the children of Israel might pass from physical bondage to national **freedom,** a freedom which led to and ended in spiritual **slavery.**

The tribes of Simeon and Levi were passed over that the Messianic promises might be realized through **that of Judah,** and the children of Israel pass once more from spiritual bondage to freedom.

Thus the act of passing over, of Hebraizing, so to say, was a prominent feature in the symbolical history of the **Jews.**

The last Supper, a Passover and a Mass.

The last supper of Jesus of Nazareth was **a Paschal** celebration. It was the celebration of a Passover, the institution of a passing over.

Moreover, it was a celebration of a peculiar character, whose characteristics point to the real nature **of the** passing over whose institution it symbolized.

One of the meanings of the Hebrew verb *pasach* is very suggestive in this regard; for it is sometimes used in the sense "to palm off on" or pass off one

for another, which was precisely what happened
when Jacob was passed over Esau that he might
fraudulently obtain his father's blessing ; and again
at the Passover in Egypt, when the blood of the
" Passover" was palmed off upon the destroying
angel as the blood of the first-born he was commanded to destroy, who was thereupon held by him
to have been slain and be already dead.

This supper, eaten at Jerusalem, was closed as a
celebration of the Mazza, that is as a Jewish Mass.

Now to close the Paschal supper at Jerusalem
with the Mazza celebration was, while passing one
thing off for another, to break, to defy the law as
authoritatively interpreted.

And that this celebration was regarded as a breach
and defiance of the law is suggested by a statement
in the apocryphal Gospel of Joseph of Arimathea.
For if Judas was the near relative and paid spy of
the high-priest, who followed Jesus to report him as
a breaker of the law, his rising instantly from the
table on receiving the sop, and proceeding at once
to inform his employer of what had happened,
shows how the act just accomplished would be and
was interpreted.

Thus the passing over which then took place was
a passing over the law ; so that the institution associated with it was the passover or supplanter of the

legal celebration ; and the commemoration added thereto that of **the** passing over **from** the bondage of the law to the freedom of the divine sonship.

*The Roman **Mass** comprises an amalgamated Jewish Ritual.*

The last supper of Jesus of Nazareth, whatever its **actual or** attributed significance may have been, **is thus seen** to have culminated in the celebration of the Mazza.

This celebration of the Mazza, whatever its conventional meaning **and** value may **be, is** renewed, and commemorated, and perpetuated in and **by the Catholic** celebration **of the Mass.**

Bearing **this in** mind, it **is significant, and** perhaps neither **unexpected nor surprising,** to find that the ceremonial **acts and representative ritual** of the Roman Mass are so like unto as to be reflections, **if** not reproductions, **of** the ceremonial acts or representative **ritual of the** Jewish celebration.

Remembering this and **the** two-fold character of **the Jewish** celebration, **and** viewing these actions **as** such **reflections or** reproductions, **the Roman** Mass **is** found, **as was to be expected, to** have combined and blended the **ceremonial ritual acts of** the Jewish diurnal blessing **and breaking of bread,** and blessing **of the cup, with those of the** annual celebration of the Mazza, or Jewish Mass, in its own single celebration; and this in such wise that either modifies the other, so as to form a congruous whole.

The Roman Mass of the Pre-sanctified.

This is clearly brought out by comparing the ceremonial ritual of the Mass of the pre-sanctified, as the Roman Catholic Good Friday's Mass is termed, with that of the ordinary daily masses of the year.

The Mass of the pre-sanctified is clearly shown by its ceremonial acts to have taken the place of, and so to reproduce, the annual celebration of the Mazza; while the diurnal masses replace the daily breaking of bread. For the Mass of the pre-sanctified, as its name implies, is celebrated with a mazza, or unleavened altar bread, which was consecrated for the purpose on the previous day; whereas all other masses are celebrated by the breaking and eating (by the celebrant) of an altar bread blessed and consecrated at the service at which it is to be consumed.

The Roman Consecration represents the Jewish Dedication.

The consecration of the host is effected by the taking of the mazza, or wafer altar bread, in both hands, and holding it in a prescribed way, and while so holding it pronouncing the words, "This is my body;" after which the thus consecrated host—as the mazza or wafer so set apart is termed—which is to take the place of the "Body" at the Mass of the pre-sanctified, is carefully folded up in a white linen cloth, and borne to and hidden away in the place appointed for the purpose, incongruously termed the sepulchre, since the crucifixion it is held to follow is not supposed to take place until the morrow, when it is solemnly fetched forth, and borne to the altar, and formally broken and consumed.

Here the consecration represents the Jewish dedication, when the selected mazza is set apart as the representative Paschal Body of the celebrant ; and then the folding up, and the concealing, and afterwards the fetching, breaking and consuming (without blessing—that is, consecration), are exact copies of the Jewish ceremonial.

But the act of consecration is preceded by and combined with the ceremonial ritualistic acts of the diurnal blessing and breaking of bread, and of the blessing of the cup.

The Jewish Ceremonial at the Breaking of Bread.

The Jewish diurnal ceremonial at the breaking of bread is always performed in a prescribed way.

The bread, chosen for the purpose and as shapely as possible, is first indented with a non-cutting instrument, as the edge of a plate, in the form of a rude cross, that it may break evenly and without crumbling.

The Good Friday cross-buns may be a reminiscence, or even a survival, of this custom—save that they are indented before baking.

Then the celebrant spreads both hands over it with the fingers extended and apart—to signify the ten species of grain of which bread that can be blessed may be made—and, slowly and reverently pronouncing the blessing, lifts it up with both hands, that all may see ; and then formally breaking it, and breaking off and taking a small portion himself, just as the Roman priest breaks off the fragment which he puts into the consecrated wine in the chalice, proceeds to break off a portion for, and pass the broken bread round to, or place it before each one at table, that all may take and eat thereof, and so partake of the one bread with him. And this passing round is from left to right, just as the Roman priest gives the consecrated wafers to communicants at the altar rails—when he passes from his left to his right.

Roman Ceremonial of the Mass identical with the Jewish.

The ceremonial acts at the blessing and breaking of bread in the Roman Church are practically identical with those of the Jews.

When about to say or sing his mass, the priest selects a mazza or wafer altar bread of perfect form and frees it from all loose particles or crumbs, and, before commencing the service, indents it with the edge of the paten, also in an imperfect crucial form, that it may be broken evenly, and a piece broken off therefrom with a clean fracture, to be put into the chalice.

Then, while the as yet unconsecrated mazza or wafer is lying in the paten on the altar, he spreads his hands over it, with the fingers extended and apart, as he pronounces the equivalent of the Jewish blessing ; after which, taking it in both hands in the prescribed way and concentrating his attention on the act he is performing, he slowly, and pausing between each, utters the words of consecration— *Hoc est enim corpus meum*—and, first genuflecting, immediately uplifts the now consecrated host with both hands, his head reverently bent, just as does the Jewish celebrant, though now not that all may see, but that all may, like and with himself, devoutly adore. And in each and all of these ceremonial acts the Roman priest does as did and does the head of each Jewish household at the commencement of the first or principal meal of the day.

So again, in consecrating the Roman chalice, each ritual act in succession is precisely that of the ceremonial blessing of the Jewish cup.

Even at the *lavabo*, or washing of hands before the blessing and consecration, the ceremonial usage is identical, the water being poured over the fingers to carry away any impurity; and these are then held with their tips uplifted till duly dried, to prevent the water running back and re-polluting their surface.

While in the ablutions of the chalice, after partaking of the consecrated wine, the first, which is of unmixed wine, represents the cup of blessings; and the second, of wine and water, the cup of cursings, at the celebration of the Paschal supper.

Roman Dry Masses.

The Roman Church attaches so much importance to these ceremonial practices, that its newly ordained or about to be ordained priests are taught them in a series of so called " Dry Masses," at which the words of consecration are omitted, that the would-be celebrant may, by this training, acquire a perfect knowledge of the ritualistic observances **to** the performance of which **he** is ordained.

The Roman High, Low and Pontifical Masses, Jewish in Type.

Even the distinction between low and high Mass and an episcopal function, follows that between the Jewish diurnal and festal celebrations and those at which a rabbi of distinction officiates—the modifications introduced in succession in the ritualistic acts being respectively precisely similar.

The Roman a Transcript of the Jewish Mass.

It would **thus appear that the Roman** Catholic celebration of the Mass is a reproduction **in a** modified form of the Jewish celebration of the Mazza.

The ritualistic similarities between these celebra**tions** are so abundant and marked, as clearly **to** establish the derivation and descent of the one from **the other.**

The Jewish father of a family chooses a bread of shapely appearance, and unbroken ; though in cases of necessity a broken bread can be used.

The Roman priest selects an altar bread of perfect form, and carefully frees it from loose particles ; but if only imperfect breads are at hand, he selects from these the most perfect.

The Jew indents his bread in a rudely crucial form with the edge of a plate.

The Roman priest marks his wafer in a similar manner with the edge of the paten.

The Jew is required to wash his hands before blessing the bread, by the pouring of water over them, and then to hold them uplifted till thoroughly dried by the napkin used for the purpose.

The Roman priest is enjoined to wash and dry his hands before consecrating his altar bread, under precisely the same conditions.

The Jew is instructed how to direct his eyes during, and to fix his attention on, the act he is performing.

So also is the Roman priest.

The Jew places both hands with fingers extended over the bread he is about to bless, and, having pronounced the blessing, immediately raises it with both hands from the table, that all may see.

The Roman priest places both hands similarly over the wafer about to be consecrated, while saying the prayer substituted for the Jewish blessing ; and immediately after the consecration uplifts it with both hands above the level of his head, not that all may see, but that all may adore with him.

The Jew at an ordinary meal prepares the cup and pours the wine into it himself. But upon high festivals this is done for him by servers, who hand the prepared cup to him. And the same servers on these occasions prepare and hand him the bread.

This also is the custom in the Roman Church.

The Jew having reverently blessed the cup, lifts it up with his right hand, carefully steadying it with the left placed under the right to support the stem.

The Roman priest, after consecrating the wine, elevates the chalice in a similar manner.

The Jew having formally broken the bread, breaks off a small piece, which he retains and eats.

The Roman priest also, after having formally broken the consecrated wafer, breaks off a small piece. But instead of eating the fragment thus broker off, he deposits it in the chalice.

With this the analogy ceases; for while the Jew merely eats the fragment of bread he has retained, with a little salt, and drinks from the cup, passing both bread and wine round that all at table with him may do as he has done—eat of the one bread and drink of the one cup in common, and so be all in communion with him and with each other—the Roman priest eats the whole of the bread he has broken, and drinks the whole of the wine himself; the ablutions following representing the third and fourth Paschal cups.

Sundry Differences between the Jewish and Roman Celebrations.

The identity in ceremonial ritual between the Jewish and the Roman celebrations speaks for itself.

But with this identity there are two wide differences. For the Jew can only celebrate the Mazza once annually, on the evening of the 14th Nissan, the equivalent of Good Friday; while the Roman priest can and does celebrate the Mass daily. And the Jew does not and cannot adore the blessed bread and wine, since to do this would be to worship material elements, which is forbidden by the law; whereas the Roman Catholic must worship and adore these.

The consecrated Elements not always worshipped at the Mass.

Evidence is not wanting, however, to show that, whatever the Roman Catholic may have done, the Catholic did not always worship the consecrated elements.

The custom of the Greek Church is conclusive here; for though it reserves the consecrated bread, its members do not worship the same during the Mass or afterwards. So far are they from this, that they do not even show it the same reverence they give to their sacred pictures and relics.

The custom of the Anglican Church is not less conclusive. For in it the consecrated bread is neither reserved nor worshipped, save by those with Romanizing tendencies.

Not even in the Roman Church.

But even in the Roman Church itself evidence exists that, whatever reverence may have been shown to the consecrated elements, there was a time in the history of that Church when they were not worshipped.

This is found in a change which has taken place in the ordinary of the Mass.

To those familiar with the service of the Roman Mass it must sometimes seem strange that the *Ite missa est*, said or sung by the officiating priest at the close thereof, precedes the benediction.

It is strange ; for these words—now interpreted, " Go ye ; it is sent," and read in the sense, " Go, you are dismissed"—as then uttered seem to invite the worshippers to depart without receiving the benediction.

But were these words always so placed ? And did they always bear the same sense ?

Hardly ! For they have been found to precede

the Canon of the Mass in some uses; and were then evidently addressed to catechumens and other un-baptized persons, who were not permitted to be present at the celebration of the " Mysteries"—as this communion service had already come to be called—because not yet admitted to communion.

These were then dismissed with the intimation, "Go, it is the Mass." So that this dismissal, as then used, was given before and not after the Mass; and was then as appropriate as it was intelligible.

The Mass at first only a social Communion Service.

But, for such a dismissal to have been possible, the Mass must have been regarded simply as a communion service, at which all present partook of the blessed and broken bread and of the blessed wine ; at which the only irreverence contemplated was that of being present without partaking.

This view of the service embodied a partial truth with a primary error ; for it shows that admission to Church membership was then required as a con-dition antecedent to admission to communion. But beyond this it indicates that the consecrated ele-ments could not have been worshipped at that time, since non-communicants were excluded from the service, instead of being commanded to be present, as was later the case.

When the irreverence of attending the Mass without joining in the communion was permitted and made obligatory, the Latin Church practically admitted that, according to its then and thus introduced novel theory, it had hitherto been guilty of the criminal irreverence of prohibiting a worship it at length claimed as the due of the consecrated elements.

When this grave alteration was made, the necessity for removing the dismissal to the non-communicants from before the Canon to the close of the service was recognized, that it might be accepted as a permission to all to withdraw. And with this the Roman use received its present form.

The Change in the Meaning of the Institution.

Does not such an alteration point to a change as having passed over the attributed meaning and intent of the original institution?

The nature of this change is self-evident.

Before it took place, all present at the celebration joined in the feast and shared in the meal, or were communicants.

After it took place, only a chosen few joined in the feast and shared in the meal, or were communicants; the remainder of the congregation becoming simply worshippers.

The Meaning and Process of this Change—a growing Reverence.

The meaning and process of this change are not far to seek.

The growing reverence for the act, now imputed to the elements shared at the Mass, at length required that they should be worshipped—worshipped by all, even by those pronounced unworthy to partake of the same.

This growing reverence was to cause, had caused, a yet further change in practice.

The communicants were no longer permitted to handle the consecrated bread. It was now placed in their mouths by the distributor. And the cup was withheld from them in the Latin Church.

This growing reverence had already caused the bread to be no longer broken for the people. It was made into small mazzas of the required size—nummular mazzas or white wafers.

A larger mazza or wafer of similar description was consecrated by the priest for himself; and this was the mazza that was formally broken.

Thus the breaking of the bread became a mere form—this through reverence, lest crumbs should fall to the ground.

The cup had been similarly withheld—lest its contents should be spilt.

The successive Steps in the growing Reverence.

The first step in this reverence was the careful handling of the mazza or wafer that was to be consecrated and broken.

Then its careful marking or indentation where it was to be broken, to cause a clean fracture, and so prevent crumbs.

But especially the careful cleansing of the chalice *after* its consecrated contents had been drank.

The mysterious attributed Consequences.

The method of consecration, the spreading of the hands of the consecrator over the consecrating, the uplifting of the consecrated elements—in which this reverence increased until it culminated—all tended to the conviction that some mysterious effect resulted from and through the consecration ; which was at length believed to be a change, a supernatural and magical change in the substance of the elements that had been consecrated—such a change as demanded that they should be worshipped.

And hence it came to be believed that the consecrated elements always had been uplifted that they might be reverently adored.

And hence, when they were uplifted, all were enjoined reverently to adore and worship them.

And upon this, all who had been previously excluded from the Mass were commanded to remain and take part in this act of worship.

Reverence—misinterpreted.

And yet the several successive acts of reverence which led up to and confirmed the view that a change was produced in the substance of the consecrated elements by the act of consecration, and were therefore held not merely to sanction but to demand the formal worship of the same, were simply borrowed from, and absolutely continuations of, the Jewish practice at the blessing or consecration of bread and wine. So that, since the Jews contemplated no change in the consecrated elements, offered no worship to them, were precluded by their faith from worshipping the divine in and through the material, the reverence with which they treated the blessed bread and wine could not, because continued in the Christian blessing and breaking of bread and pouring out and blessing of wine, authorize the view that the act of consecration produced a change in

H

the consecrated elements, still less a change which entitled them to be worshipped.

Thus the reverent treating of the consecrated elements teaches nothing in this regard ; and, in so far as it has been held to sanction the Roman Catholic belief here, has had a force imputed to it which it did not possess.

The Ritual of Institution.

The institution of the Christian communion service, whatever its original meaning and intent may have been, passed, as to its form, from the Jewish to the Catholic Mass through the last supper of Jesus of Nazareth.

The Jewish ceremonial ritual is, in the main, perpetuated in it.

The inference, therefore, is, that this ritual was the basis of the institution.

That it was the basis of the institution, evidence is not wanting.

The Jewish ceremonial Ritual used by Jesus of Nazareth.

This evidence is found in the statement of the evangelist, that Jesus said, after blessing and passing round the cup at his last supper—which cup, as following the cup of blessings, was the fourth Paschal cup—" I will no more drink of the fruit of the vine until that day when I drink it new in the kingdom of God." For he had just pronounced the words of the blessing of the wine, the Jewish formula for which terminates with the acknowledgment, "who createst the fruit of the vine ;" so that the peculiar idiom, "fruit of the vine," would seem to have been suggested by the words he had just repeated.

An Inference, a Declaration and a Record.

At any rate, we find in this remarkable statement an inference, a declaration and a record of great significance.

The inference is, that he drank of the cup before passing it round, as both usage and prescription required ; just as they required that he should take of the bread before offering it to his disciples, that they might all partake thereof.

The declaration, that he expected to drink wine in his Father's kingdom.

The record, that he still treated the blessed or consecrated wine *as wine*, which is a very, important fact.

The Roman held to be the Mass of Jesus.

It is essential to remember, in considering this institution, that the Mass is held to be the doing of

that which Jesus of Nazareth did at his last supper ;
a doing in commemoration, first of his doing, and
then of his dying—as his legacy to his disciples ;
and to be his memorial and the celebration of his
memory.

What Jesus did at his last Supper.

We are told what Jesus did.

After supper, that is *at the time appointed for the
eating of the Paschal Body—of his Paschal Body—*
he took a bread, a mazza, for no other bread was
permitted at the Paschal season, and blessed, and
broke, and gave it to his disciples ; placed it before
them, according to usage, and said, " Take (so that
he neither placed it in the hand nor in the mouth),
eat." And then (that is after, and only after, he had
bidden them take and eat—after they had eaten or
constructively eaten, as he had commanded—at the
very least, as they were taking to eat) added, " This
is my body." So that if these words, so called of
consecration, did more than signify the meaning of
the act, did more than signify that the broken mazza
represented his Paschal Body, which he ought then
and there to have given them, he commanded them
to eat that which, though he had blessed, he had
not yet consecrated.

Then he took the cup, and, having blessed it,

passed it round to his disciples with the words, "Drink ye all of it" (all, as though foreseeing that some would thereafter be deprived thereof); adding (again after having commanded the drinking), "This is my blood of the New Testament which is shed for many" (St. Luke, "for you") "for the remission of sins."

For the remission of sins. These words are suggestive; and, when the various readings of the utterance are considered, it is hardly possible to avoid the conclusion that, as uttered, it conveyed to its hearers the sense—This, which is poured out for you, is my blood of the New Covenant of the forgiveness of sins.

The act is the interpreter of the words and the witness to their bearing here.

The Meaning of his Institution.

These words, read them as one will, imply, what they must when uttered have clearly expressed, the meaning of the institution.

Under the Jewish law there was no forgiveness. Sin, once committed, must be expiated. An eye for an eye, and a tooth for a tooth, were its prescriptions. This was the Old Covenant of expiation and atonement.

This unforgiving Covenant Jesus then and thus

passed over and set aside; substituting the New Covenant of the forgiveness of sins as a step towards universal love.

The Catholic Communion of Jesus of Nazareth.

This communion of Jesus was called catholic, or **universal,** because all who so desired were to partake thereof, in contradistinction to the commandment and custom of the Jews only to break bread, to eat and drink, with those of the household of the faith. And **to do** as he had done, to break bread with all, even with such traitors as Judas, was what he commanded when he said, " Do this in remembrance of me."

The agapés, or love-feasts of the early Christians, were the natural outcome of this teaching ; and **it may well have been** that the licentiousness imputed to these **assemblies originated in** the minds of the **imputers,** and was due to the growing antagonistic spirit of asceticism, which made its votaries more and more intolerant of any giving way to the affec- **tions,** however innocent.

The Institution, the Supercession of Sacrifice.

The fulness of the supercession, of the abolition of the Old Covenant here is shown in the superces- **sion and abolition of the sacrificial** act, by the sub- stitution of bread and wine for the body and blood of the Paschal lamb, that the very idea of sacrificial expiation and atonement might be blotted out from the minds of those who accepted his teaching and followed his example.

This supercession was by substitution, in condescension to that weakness of the nature of man, due to his evolutional creation, which makes it so difficult for him to free himself from the influence of hereditary training and habitual use ; that, by transforming the customary act, the mental attitude developed by it might be gradually changed, until, with the passing away of the original act, the idea connected with and associations springing from it should be blotted out together.

It was by a misguided extension of this method, by an inverted misapplication of it, that the doing away with the idea of the necessity for atonement by the commanding of forgiveness, was changed into the conception of an atonement accomplished once and for all, with all the abuses which have arisen therefrom.

The Idioms of Institution.

The words used in the supercession, moreover, lead to the recognition of an idiomatic usage of the Hebrew sacred Scriptures ; for David is reported to have said (2 Sam. xxiii. 17), on refusing the water

from the well of Bethlehem by the gate, procured
for him at the risk of the lives of the brave men
who had fetched it because he had expressed a
longing for the same—" Is not this the blood of the
men?"   Or, as in 1 Chron. xi. 19, "Shall I drink
the blood of these men?"

But, indeed, this idiom appears in the institution
of the Passover (Exod. xii. 13); where, however, it
has been overlooked and mistranslated even in the
Revised Version ; for Jehovah says, *not*, " The blood
shall be for a token to you," *but*, " Your blood [shall
be] for a token [to me]," as is confirmed by the
context.

The Hebrew phrase here is, *Had-dam lacem*, "the
blood of you" or "your blood ;" just as, in the head-
ings of the individual psalms, *Mizmor l'David*, "a
psalm of David."   And it is as improper to say,
" the blood to you," as it would be to read, "a psalm
to David."

What the Roman Priest does at his Mass.

We have seen what Jesus said and did at his
final celebration of the Paschal supper.

We have now to see how the Roman priest acts
at his celebration.

The Roman priest turns his back upon the people
when he says or sings his mass.

He eats the whole of the mazza (or wafer) he has blessed and broken, merely permitting those present at the time to worship the same.

He drinks the whole of the consecrated wine.

When there are communicants, he takes from the tabernacle a pyx containing reserved mazzas—mazzas reserved from some previous mass—and gives these, as far as his mass is concerned, unblessed, and certainly unbroken mazzas, one to each of the would-be communicants, placing them on the tongue.

But in so doing, so far from doing what Jesus did, he, in each and every particular, does the exact contrary.

The Roman Priest does the exact Contrary to Jesus.

The Roman Catholic priest does exactly the contrary to Jesus in his communion.

Does not pretend to deny that he does exactly the contrary to what Jesus did.

Rather justifies himself for so doing ; saying that his communion is a communion with Jesus, and that all who are admitted to communion with Jesus are in communion with each other ; so that it is the fault of those who are not admitted to communion with Jesus that they are not in communion with those who are—forgetting that the traitor Judas

was not excluded from his **community and com-**
munion.

The Universal changed into the Exclusive.

But by making the social communion of Jesus a
religious act ; by declaring the consecrated mazza
his body, the consecrated wine his blood ; by requir-
ing all to worship that of which only the few are
permitted to partake,—has not the Roman Church
changed the catholic, universal and all-embracing
communion of Jesus **into an exclusive** community,
and turned that which he intended to be a symbol
and bond of union, into a **token of separation, of
division, of disunion** and strife ?

Such certainly has been the **effect of changing a**
domestic **into a** formal act. Such **the** fruit of converting a social communion **into a ceremonial rite.**

The Roman Priest consecrates his own Body at Mass.

And yet the priest, who claims to enter into **com-**
munion with Jesus by eating his body and drinking
his blood, who claims to admit others to communion
with Jesus by giving them his body to eat, actually
eats and drinks that which he has formally declared
to be his own body and blood—actually gives to
others to eat that which he has by consecration
made, technically **and** by dedication made and

affirmed to be his own body; for in consecrating he says, "This is *my* body," "This is *my* blood," or words to that effect; and by so saying claims that they are, and by imputation makes them, what he declares them to be.

And even doing what he does as the representative of Jesus would only make them, in conformity with his own declaration, a representative body and representative blood.

His own representative Body.

In acting in conformity with his declaration he would be doing rightly, according to the practice of the Jews, as long as he recognized that the body he gave was a representative body, representing the body of his Passover, which was by dedication made the Paschal body of the giver.

But if so—and this, again, is a question of fact which each can verify for himself—is not the fact that the Roman priest consecrates, as Jesus did, by saying, "This is my body," "This is my blood," direct and conclusive evidence that when the custom originated, the body and blood given and taken were known to be, and given and taken as, the Paschal body and blood of the giver?

And is not this a further proof that when a change in practice was made, while it was making,

so to say, with a growing change in faith, the catechumens and others then held to be not fit for communion were excluded, because it was still understood that all present should partake? And that,
when at length the change in faith was fully accepted
by those in authority, all were required to be present
at the Mass, and worship that of which they were
not permitted to partake—the form of consecration
then coming to be regarded as something very like
a magical incantation.

Spiritual Evolution in the Catholic Church.

In the Catholic Church a process of spiritual
evolution has gradually converted the natural into
the supernatural by changing the social into the
religious.

The effects of an antecedent, an analogous evolution, had misled here. Antecedent misapprehensions
had misguided the workers and victims of the evolution.

An instance of these misapprehensions must be
noticed here, owing to its bearing on the general
question.

Attributive Divinization by Ex-deification.

Divers gods are spoken of and named in the
Book of Genesis.

These have been skilfully dealt with so as to make their names attributive designations of the one God of the Jews.

In this way "the god *Shaddai*" became "God Almighty ;" "the god *Helion*," "the most high God."

Under this view, Melchizedek, priest of the god *Helion*, became a priest of the most high God.

This priest came forth with bread and wine to render homage to Abram in the name of his god, Helion, and to offer him tribute.

This priest, under misapprehension viewed as a priest of the most high God offering bread and wine, at once became a typical character to a Church in a state of transition to a priesthood offering bread and wine.

Ecclesiastical Evolution in the Roman Catholic Church.

In such a state was the Church which became Catholic and Roman. And the several successive steps through which this transition in evolution passed in her appear to have been these.

The *Peter* or "First-born"—which is what this Hebrew word means ; that is, the *Presbuteros*, or "Elder" of the family, household or domestic circle— was the breaker of bread to that circle, unless a guest or guests were present, when the most worthy, at the invitation of the *Peter* or *Presbyter*, was the breaker of bread.

When domestic gatherings took place, the Peter of Peters, Presbyter of Presbyters, or Elder of Elders, was the breaker of bread, unless guests were present, when the one highest in rank took his place.

When congregational gatherings took the place of domestic assemblies, the Peter of Peters became the Presbyter or Elder of the congregation—the official celebrant of its communion and other services.

When the official celebrant was elected to his office, on the rule of seniority being set aside, he came to be looked upon as of priestly rank ; and had to be confirmed in his appointment, and then ordained to it by the overseer of the district or diocese.

The overseer or *Episkopos*, like the apostles, had no congregation of his own, but went from place to place, preaching in synagogues and elsewhere to Jew and Gentile, calling others to the faith, and confirming those already therein by joining in their gatherings and renewing their teachings.

When the Peters became priests, then the overseers became bishops, archbishops, patriarchs and the like ; and the supreme head in the see of Peter, as the Roman see came to be called, exclusively appropriated the title Peter (Pater), Papa or Pope.

This hierarchy rested on the idea of an accepted priesthood, of which the individual priest was the unit.

Its foundation was attributed to the risen Christ.

Of this hierarchy all were individual priests.

As priests they required a sacrifice.

As priests after the order of Melchizedek they must offer bread and wine.

These offerings, this sacrifice was found in the commemorative sacrifice of the Mazza—a celebration which had only been a commemorative sacrifice in this, that to the followers of Jesus it commemorated the abolition of all sacrifice—which then became the sacrifice of the Mass.

But there could be no sacrifice without a victim.

This victim was found in the Paschal body and blood of the celebrant of the Mass, now transformed into a sacrifice, which was regarded as the body and blood of Christ, whose sacrifice on the cross was thus constantly renewed and perpetuated.

The holiness of this victim required that the body and blood thereof should only be partaken of by the holy.

But to be holy, would-be partakers must be made holy.

They must be cleansed from the stain of original, that is of imputed sin, by baptism.

They must be purified from actual sin, committed subsequent to baptism, by priestly absolution.

They must renounce their own will, and then, imbued with the spirit of penance and asceticism, they might venture to become partakers of the body of the Lord at the holy sacrifice of the Mass, which consummated the attributed holiness. For through this partaking, worthy partaking, his holiness was imputed to them.

And finally, this victim, under this evolved view believed to be really present in the consecrated mazza, was necessarily worshipped at the holy sacrifice of the Mass.

Thus, as it would appear, was the holy sacrifice of the Mass made what it is, the centre and soul of Catholicism.

And yet this now and hence called holy sacrifice of the Mass was, at the outset and as instituted by Jesus, a social communion or feast of love, at which a mazza was used to replace the body of the Paschal lamb hitherto sacrificed by or for the celebrant of the feast ; its intent to remind the followers of Jesus that sacrifice was to pass away from them for ever.

The Mazza lost sight of in the Mass.

Is it due to the transformation thus set forth that
the meaning and derivation of the designation, Mass
have been lost sight of?

They ought not to have been, for in the New
Testament, as in the Old, mazzas are repeatedly
mentioned ; the feast of the Mazza is spoken of, the
celebration of the Mazza set forth.   But unfortu-
nately, following the Septuagint, on every occasion
when mention is made of the mazza, the word mazza
is, in all versions, translated instead of being preserved in the text, and so has passed through its
Greek representative into azyme, and been rendered
" unleavened bread."

And yet the word mazza is an ecclesiastical term
which, in the interests of unsectarian theology, it
would have been well to have preserved in the translation of the Bible, as, in its modified and arbitrarily
meaningless form, it has been outside thereof—in
the traditional name of the Christian Paschal, and
then of the Catholic daily breaking of bread.

As thus used, it is a term familiar to all Catholics,
to all Christians ; but, through the non-recognition
of its source, its relations to the same have, with its
meaning, been lost.

Had this term been preserved in the Bible—had

I

it been transferred **to the versions of** the New **Tes-**
tament—had it been reproduced therein, whether **as**
matsah, mazza, massa or mass, instead of translated
"unleavened bread"—it would have been palpable
to all that the Christian breaking of bread was an
adaptation of the Paschal celebration, combined
with a continuation in a modified form of the Jewish
diurnal custom in that regard ; and that the celebration of the Mass was a transformation of the
celebration of the Mazza.

NOTE.

The act of breaking bread was to the **Jew** an act of domestic
worship. When **a** meal was about **to commence, the** head **of**
the family (or most distinguished guest at his request), having
previously **washed his hands (as all** were bound to do before
placing **themselves at table), reverently** taking a whole bread
(though **a fragment may be used in case** of need), and partially
cutting or denting **it,** that **the fracture may** be a **clean** one,
places it before **himself, and** covering it with both hands
(**with** fingers extended and apart) **blesses** or consecrates **it** by
saying the words, " Blessed art thou, O Lord **our God,** King
of the world, who producest bread from the earth." To which
all respond " Amen."

Then taking up the thus consecrated bread **he** breaks off
the partially incised fragment, and dipping it in salt (or other
prescribed and prepared condiment) straightway **eats** the
same in silence.

He then breaks **off and** places a portion before each of the
assembled party, that all may themselves take and eat of
the consecrated bread, which should be consumed in silence,
before any other food is taken.

He then **proceeds to** bless the cup. Filling and taking it in both hands, he raises it a palm's height with the right hand (steadying it with the left hand placed under the right) that all may see ; and, fixing his eyes upon it, after a pause reverently consecrates it with the words, "Blessed art thou, O Lord our God, King of the world, who createst the fruit of the vine."

During the consecration, all should attend and repeat the words in a low voice.

The bread and wine are thus blessed at every meal, and fragments of the consecrated bread are reserved and left on the table (which is regarded as a domestic altar), that the sick, the poor, or those coming late, may partake thereof.

At this blessing, the use of the form of words prescribed is imperative, but each has his own way of breaking—his own ceremonial ritual, so to say—and may be recognized thereby at the breaking of bread ; as was the risen Christ by Cleopas and another.

The Jewish Passover was a festive meal. Hence at the Pascho-Mazzal supper bread and wine were blessed, as at other meals.

But there were differences in the celebration between this supper and other festal as well as ordinary meals.

Differences in the bread—for unleavened or "sweet" bread was used instead of the leavened or "soured" bread of other seasons.

And three breads took the place of the one, and were solemnly elevated, as the Paschal commemorative oblation, after the larger half of the middle one had been reserved and concealed.

Differences in the wine (red was preferred)—which must be the best within the means of the celebrant, or attainable ; for at the Paschal supper each has his own cup, which was replenished for him four times, and took the place of the one cup passed round at the ordinary meal.

Of these cups, the first, duly blessed, was drank before the elevation of the bread, and the second before the blessing of the bread.

From the second cup, which represents the Paschal blood, each with his finger sprinkled in commemoration of the delivery from the plagues of Egypt. And after drinking the contents, the cup itself was carefully cleansed.

Then the upper bread was blessed, and **each of** the three **was** partaken **of in the** prescribed **manner;** after which the supper was proceeded with.

After supper, midnight approaching, the celebrant withdraws the reserved and concealed half-mazza from its hiding-place, and, having eaten a portion thereof himself, places a similar portion **before each,** passing from left to right, that **all** may partake thereof.

This is the representative body of the Passover, **the Paschal** body of the celebrant.

After this, no more is eaten; but the cup of blessings is **at** once taken, and is followed by the fourth cup—the **cup of** cursings as it is sometimes **called, because on drinking it the** Jews invoked the Divine vengeance on their enemies. Sometimes a fifth cup is taken—the inebriating **cup of future** deliverance.

The taking of food was called by the Jew the breaking of bread, whether this partaking were at an ordinary or festive meal, because **the** first act **of** the ordinary meal was the blessing, breaking and partaking **of bread;** just as the second **act was the blessing and** passing round **of** the cup. So that **when** the breaking of bread is spoken of in the Scriptures or elsewhere, the partaking of an ordinary meal is indicated, **unless a** festive celebration is spoken of. Hence when the **apostles or** disciples (who were converted Jews) are said **to have been** in the habit of breaking **bread** from house **to house, the** lesson shown by their example **is that** they made **no distinction of** persons, but **were in equal social** communion with all, **taking their daily** meals from house to house.

Hence **the daily** breaking of bread, transmitted from the Jew to the Christian, was **a** domestic rite, which gave its name to the ordinary meal because that meal was sanctified **by** the **rite, just as afterwards, when the** " breaking of bread" became the celebration of a Mass, the Christian meal was sanctified by a preliminary prayer or grace; and the designation was used of all meals, because by the act all meals were sanctified. In no case did it designate a festal meal, for each feast had its own proper and characteristic name, and was periodic in its recurrence.

In the elder Buxtorf's *De Synagogâ Judaicâ*, ch. xii., xviii., a detailed account of the Jewish domestic ritual is given.

"THE PETER."*

A PROBLEM IN BIBLE NOMENCLATURE.

Why was Simon called Peter? His declaration, "Thou art the Christ, the Son of the living God" (Matt. xvi. 16), seems to demand the antithetical declaration, "Thou art the Peter; and on this, the Peter, I will build my church,"—"the Christ" and "the Peter" being the antitheses either of the other.

Was this antithesis in the mind of Jesus?

Who can doubt it? But, if so, the antithesis drew its significance from the official relations of "the Christhood" and "the Peter" to historic Judaism.

But was Simon called Peter? St. John (i. 42) says that he was "called Cephas, which is by interpretation Peter;" and thus seems to settle the question in the sense that the Christ-given name was Cephas, and not Peter.

But then the same evangelist does not again call

---

* Reprinted from *The Leamington Spa Courier.*

him Cephas, though naming Simon frequently, the designation subsequently used in his Gospel always being either Peter or Simon Peter; and though Simon is spoken of by name some ninety-eight times in the Gospels, he is not called Cephas save on the one occasion when this designation is attributed to him; while of the eight places in which Cephas is mentioned in the Epistles of St. Paul, four have the various reading Peter.

Moreover, Simon calls himself Peter and Simon Peter, or is reputed to do so, in the Epistles which bear his name; and is called Peter or Simon Peter some fifty-eight times in the Acts of the Apostles.

It seems incredible that one who was habitually addressed as Cephas should have been as habitually designated Peter in writing, and the question necessarily arises, Could Simon have been called Cephas?

St. Matthew says twice (iv. 18, x. 2) that he was called Peter, as also does the writer of the Acts on four several occasions (x. 5, 18, 32, xi. 13); while St. Mark (iii. 16) and St. Luke (vi. 14) declare that Jesus called him Peter.

The weight of testimony here seems overwhelming; and when it is remembered that the Revisers of the New Testament have rejected one interpreting verse (v. 4) in the same Gospel of St. John, whose statement is the source of the difficulty here,

and have bracketed an entire narration therein (vii.
53—viii. 11) as an addition to the text, the unrelia-
bility of an assertion in direct opposition to what
is deliberately affirmed by two other evangelists
(whose declarations are confirmed by the not otherwise disputed testimony of the Gospels and Acts,
as well direct as indirect) becomes evident.

But in admitting that Simon was called Peter
and not Cephas, we are obliged further to admit
that the name Cephas was imputed to him with a
motive and for a purpose—to identify the word
Cephas with the name Peter, in order to make it
appear that *Peter* was derived from the Greek *Petros*
(which was thus made out to be a translation of
Cephas), and could not therefore be an original
Hebrew word of which *Petros* was the Hellenic
form ; thus to attribute to *Peter*, through *Petros*, the
meaning of the Syriac word *Cephas*.

And yet to say that Simon Peter was called
Cephas or *Petros* (a stone) because *petra* means a
rock, in order to make it appear that the Christ-
given type of the free Christian unit lost his typical
individuality in a functional office, under which he
was to represent the Church to Christ, and Christ
to the Church, and so become the vicar of Christ
and founder of a vicariate on earth, is to follow a
line of reasoning under which it might ·also have

been affirmed that Simon was called Peter because *pater* means father, which is by interpretation *papa* or pope. Were those so interpreting withheld here by the unmistakable words of Christ, "Call no man your father on the earth, for One is your Father, which is in heaven" (Matt. xxiii. 9)?

And yet this is precisely the way in which *Peter* has come to have the meaning "stone," and thence "rock" attributed to it; for the one meaning is gained through the other, and eminent commentators have not been wanting who have suggested that Simon was called Peter because he was a stumbling stone.

In reading the Gospel of St. Matthew, the tradition that this Gospel was written in Hebrew, confirmed as it is by internal evidence, should not be overlooked. And it should also be remembered in this regard that the same internal evidence shows that it was not translated into Greek by its Hebrew author. Hence, whether in the process of translation or otherwise, changes have found their way into the text, as in vi. 6, where the reading has been altered from "pray to thy Father in secret," to "pray to thy Father which is in secret."

Such changes throw doubts on the authenticity (in detail) of the written forms in which the substance of certain declarations have been preserved and handed down. Thus the question of Jesus, given in the Authorized Version (Matt. xvi. 13), "Whom do men say that I, the Son of Man, am?" which can also be read from the Greek as, "Whom do men say that I am—the Son of Man?" has been rendered by the authors of the Revised New Testament, "Who do men say that the Son of Man is?"

From these variations we learn that the purport of the question, as separated from its form, was, "Whom say men that I am?" And the subsequent question, "Whom say ye that I am?" lends colour to the suspicion that the words, the Son of Man, have been added to the original to give strength to the declaration of St. Peter.

However this may have been, the acknowledged variations in the form of the question show that analogous changes may have taken place in the form of the declaration made by Jesus (only the omission of the article and a change in gender, be it observed); so that "the Christ" may have said, "Thou art the Peter; and on this, the Peter, I will build my church."

But if so, then Jesus, the Christ, called Simon the Peter because on that which Simon was, "the Peter," he proposed to build his church; for Simon was as much the Peter, whatever the Peter may have been, as was Jesus the Christ.

In what sense, then, was Simon the Peter?

Jesus was declared by Simon to be the Christ. Now to be the Christ in the Jewish sense was to be anointed to or vested with the official position accruing to the name.

Two official Christs were known to the Jews. The Christ priest, the duly anointed high-priest, who was called "the Christ;" and the Christ king, the duly anointed king, also called "the Lord's anointed," or Christ. And these were the spiritual and temporal rulers of the Jews, in whom all authority, spiritual and temporal, was vested.

Now Jesus never held either of these offices in Judaism; was never anointed to or vested with the authority of either.

Hence when he suffered himself to be called the Christ—to be called that which (in the eyes of those who knew that to be the Christ due official unction and vesting were needed) he never was—he signified that in him the official Christhood passed away; as was indeed the case.

The Christhood was to the Jew the official organ of sacerdotal sovereignty. It had, moreover, a special relation to the primitive sacerdotalism which had grown up through domestic worship.

In patriarchal times the head of the family, who became the head of the tribe, and so on, was the first-born or elder ; and, according to the Targums of Genesis xlix. 3, the law of primogeniture vested the first-born with priestly and sovereign rights.

When the Christhood was established, it assumed and absorbed the rights of primogeniture, so that the privileges of the first-born passed away in it. And that the very memory of these might be blotted out in a deceptive transformation, the first-born was devoted to Jehovah, and, now no longer free, had to be redeemed at a price from the sacrificial knife and smoking altar, which was otherwise his doom. Thus did one usurpation—the usurpation from which Abel sought emancipation—melt into another.

The Christhood was at first one in Israel, and it was only with reluctance divided into two by the appointment of the Christ king.

But the Christhood was only established for a time, and with a purpose.

This time had run its course ; the purpose was fulfilled ; the official Christhood had done its work when Jesus commenced his divine mission.

The aim of that mission was to free the spiritually enslaved Jew, and restore to him the privileges of the children of God.

This freedom and these privileges had ever been symbolized by and identified with the rights of primogeniture—those rights of the first-born, born unto freedom—which had disappeared in the rule of the priests.

Such being the facts of the relations in which he found himself, and of the case with which he was dealing, would it have been strange had Jesus—the Christ who abolished official Christhood by showing forth that it had passed away in himself—in restoring the freedom of the children of God to his followers, and giving in the person of Simon the symbol of that restoration, used the symbolical words, "Thou art the Peter (the first-born, the free); and on this, the Peter (the first-born, the free), I will build my Church, and the gates of hell (the powers of darkness working through persecution unto death and its jaws, the grave) shall not prevail against it"?

This much is certain, that Simon was the first-called or first-born of the followers of Jesus, and that the Hebrew word *Peter* means "first-born" and "free."

THE KEYS.*

A PROBLEM IN BIBLE SYMBOLISM.

WHEN the Christ said unto the Peter, "I will give unto thee the keys of the kingdom of heaven, and whatsoever thou shalt bind on earth shall be bound in heaven, and whatsoever thou shalt loose on earth shall be loosed in heaven" (Matt. xvi. 19), did he utter a vain and empty phrase, as some seem to suppose? Did he transfer the teaching authority of the Jewish Rabbis to his first follower, as others assume? Did he give a new, a special power to Peter and his successors, as sacerdotalizers affirm— a power of dictating to others by defining doctrine and prescribing discipline; a power which might so easily degenerate into and become or be made the instrument for re-binding heavy burdens, grievous to be borne, and laying them on the shoulders of men?

The latter force has been largely imputed to his

* Reprinted from *The Leamington Spa Courier*.

words: and yet the Christ must have used them in their obvious and natural sense while restoring to the Peter—the free individual Christian—that God-given freedom, liberty of conscience, of which sacerdotalism had robbed the Jew. How, indeed, under the circumstances, could he have used them in any other?

The Scripture symbolism of the keys is three-fold. "These things saith he that is holy, he that is true, he that hath the key of David, he that openeth and no man shutteth, and shutteth and no man openeth" (Rev. iii. 7). "And the key of the house of David will I lay upon his shoulders: so he shall open and none shall shut; and he shall shut and none shall open" (Is. xxii. 22). "Ye have taken away the key of knowledge" (Luke xi. 52). And this three-fold symbolism figures the divine, the transmitted, and the teaching or interpreting authority.

The idiom thus rendered, which is the Scriptural one, significantly associates the keys with their proper function, that of opening and closing.

Outside the Scriptures, the familiar Talmudical idiom, "bound and loosed," common to all rabbinical teachers, is found, and as significantly associates those who employ it with their assumed function.

The judgment pronounced by the Christ on the Scribes and Pharisees, according to St. Matthew (xxiii.), clearly sets forth his mind as to the Jewish official teaching and its fruits.

These were the literal and practical interpreters of the law. Yet he said unto them, "Woe unto you, Scribes and Pharisees, hypocrites! For (and here he uses the idiom of the keys) ye shut up the kingdom of heaven against men : for ye neither go in yourselves, neither suffer ye them that are entering to go in" (ver. 13).

Throughout the discourse in which he pronounced this judgment, as handed down in the Gospel, he associated the Scriptural idiom of the keys with the Talmudical idiom just noticed. His motive for doing so is palpable here. He condemned the usages set forth in either.

In addressing Peter, he again combined the Scriptural with the Talmudical idiom, by associating the symbolism of the keys with the function (which was not their function) of binding and loosing. Was his mind the same in these regards on this occasion also ?

He spoke with deliberation. Each word that he uttered was duly weighed, and must have been intended to convey its own proper meaning. The gift of the keys signified one thing. The gift of the power of binding and loosing another. Both of these gifts were made to Peter. But they were

made to him, or rather the account of the giving
has been transmitted to us, without the intimation
in whose regard he was to use them.

And yet whether he was intended to use these
gifts in his own regard or in that of others must
have been signified ; so that the unrecorded intimation has to be sought for in such side lights of the
context of the narration as indicate the intention of
the giver and the circumstances and surroundings
that called forth the gifts.   Hence, to learn the
intent of the Christ here, these must be duly weighed.

But to do this, knowledge of rabbinical usage
is indispensable, and familiarity with Talmudical
idioms absolutely necessary.

The Rabbis thought that they were, and suffered
themselves to be called, "The light of the world"
and "The salt of the earth," because they were held
to be the depositories and transmitters of the traditions of the ancients, and were therefore looked up
to as authoritative interpreters of the law.

Was it with reference to this that Jesus told
his disciples that they, the representatives of the
unlettered—of those unversed in the prescriptions
of the law and unfamiliar with the traditions of the
ancients—were (through the freedom resulting from
this ignorance) the light of the world and the salt
of the earth ?   And did he so declare them to show

that the official light and the official salt **were to** pass away, because official light was darkness, official salt savourless and only good to be cast out and trampled under foot?

Certainly, in **thus** transferring **to the individual** Christian the authority claimed and exercised by the Rabbis over the unlearned Jew, that each of his followers might **be** a "Peter" or "free," he caused the power that had accrued to the Rabbis to pass away, as far as they were concerned. And this was the intention of that transfer.

In combining the transference of a power that had been exercised over the individual Jew to **the** individual Christian with the gift of the official power of the Rabbis—the power of binding and loosing—he as certainly had **a** further, which must have been an analogous intention.

But the transference of the power was the freeing **of** the individual. Was, then, the gift of a further power, the gift of the right to use the freedom thus bestowed? All the analogies of the case declare that it was.

To ascertain the intention of the Christ here and determine the meaning of his words, the force given by the Rabbis to the Talmudical idiom through which the further power was imparted must be considered. This is to be gathered from the Talmud, through the usage therein **set forth.** And here we reach solid ground.

The Mishnah comprises a more or less classified series of rabbinical **decisions,** or cases of conscience growing out of the prescriptions **of the law.** In these, after stating the circumstances of **the** case under consideration, the decision is given as binding on or loosing to the conscience of the subject. **And** this decision is invariably expressed in the formula, *asur,* "bound," or *patur* (mark the association through the Hebrew between *Peter* and *patur*), "freed"— which decision is final. But this usage **made the** individual Jew, in all cases of conscience, the subject of the Rabbi.

This was evidently in the mind of the Christ **on** this occasion. The association of the Talmudic with **the** Scriptural idiom may be held to prove the fact ; and his **will was to free his** followers from **this** subjection.

But if this **was his will—as who** can doubt, seeing that the freedom **he** conferred followed the gift— was he not led to express **it** because the freedom he bestowed was essential **to his** followers, that their unfettered consciences might **be** opened **to that** **Divine** action **by** which God **speaks through the** individual conscience **in a** voiceless utterance **to the soul ?**

And yet, if such was his will, such the motive that impelled him to declare it when, in the Peter, the first-born, the first emancipated, he gave the symbol of his Church ; and in the Peter, the free, the type of the individual Christian, did he not thus confer a power which each was to use in his own regard and not in regard to another, and thus restore that liberty of conscience which was the birthright of all, that nothing might come between that conscience and its Divine Ruler ? For the unfettered conscience is the channel through which the heavenly Father warns and guides his earthly children.

One thing is certain. To have done otherwise, to have given to Peter and his successors a power of binding and loosing over the consciences of others, would have been to have taken away with one breath what had been given with another.

THE CHURCH.*

A PROBLEM IN BIBLE UNITY.

THE Revisers of the New Testament did a good work when, by removing John v. 4 and 1 John v. 7 from the text, they made it plain to the public mind that the sacred Scriptures had been tampered with in a doctrinal sense. Had they gone a step further, and admitted collectively, what they would hardly venture to deny individually, that the Epistle to the Hebrews was not written by the apostle whose name it bears, their work would have been more faithful. They excuse themselves here by the plea that they were not expressly directed to extend their revision to the titles of the several books. But they were directed to make a faithful revision of the text; and no revision can be faithful which does not correct misquotations from the Old Testament. Now in the Epistle to the Hebrews (viii. 9), the Revisers maintain the reading, "And I regarded

* Reprinted from *The Leamington Spa Courier.*

them not, saith the Lord ;" whereas the Authorized Version translates the prophet's words, " Although I was an husband unto them, saith the LORD" (Jer. xxxi. 32). Then they correct the rendering of Heb. x. 5 into, "But a body didst thou prepare for me," although the Authorized Version has it, "Mine ears hast thou opened" (Ps. xl. 6) ; and that of Heb. x. 38 into, "And if he shrink back, my soul hath no pleasure in him," where the Authorized Version reads from the Hebrew, "Behold, his soul which is lifted up is not upright in him" (Hab. ii. 4). But in each of these readings they re-affirm an original error. It must be confessed they were in a difficulty here, for the misquotations form an integral part of the connected argument set forth in the Epistle. But then they show that the writer of the Epistle can hardly have been the apostle Paul, since he has quoted from a corrupted copy of the Septuagint, and based an elaborate argument on falsified renderings of the Hebrew text. His testimony on any point is thus open to question ; and hence his attribution to Melchizedek, that he was priest of the most high God, can carry no weight with it as against the direct statement of the Hebrew text that he was priest of the god Helion (Gen. xiv. 18).

It has been admitted by the Bishop of St. Andrews, one of the Revisers of the New Testament, with regard to the nomenclature of the orders of the Christian ministry (I quote from the *Standard* of September 23rd, 1881), that "in dealing with the words which relate to that important point, the result, unsatisfactory as it is from unavoidable necessity in our present Version, has certainly not been rendered less so, but rather the contrary, in the Revised. I say unavoidable necessity, because each of the English names — Bishop, Presbyter, Deacon—has now a fixed and distinct meaning, not only in itself, but in relation to the others ; whereas not one of the Greek words from which they are derived, and to which, accordingly, they might be supposed to correspond, has in the New Testament any such fixed and definite meaning, either in itself or in relation to the rest. The nomenclature was then in a transition or (so to speak) fluid state, which it is now impossible for us to represent accurately in translation, or otherwise than by description." This is suggestive, especially when it is remembered how easily the Hebrew *Peter*, "first-born," would pass into the Greek *Pres-buteros*, Presbyter or "elder." Now this period, when the nomenclature of ecclesiasticism was in a transition or fluid state, is included in and covered by a yet longer period, during which the history of

Christianity is lost in an all but impenetrable darkness. The few gleams of light that do pass through indicate that this was a period of struggle, ending in a period of compromise.

But a period of compromise is only a period of truce, during which the contending parties agree not to disturb one another ; and continues but till the one has absorbed or is able to cast out the other.

The struggle here was practically between those who came in the line of the priests, and claimed that the kingdom of God was to be sacerdotal in character, or administered, that is governed, by priests ; and those who came in the line of the prophets, and taught that God's kingdom consisted in the divine ruling of the individual conscience.

From this period of struggle and compromise a priestly Church emerged ; and in the hands of this Church, the New Testament in its present form.

This Church presently became dominant and persecuting ; the extirpator of heresies, as it termed the teachings of those in the line of the prophets ; the destroyer of all scriptures which did not agree with, or could not be conformed to, its own doctrines. And it is to the unsparing zeal of this Church that the loss of all early MSS. is due ; for it termed all copies of the Gospels corrupt, all Chris-

tian writings heretical, that were not in accord with
its own views.

Thus the New Testament in its present form has
reached us through a priestly Church, which suffered
no unapproved, that is no early, copies to remain.
And in the hands of this Church it has been moulded
to sacerdotalizing views, and interpreted in a sacerdotal sense.

The great struggle between the sacerdotalizers
and those who resisted sacerdotalism was as to the
ruling of the individual through the conscience.

The sacerdotalizers affirmed that when the risen
Christ said, "Whose soever sins ye remit, they are
remitted unto them ; and whose soever sins ye
retain, they are retained" (John xx. 23), he commanded auricular confession to a priest, with a view
to priestly absolution.

But then those who resisted sacerdotal pretensions pointed out that St. James (v. 16) interprets
this, "Confess your sins one to another ;" that the
living Jesus constantly taught that each was to
forgive his brother that brother's trespasses against
himself ; and that it was only when the sin was
aggravated by persistence, and became an offence
against the community, that the Church, the offended
community, should be appealed to, and is then permitted to leave unforgiven an unrepented sin against

itself: this to make it clear to all that the failure to return to unity and harmony rests with the original offender.

To fully take in the doctrine of Jesus on the subject of the forgiveness of sins, it is absolutely necessary to grasp the Jewish interpretation of the law in this regard.

According to the Rabbis, sin was absolutely unforgivable; so that, once committed, nothing but expiation remained. To demand an eye for an eye, and a tooth for a tooth, was to fulfil the law; while not to require the legal expiation was to break the same; and the rigorous enforcement of this view had made the Jewish character what it was.

In doubtful cases the Rabbis were appealed to, and bound or loosed—such was the official term—declared that the sins in question had or had not been committed, according to the circumstances. And, their decision given, the sinner was bound to expiate; and the one against whom the sin had been committed could not forgive the same, but was bound to exact due atonement, under the penalty of becoming himself a sinner.

In contradiction to this doctrine, Jesus taught that God will have mercy and not sacrifice, and that man had the power of forgiving, each one his brother his sins—the sins that brother had committed against himself. And to enforce this teaching and bring it home to all, he incorporated the same, as a petition, in his own prayer—that prayer which all are expected to use—that those using it, by asking God's forgiveness as or because they themselves forgive, might thus have the absolute necessity of forgiving sins constantly kept before them. And hence his gospel was called the New Covenant of the forgiveness of sins.

But if this was the teaching of Jesus, then should not all his charges on the subject of the forgiveness of sins be interpreted in conformity therewith?

The word *Ekklesia* only occurs three times in the Gospels.

It is used by St. Matthew alone, and, if his Gospel is a translation from the Hebrew, represents a Hebrew word—the word used by the Christ.

In the Septuagint it is of frequent occurrence, being synonymous with *Sunagôgé*, and stands for the whole people of God.

Its synonyms in the New Testament are "The kingdom of God" or "The kingdom of heaven"—terms susceptible of a double significance—though, when it is remembered that Jesus said, "The kingdom of God is within you," is it not manifest that he referred in it to the Divine rule over and through the individual conscience?

Many of the expressions used in the New Testatament are capable of a double interpretation in a similar manner.

Such expressions point to the period of compromise, and were the terms through which compromise was rendered possible.

Single words were so used. The Hebrew *Peter* became the Greek *Presbuteros,* a simple "elder" until the **free** Peters passed under the rule of the transformed presbyters, now become priests. Similarly *diathèkè* was used for Covenant and Testament.

In *Ekklesia* such a suggestive word is found—and suggestiveness rather than precision was sought **in all terms of** compromise; **for** *Ekklesia* primarily means "called out," while referred to *kleis,* "key" (with which it has been so closely associated), and interpreted through the Hebrew, it signifies "disembodied," **or shut out of** a body or community.

Read through these indications, which is the more **reasonable** conclusion—that the Church **of** Jesus, or kingdom of God founded by him, consisted of **those** called out of the world to be subjected to a body ecclesiastical, or of those called not only out of the world but also out of sacerdotalism; that the unity and catholicity thereof might consist in this, that all were called from external mediation of every kind **to** individual freedom—this that God might rule in all, speaking through conscience in a voice-less utterance to each of his children?

The Church of Jesus was to be in the line of the prophets; of those who, guided by Divine inspira-tion, communed direct with God.

The righteous Abel was the first of this line, for he made his offering himself and not through his brother, the first-born, presbyter or priest; and, approved by God for so doing, was slain by that brother.

Was this historical symbolism prophetic? Did it foreshadow the relations of the two ways of deal-ing with God for all time, while significantly indi-cating that which was conformed to the will of the Heavenly Father?

NOTE.

The problems respectively designated Melchizedek, The Peter, The Keys and The Church, formed part of a series of articles published in *The Leamington Spa Courier* as a review of the Revised edition of the N. T. On referring to the Revised edition of the O. T., published four years later, the reader will find that the Revisers maintain the readings of the Authorized Version of Jer. xxxi. 32, Ps. xl. 6, and Hab. ii. 4, and thus admit that in the Epistle to the Hebrews a falsified rendering of the same has been handed down. Such a position carries its own moral. The problem could only be solved in one way, and from this solution the Revisers evidently shrank.

THE DIVINE PLANE.

A PROBLEM IN BIBLE PNEUMATOLOGY.

THE Jews are held to have been the first believers in and upholders of the Divine Unity. But even in the children of Israel this belief had its beginning, the affirmation thereof its starting-point.

When the orthodox Israelite repeats, as he does daily, his *Shema,* in the sense, " Hear, O Israel, the Lord our God is one Lord"—he thinks he attributes to the Hebrew words he utters the meaning they were used to express by Moses in his solemn address.

But the Hebrew lawgiver held a peculiar position in Israel. He had done battle for Jehovah with the gods of Egypt. In this battle, which was a prolonged and severe struggle, Jehovah had conquered and freed his people from the bondage in which they had been so long held.

The battle in which he had been engaged for this purpose had been a real battle. None knew this better than Moses. None knew so well as he how great was the power of those with whose priests he had contended.

He had learnt in this way that Jehovah was the God of gods; for he never denied the existence of other gods. "Thou shalt have none other gods before me," was the commandment he received and delivered. Hence in the name of Jehovah he forbade the children of Israel to serve other gods, to make images or likenesses of other gods, of their symbols, and so forth.

This God of gods, who by baptism in the *Jaboc* had converted *Jacob*, the "Crooked," into "Israel," the "God-straightened," had chosen the descendants of the God-straightened to be his own peculiar people; had delivered them from bondage to the servers of the gods which had vainly resisted him; had miraculously preserved them in the desert; and was now leading them to the land he had promised their forefather, Abraham.

With the knowledge of all this before him, is it strange that the lawgiver should have exclaimed, "Jehovah is our God, Jehovah alone"? For this is the idiomatic and natural sense of the Hebrew words he used.

But if the words by which Moses said, "Jehovah is our God, Jehovah alone," have had the meaning imputed to them, "Jehovah is our God, Jehovah is one," then it becomes evident that, while a change has taken place in the Jewish conception of God, the Divine Unity affirmed by the Jews is a unity which does not exclude the existence of other gods —the gods of which Jehovah is claimed to be the God, the gods which he had forbidden his people to serve.

What were these gods, these *Achar*, of which Jehovah, the *Achad*, is claimed to be the God ; of which he had proved that he was the God by overcoming them, and snatching his people out of their grasp ; which he had forbidden his people to serve ?

The Greeks believed in the existence of familiar spirits, which they termed *daimons*. But in this belief they were anticipated by the Hebrews, who held that there was a class of personating spirits which they designated *demions*, "personators."

Were these demons one and the same class of spirits ? And was their Greek name merely an adoption or adaptation of the original Hebrew designation, as the *genii* of the Latins seem to have represented the Aryan *Jins ?* And were these familiar personating spirits ministering agents of those other gods which Jehovah forbade his people to serve ?

Admitting, with Jehovah, who expressly asserts it, the existence of other gods, which, inasmuch as they claimed to be gods and sought to seduce men into serving them, were personators of the One God, were these other gods simply a higher class of personating spirits—an order of spirits which had acquired and exercised greater powers? And is not personation the key to the mystery of the spirit state?

But once granting this position, how are we to know that Jehovah was not a personating spirit, a spirit which arrogated to itself that it was, and thus became the personator of the One unknown and unknowable God? Nay, how do we know that the spirit calling itself Jehovah, in arrogating to itself his attributes, did not thus cause its own designation to be imputed to the One who is in reality as nameless as incognizable?

That the spirit Jehovah is a personator, itself admitted in acknowledging to Moses that it had appeared to the patriarchs as the god *Shaddai.* With the same breath it assumed the name Jehovah; and it is on the faith of the assertion of this personator that the names *El, Eloah, Elohim* and *Shaddai,* have been read and interpreted in juxtaposition with Jehovah as "the Lord God Almighty;" and when the name Jehovah became ineffable or unutterable, the designation *Adonai,* "Lord," was substituted for it, and it was read as the Lord; and it was owing to this substitution that "the Lord" passed from the Jewish to the Christian "Word" and world as a designation of God.

The god now calling itself Jehovah had previously caused to be attributed to itself, and so absorbed and appropriated, the analogous designation of another god, the god Helion, as is seen when the narrative of the meeting between Abraham and Melchizedek is rightly read and understood.

In this narrative is found one of the several contradictions to the statement made by Jehovah to Moses, that this spirit had not revealed itself to the patriarchs as Jehovah. Was this because another spirit, a spirit of whose assumption of the name this spirit had no knowledge, had previously called itself Jehovah? And should a distinction therefore be drawn between the spirit which called itself Jehovah to the patriarchs, and the spirit which gave that as its name to Moses? And when this spirit, or its representative or successor, receives the title "most high," has it not gained this attribute through the absorption of the god Helion, just as it acquired the attribute "almighty" by personating the god Shaddai?

Regarded from this point of view, is the history of personation amongst the gods this, that one god melts into and is absorbed by another, which assumes its attributes and powers only to be itself absorbed by and disappear in another shadowy impersonation? And are the names under which these personating spirits severally and successively reveal themselves to man chosen by them because the attribute to exercise which they reveal themselves or appear has been already associated with the name they therefore assume?

The permutations through which the name Jehovah has passed are very remarkable in this regard.

The word now read Jehovah first appears in Gen. ii. 4, where it was used as a verb in the sense "caused to be" in the sentence, "By a succession of formations God caused heavens and earth to be;" and it may have been in consequence of this use of the verb, and the associations which gathered round it, that the fitness of the word for the purpose caused it to be subsequently assumed and revealed as a divine name; while this assumption and revelation, by an inevitable reaction, caused it then to be so read in this passage.

However this may be, the spirit that revealed itself to Moses as Jehovah used the name in this sense when, speaking of the promised release of the Israelites, it said—not "I am that I am," but—"I shall cause it to be, I who cause to be;" adding, "Say unto the children of Israel, *I shall cause it to be* hath sent me **unto you** ;" **thus giving the** accomplishment of the promised release as the proof that **it** was to be the releaser.

The word Jehovah, when read from the unpointed Hebrew, draws its verbal **sense** through the vowel sounds by which it is interpreted and uttered ; and **thus,** according to the way in which it is pronounced, **says,** either " **He** caused to be," " He causes to be," " He will cause to be ;" and it was owing to this that its peculiar fitness to become the divine name was due, for it thus combined past as well as future with present relations in a single unutterable word-sign, which was thus a veritable symbol. But as a symbol it had, could have, no proper vowels of its own, and the recognition of this fact caused the name to become ineffable.

It was thus inevitable that the symbol subsequently known as Jehovah, and possibly previously as *Jao* or *Jahveh*, should become ineffable, because this very peculiarity caused its utterance as a name **at once to** deprive **it of** its comprehensiveness ; for the given sounds limited its significance to the then and thus declared relation, and so reduced the attribute it represented from infinite and eternal to temporal proportions.

Hence the Jewish teachers forbade its utterance **as** an irreverence, when it became and was termed

the ineffable name; so that even the high-priest
(Messiah or Christ, as he was called) was only permitted to invoke it once a year, on the great day of
atonement, when, to avoid giving it vowel sounds,
the Hebrew letters of which it was constituted were
separately intoned *Jod, Hé, Ouv, Hé*. On all other
occasions it was in consequence read *Adonai*, Lord;
and it is through the attributed vowels, *o* and *a*, of
this word that it has been rendered and is read as
J'hovah.

After it became unutterable, it was for convenience
abridged, and used in the form *Jah*, until this also
was assumed as a divine name, when it was read
Jod Hé, in which the two letters *Jod* and *Hé*, constituting the abridgment, were expressed. Later it
was written *Jod Jod*, and finally it gained its simplest
form, *Jod*, from which the word *God* appears to
have been derived.

The name Jehovah has also been associated with
other names in connection with special manifestations, as *Jehovah Ireh, Jehovah Nissi, Jehovah
Shalom.*

Do these transmutations, in association with the
many other names held to designate Jehovah, represent a forgotten Hebrew Pantheon in which the
many have been subsequently read as the one?
Their combination, as a unity or associated use,

can only be interpreted in one of two ways; for either a single spirit has revealed itself under many aspects and in different guises, adapting its revelations to the passing moods of the mind of man, and reflecting while seeking to mould that mind, or many spirits have claimed in succession to be the one spirit whose attributes they have in this way assumed. In either case, a system of personation is the one aspect of the divine plane presented to the student of the Hebrew sacred Scriptures.

The thoughtful inquirer will find it difficult to close his eyes to the fact that a vast system of spirit personation underlies and is at the root of Judaism. The earlier Eastern races, the Babylonians, the Egyptians, the Greeks and the Latins, all believed in spirit personation. None believed that the forms in which the gods appeared were their own forms. In their eyes these apparitions were mere assumptions of form—assumptions for a purpose.

What was the purpose which underlies spirit personation, as handed down in the Jewish and Christian Scriptures?

Does not the history of Abraham show what that purpose was?

The patriarch, urged by the inner light which guides the uncorrupted heart and mind, turned from the religious systems of those amongst whom he had been brought up, and from the gods they served, to the Father of all, whom he sought in nature, away from the haunts of man. For this reason he was called *Ab ram*, "He exalted the Father." And it was in this exaltation of the Father that Jesus saw the anticipation of his own teaching. And it was because of this exaltation of the Father that he said, "Your father Abraham rejoiced to see my day," in which, after the manner of the Rabbis, he played upon the names Abraham and Isaac.

But the very fact that Abram abandoned the service of the gods to exalt the Father attracted the attention of the spirit world—of the gods from which he sought to separate himself. And one of these, taking advantage of his aspirations after nature, led him forth to the land which it thereupon made the land of promise ; where, succeeding in fully beguiling him, it revealed itself as or personated the Being to whom the yearnings of his heart had tended. And Abram believed. But in so believing he was deceived. And the personating spirit, to mark the completeness of its triumph, changed his name *Ab ram*, "He exalted the Father," into *Ab ra ham*, "Father saw a multitude," in which the exaltation of the Father disappears—disappears in the " exalted Father," as *Ab ram* was subsequently read.

In this way the patriarch was recalled from the natural to the supernatural.

But even so he was not to be beguiled into a formal religion.

He had been brought to believe in Jehovah, and to serve that god by obedience and sacrifice, even to the extent of sacrificing the child of promise, had not his uplifted hand been arrested ; and, so serving, he was left in the faith thus implanted in him, which, however, was revived from time to time by the repeated apparitions and renewed promises of the spirit that had inspired it.

The purport of spirit personation in Judaism and Christianity was to draw man from the natural to the supernatural, that the longings of his nature might be turned into spiritual aspirations. And the supernatural is in constant warfare with the natural to this intent.

But there is also a warfare between spirits *inter se,* each of the more powerful ones seeking to build up a spirit kingdom for itself, and therefore seeking a following amongst men.

The history of some of these struggles, with their varying successes, occupies no small portion of the Hebrew Scriptures.

The Jews were constantly falling into idolatry, constantly worshipping those other gods they were forbidden by Jehovah to serve. But in this forbidden service they did not worship mere idols, as it has been made to appear, but those the idols represented, the personating spirits with which the personating Jehovah carried on the actual warfare.

Could that be the divine plane on which such a warfare was possible?

The divine plane is to man the plane on which he has been placed by God through nature; that plane on which the Creator of the natural carries on the workings of the visible universe. This plane is only to be reached by man through the duly controlled natural use of his natural life.

THE HUMAN PLANE.

A PROBLEM IN BIBLE KOSMOGONY.

Is man a created being, or a being in process of creation?

He comes into the world by natural generation, lives a seemingly aimless life on earth, and, passing away at death, so finishes a brief career; and, thus viewed, is simply a created being—a being created that he may live for a short space and then vanish.

But man's inner vision causes him to look beyond the grave for that outcome of his life without which it would appear to be a failure. For man has aspirations which cause him to consider himself something more than the intelligent and intellectual animal he appears to be; and these aspirations have led to the teaching which has been fortified by external indications, and thus assumed the force and character of a revelation, that the perishable human is simply a veil for the imperishable—the divine human which proceeds therefrom at death to another and higher state of existence. Hence the perishable has been even regarded as a prison-house for the imperishable, and the life of man on earth as simply a passage from one state of being to another.

Whence came these aspirations to man? Whence the revelation which has given them shape and colour? Why does he believe that his unstable body is the perishable vesture of an imperishable spirit which passes therefrom at death as a living soul?

If such be the case, then the life of man has a meaning in it; a meaning which does not appear upon the surface; a meaning, the knowledge of which has been withheld from him. And yet a very little reflection will show, to those who reason from the known to the unknown, that this meaning is, that his life is part of that natural process called the Creation, by which the perishable is gradually converted into the imperishable in the divine kosmos.

Man can have no knowledge of God, save through his working and his works. It has been assumed that God has revealed and reveals himself to man from time to time, otherwise than through his working and his works; indeed, the whole fabric of religious worship rests upon this view, and the believers in the supernatural, the spiritual, the revealed, treat the believers in the dignity of the natural with contempt, and regard nature in all its manifestations as a fallen state.

And yet even those who believe that God works by supernatural means and reveals himself in spirit guise, admit the existence of other spirits which delight in misleading and deceiving man.

But, so admitting, how can they know that any spirit is what it claims to be?

The ancients were well aware that some of the spirits which sought to communicate with man were not what they represented themselves, but were simply acting a part, *for a purpose.* These they called *demons*, that is, "personators."

Catholic mystical theologians are familiar with the fact that this spirit personation goes so far that personating Christs appear from time to time, and seek to influence those to whom they appear; and some of their chief difficulties in dealing with those subject to such apparitions is the discerning of the spirits, or determining whether a given apparition be of the risen or a personating Christ; and so of all other individual spirit appearances.

Is it not strange that persons so believing have never asked themselves the question, Was the Jehovah of the Hebrews what it represented itself to be? Was it not rather a personating spirit, or more probably a series of such spirits which appeared from time to time, and acted and taught under the name Jehovah, and hence taught differing doctrines, and even contradicted each other's teachings upon occasion?

Those who have learnt to distinguish the difference between things spiritual and things divine, between God and functioning agencies, between God and spirit, are alone aware of the deep significance of that which underlies this question.

Man looks upon the infinite and calls it space. He gazes on the heavenly bodies revolving therein, and calls them the sun, the moon, stars, comets, and so forth. By dint of studying their several motions, he learns to distinguish between fixed and moving stars. By closer attention, he finds that the moving stars are passing round the sun with the earth on which he dwells, and then he calls these planets. After further study, he discovers that the moon is revolving round the earth, and is its satellite. He then realizes that the sun, or central body of the planetary system, is itself in motion. And finally he determines that the fixed stars are so many suns —centres of other systems akin to the solar system of which the earth is a member; and that all are, like it, in motion, and probably revolving round some remote centre by whose influence all their movements are directed—the whole constituting a vast circulating system.

So gazing, so studying, so learning, man evolves what he calls science, lost in the meshes of which he forgets to ask himself the meaning of all that he observes. He does not even pause to consider what space is ; what the heavenly bodies ; what the combined function in which all are taking part.

And yet that a function is going on ; that space is that wherein this function is fulfilled ; and the heavenly bodies the instruments or organs whereby it is discharged, he cannot doubt.

The ancients were more far-seeing. To them it seemed impossible to distinguish between infinite space and the infinite Being who must occupy that infinite space. Hence they looked upon space as the vesture of the Infinite—the incognizable substance of God. And, so regarding these inseparable relations, is it strange that one of the names given by them to the infinite and eternal Father of all was "Space"?

To them the universe was the outward manifestation of the Divine ; the heavenly bodies simply organs of God carrying on the several functions of the divine life ; the whole, the expression of the working of an impersonal God, whose boundlessness and incognizable nature carried with it the semblance of non-existence.

This was the view of men who reasoned more closely than have done and do their successors of more recent times. What if their view should, after all, have been the correct one? Is there anything unreasonable in the conception that space—that wherein all is—is the **primary vesture of God?** Is it irrational to suppose that the heavenly bodies, which are discharging **their** respective functions therein, are discharging them with reference to that primary vesture; **and are therefore the organs of** him who has clothed himself in that vesture?

The life of God is a hidden life; a life unseen of man. But it is none the less a life carried on in space, and therefore a functional life. **That is to** say, the life of God carried on in space is carried on through space, or acts not only therein but thereon; and so acting produces changes in space, which necessitate and are themselves the starting-points of further change. But this is functional action; **for** the nature of functional action is this, that it springs from one series of changes and produces another through the organs on which it depends—springs from **the** one to produce the other.

Now functional action, as observed on the earth, is produced by or depends upon the influence of the sun and other heavenly bodies.

These act upon the earth in space and through space.

But do they act only on the earth—only on each other? Or does the influence proceeding from each and passing through space act thereon?

Why should it not?

How could it help doing so?

But, if it does, then the primary action of the heavenly bodies must be with reference to that wherein they are acting, and they must be the functioning organs of that wherein their functions are discharged—of space itself; of that which space contains, and clothes, and represents, and is.

What if the ancients were right, after all?

What if space really be the incognizable substance of the Incognizable, that is of God?

Granting this for a moment, though God remains incognizable as ever, the meaning of the makrokosm, as the outward manifestation of his hidden life, becomes intelligible, its analogy to the mikrokosm complete. And then taking the mikrokosm as the starting-point, it becomes possible to interpret the one through the other.

Man, the mikrokosm or personification of the

makrokosm, is an organized being whose life is maintained by the circulation of cells—the corpuscles or globules of the blood.

Is God, the makrokosm, an impersonal Being whose hidden life finds its functional expression in the circulation of cells—the heavenly bodies?

Were this the case, man would indeed be made in the image of God and be his very child—the personification of the Impersonal.

When we say that man is the child of God and a reproduction of the image of his Father, do we mean that he is simply the offspring of the mind of God, and merely made by him as the potter fashions the clay? Or do we hold that he is functionally generated by his Father?

The ancients thought that the makrokosm functioned in this wise.

Regarding the heavenly bodies as members of an infinite circulation, infinite in time as in space, and viewing them as circulating organs which discharged important functions in regard to space as they moved therein, their observations led them to conclude that constant changes were taking place, as well in space as in the individual circulating bodies —changes in virtue of which the imperishable properties and qualities of space were maintained, while the maintaining organs were constantly passing away and being as constantly replaced by others in due course. But even here they drew a distinction; for while, according to them, the planetary worlds were perishable, the solar bodies were **persistent.**

Reasoning from these data, and guided by astronomical observations duly interpreted, they believed in the existence of a central sun, and taught that, with reference to that branch of the circulation of which the solar system was a member, two intermediate suns revolved between the central and the terrestrial suns; and this in such wise that while the solar system passed round the nearest of these as its central body, this, with all the systemic members **of its** complex system, circulated round the next, which carried the whole vast system with **it** round the **central sun ; and** these several suns they held to be the male organs producing what we **call** the Creation.

Of these organs, that nearest to the central sun passed round that body on a polar plane, while the compound system circulating round it moved on an equatorial plane.

These suns were, in their eyes, electrical organs— organs from which streams of electrical influence were constantly passing.

They maintained that what **to** our senses was

space, was invisible and impalpable substance ; substance unknowable of man ; substance constituted of spirit and matter in a particular state.

That action in the hidden life of God produced a change in this spiritu-material substance, thus setting free some of the spirit and matter entering into the constitution of this substance, in an elemental state.

And that, owing to this action and its outcome, the divine substance was permeated by elemental spirit and elemental matter in a free condition.

And they taught that the intent of the circulation of the heavenly bodies was to gather up the elemental spirit and elemental matter diffused in space, and re-combine the same and restore it in the spiritu-material state to the divine substance from which it had been set free.

This re-combination and restitution was, according to them, effected in one of two ways ; for the restored elements either took the form of simple substance, thus to contribute to the maintenance of the divine life, or they were converted into individual organic being—the human soul—which, as an impersonation of the divine, passed to the solar body to whose influence it was subjected, there and thus to enter into and enjoy the divine life.

The process of re-combination was a simple one.

The electrical influence passing from the central sun and permeating space brought spirit and matter into union by a process of combustion, and then gathered the product of this combustion together, by mutual attraction of the combined particles, until a globular body was formed, which, female in essence, moved towards the nearest male body or sun, but, withheld from that body by the electrical action of the central sun (which similarly electrified both and so held them apart), passed round it, and thus, as a planet, entered the general circulation.

In this circulation it had a definite part to play ; for, continuing to attract to itself the products of the combustion of elemental spirit and elemental matter continuously going on in space, it passed the same through functional processes, physical, chemical and vital, in order to return them to space in such a condition that they may ultimately re-enter the divine substance and contribute to the maintenance of the divine life. And here this simple function might have ended.

But this simple function only provided for the restoration of spirit and matter to space in the substantial union of the divine substance.

For the organic generation of the children of God a more complicated functional action was needed.

In the terrestrial system this was provided for by

the consecutive action of the several solar bodies of its system on the earth.

The action of the central sun had generated the earth.

To the polar sun, as for convenience it may be termed, the earth was a matrix, from which the fecundating influence of that sun produced the inorganic cell, which has played so large a part in the development of the inorganic constituents of the planetary body.

This inorganic cell, of which the crystal may be taken as the type, was a matrix from which the fecundating influence of the equatorial sun produced the organic cell, from which the vegetable and animal kingdoms, culminating in the human, were built up.

This organic cell became in the human the matrix from which the visible sun, by its fecundating influence, engendered the psychic cell, whose presence is limited to the human.

These several matric cells were the instruments used by the spirit of the earth—the unconscious agent of the Divine to that intent—for the building up of the respective kingdoms of which they formed the primary constituents, save and except the psychic cell, of whose existence it had no knowledge.

The spirit of the earth, like the presiding spirits of all planetary bodies, was the outcome of the primary generation of the planet whose spirit it was—the concentration of its spirit forces.

Its existence as an individual spirit was contemporaneous with that of its body, the earth, through the formation of which it had been engendered.

Its function was to preside over, direct and guide the functional action of the earth ; and in so doing it was the organ of the providence of God.

Hence it was all-powerful on the earth, within the prescribed limits of its function ; and the range of its influence was as wide as was the range of the influence of its sister planetary members of the solar system.

But its experience was simply terrestrial ; acquired during and through its planetary existence, which was its sole conscious life ; and its knowledge was limited by the range of this experience.

On earth, as the spirit thereof, its power in dealing with the products of its functional activity was only limited by the functions submitted to its control ; and as the spirit of the earth, its individual existence will cease with the passing away of its body, when it, with the spirit kingdoms it has built up, will be simultaneously dissolved.

The aim of the spirit of the earth, in the function

it presided over, was the generation, through the human, of a spirit kingdom—a kingdom of individual spirits of which itself was to be the head.

In carrying on this work it used appetite as the incentive ; gradually forming, developing and maturing the individual spirits that were to enter this kingdom, by passing them through a series of advancing forms, themselves produced in succession during the progress of the work by appetital or natural selection, until the human, through which each individualized spirit had to pass, was reached.

But in the human it commenced the transformation of its work, for now it sought, by giving natural appetite spiritual aims and incentives, to develop a spiritual nature in the individual spirits, and so repress and subdue the natural instincts which successive lives in organic and animal forms had produced.

In this it only partially succeeded—religious and ascetic influences being the instruments it used for the purpose.

Hence under these influences the spirit kingdom it was building up separated into two divisions, of which the one comprised those which by overcoming their natural appetites had made themselves wholly spiritual, and so rendered themselves pleasing to their God, the spirit of the earth ; while the other consisted of those which, by remaining more or less subject to their animal inclinations, constituted that far larger class of grosser spirits which, by retention of their animal propensities, **were** lost to the higher purpose of the spirit of the earth.

But the aim of the spirit of the earth was not the aim of God. Its purpose was not God's purpose. The children of God were not to be individualized spirits, but organized souls.

Hence while the spirit of the earth was working, and as it worked, the divine operation was going on. But this operation was essentially selective. The generation of the children of God was to be a purely natural, a functional generation. The divine kingdom into which they were to **enter** was a kingdom in which love was to be, of which love is, the actuating impulse. Only those capable of loving, and trained to love, can be admitted therein.

Hence to the children of God the human life was and is the state in which they were and are to fit themselves for loving and being loved.

Man can take with him from this earth but one possession, can acquire therefrom but one property, that gained through the affections.

Those who love each other in this world, and are to each other all that love only can make them, are alone capable of becoming children of God.

These attract to themselves the electrical influence of the central sun, as it passes through and permeates space; and this influence, finding in them living psychic cells—for the psychic cell loses its viable properties in those in whom love has no part—is absorbed by these, and through them engenders the living soul or true child of God, which, formed, and built up, and matured during the human life, by the functional processes of that life, passes from its matrix, the human body, at death, as a living soul, with all its bodily organs in their most perfect state, fitted for the enjoyment of the divine life, whose characteristic is love.

Thus the distinguishing mark of the children of God is, that they are loving and lovable—loving and lovable in the natural sense; for they are the children of the God of nature, who works by natural processes, through natural uses, that the outcome of his work may be wholly natural.

The spirit of the earth, with its subordinate spirit agents and spiritualizing agencies, is used by God in two ways in the process of creation; for it is the developer of the natural order.

In this development it uses appetite as its incentive, the instincts and propensities that grow through the selfish indulgence of appetite as its instruments— for self-seeking is the impulse by which evolution through natural selection is carried on. And then, from the thus developed natural kingdom it builds up the spirit kingdom it is seeking to form, by changing the aims and transforming the appetites through which it has hitherto worked.

But by each of these operations it unconsciously carries on and promotes the work functionally committed to it by God; for by the natural process of evolution the human form is produced, which is to be the personal form of the children of God; while by means of the spiritual process of elimination all of the human is removed and disposed of that is incapable of receiving the divine sonship.

Looking at man from this point of view, it is evident that, since to him his natural life on earth is a great opportunity, there are two ways in which he can misuse and therefore abuse that natural life.

In the first place, he can animalize himself by a reckless and self-seeking indulgence of appetite, to the detriment of others as well as of self, which is the abuse of nature.

In the second place, he can spiritualize himself, to the detriment of his organic being, by the disuse of nature through self-seeking self-denial.

Of each of these misuses, self-seeking is the distinguishing mark; and when once this is recognized it becomes apparent that the unselfish use of the natural can alone be the use that gives rise to the conditions which attract the warning, guiding and restraining influence known as the voice of conscience, by which the children of God are withheld from the animal and the spiritual, that they may be moulded through the natural.

This influence is a divine operation working through natural channels.

But if man, the man who by his use of life places no obstacles in the way of God's desire in his regard, is thus withheld by the divine from the animal and the spiritual that he may be developed through the natural, then is the natural the means by which the author of nature is engendering his children.

While, if the children of God are rescued by the divine from the spiritual, as well as from the animal, that they may be made, and become, and be wholly natural—

And if those not so rescued pass at death in the spirit state to one or other of the divisions of the spirit kingdom of the spirit of the earth—

Is it not evident that the life of man is a condition in which the spirit enters the body that it may be converted into a living soul, and so pass from the earth as a child of God?

And is it not further evident that this conversion

is the result of a **natural** process and the outcome of a natural life ?

And **is** it not manifest from this that the choice given to the spirit **of man at birth,** the option placed before him, the selection to **be** made by him in this **his decisive** opportunity, during and by the uses he makes of his natural life, depends upon those uses ; and therefore **that** the great problem to **be solved** by that life is—SOUL *or* SPIRIT ?

SUETONIUS, for Christ, wrote Chréstos, not Christos; and called the Christians Chrestianoi, not Christianoi; but this has been imputed to him as an error. And yet under this slight divergence in spelling a great truth has been veiled.

Judaism needed a functioning Christ. This was provided for in its anointed high-priest, whose official title was "the Messiah."

This Messiah became its virtual ruler.

Dissatisfied with this ruler, the Jews clamoured for a king, that they might be freed from Messianic rule.

But when a king was granted to them, he also was anointed, and thence called "the Messiah;" so that the Jews had now two Messiahs—two official Christs.

The title became in this way doubly familiar to

all, and the Messianic rule was thus preserved, when not in fact, at least in semblance.

The dissensions which followed this severance of the Messiahship, with their disastrous consequences to the nation—coupled with the belief that the Jews, as God's chosen people, could not be permanently deprived of their nationality and kept out of the land of promise—led in the course of time to the expectation, which gradually assumed a prophetic character, that a Christ would ultimately arise who would re-combine this severed Messiahship in his own person, and establish a kingdom whose high-priest, sitting on the throne of David, would rule over the people of Jehovah ; to which kingdom there was to be no end.

The establisher of this kingdom was to be "the Messiah," and was the Christ expected by the Jews.

When Jesus of Nazareth came into the world, this expected restorer had not yet appeared ; this kingdom had not yet been established.

During the eighteen centuries which have run their course since the passing away of Jesus of Nazareth, no such restorer has arisen, no such kingdom been founded ; and even amongst the Jews the expectation of such a restorer, of such a kingdom, has subsided.

During the lifetime of the Nazarene this expectation was at its height, and it was thought by many that he would prove to be this restorer.

But when at the close of his brief career it was realized that he had never sat on the throne of David, had not been an anointed priest, was not even of priestly lineage, and could not be shown to have sprung from the royal house of David, this idea was perforce renounced by those who had most cherished it.

Renounced for a time. But when the prophetic epoch, during which this restorer ought to have appeared, had gone by, and it was found that none such had manifested himself, the attention of those who had expected him was once more drawn to Jesus of Nazareth by the rapidly increasing number of his followers and the supernatural phenomena held to be wrought in his name. And the question was once more raised, Was not he the promised restorer, after all?

This question was suggested to those who looked not for a natural but for a supernatural and spiritual restorer; for the expectation had been two-fold, the expectants of two classes.

To these a remarkable opening presented itself.

They found that Jesus had been an inquirer after spiritual truth from a very early age.

That he had received the baptism of a famous ascetic teacher.

That at this baptism a spirit had descended on and hovered over him in the form of a dove, and proclaimed him to be the Son of God.

That he had thereupon retired into the desert and fasted forty days and forty nights; after which he had been supernaturally tempted.

That he had publicly changed water into wine at a marriage-feast.

That he had called his teaching the gospel, or good news.

That he had suffered himself to be called the Christ.

That he had taught that in him, as the manifestation thereof, the Word had passed away.

That he had claimed to be the Son of God.

That he had given bread and wine to his disciples as his body and blood before he suffered death.

That he died on the cross rather than surrender his doctrine of the divine Sonship.

That he had risen from the dead on the third day, and, after giving a solemn mission to his disciples, had ascended into heaven in their presence.

It was true these supernaturalizing Christians were also aware that the followers of Jesus understood all these acts and doctrines in their natural sense.

That they held that when as a child he questioned the doctors in the temple, he really questioned the authority of the law.

That when he received the baptism of John, he did so under a mistaken impulse, and as a protest against Judaism.

That when a spirit descended on him in the form of a dove, this was an attempt yet further to mislead him and supernaturalize his doctrine of the divine Sonship.

That recognizing through this his own mistake, he immediately withdrew from the Baptist, and never approached him again.

That he went into the desert to expiate his error by a prolonged fast.

That when after his long expiatory fast he was so sorely tempted, he learnt the power acts of expiation gave to spirits ever watchful to take advantage of man, and that therefore expiation was not for the children of God.

That when water was turned into wine at the marriage-feast, this was not done by him (who had sought to give a lesson of temperance to the guests, who had already drunken enough), but by a spirit seeking to delude him and others.

That when he called his teaching a gospel, he also said, in the same Hebrew word, that it was a gospel of "flesh;" because the good news he proclaimed was the recall of man from spiritual and supernatural influences to flesh and blood—that is, to God speaking through nature and the natural.

That when **he** suffered himself to be called the **Christ, it was to** show that, through him to his, Christhood had passed away for ever.

That when he suffered himself to be called "the **Word," it was because he had** become the Word to them.

That thus his teaching took the place of the written **Word,** which, in the doctrine of the divine Sonship, passed from his followers **for ever.**

That this was again shown forth in the symbolism of the transfiguration, when the lawgiver and the prophet disappeared in a cloud and left Jesus alone with his disciples.

That when he claimed to be the Son of **God, it was to** make his doctrine clear that man, as God's child, must suffer none to come between him and **his** divine Father; so that under this doctrine, **priesthood and** mediation passed away from his followers for ever.

That when he gave bread and wine as his body and blood **to** his disciples, it was as his "Paschal Body" and "Blood" that he so gave it, and in place of the body and blood of the lamb he should have sacrificed, but did not.

That he gave the representative Paschal Body and Blood on this occasion to show that, through him to his followers, sacrifice and expiation had passed away for ever.

That when he died upon the cross rather than surrender his doctrine of divine Sonship, it was that his followers might see the value of the freedom from priestly guidance and mediation he bequeathed them, since he thus died to maintain it.

But with his death his mission as the Son of Man ceased.

Dying, he returned to his Father, having finished the work that Father had given him to do ; returned to his Father's kingdom, to the place in that kingdom his Father had prepared for him.

His life had been the guide of his followers.

The teaching of that life was to be their guide for ever.

The corner-stone of that teaching had been the rejection of the supernatural for the natural, the turning from the spiritual to the human.

Hence the followers of Jesus, even if beguiled for a moment by the unexpected character of the apparition and its pretensions, had not been slow to find out that the risen Christ was not Jesus, but a personating spirit, which, appearing in his form, sought to pervert his teaching, that it might in his name once more recall man from the natural to the supernatural, that the human might again merge in and so be set aside by the spiritual.

The expecters of a supernaturalizing and spiritualizing Christ were aware of the sense in which the Messiahship of Jesus had been held during his lifetime. But they also knew that the time for the coming of the expected Messiah had passed, and that if Jesus had not been that Messiah, then were the predictions falsified, their expectations brought to nought, and their faith left without a foundation.

Some of these had been followers of Jesus.

Some of them had seen, conversed with and been instructed by the risen Christ, who made their hearts burn within them as he explained the Scriptures in the sense he desired to impress on them, though they had not recognized him at the time.

These were easily persuaded to believe this spirit and implicitly receive its teaching, because it was in accord with their own expectations and harmonized with their instinctive leanings.

These were the instruments used by the risen Christ.

They looked with horror on the natural view of the life of Jesus ; had always regarded it with aversion, and sought to give a spiritual turn to his natural sayings.

They would have corrupted his doctrine from the first. Had done so, as far as they could, even during the life of Jesus ; and failing, had quitted him in disgust. And now, under the inspiration of the risen Christ, they found that they had quitted him under a mistake ; that their view of his teaching had been the correct one ; that of the followers of Jesus who had remained faithful to his leading, a misapprehension. And in this way they became the willing and zealous instruments for the subversion of that work for which Jesus had given his life.

Already deceiving themselves, how easy it was for them to be deceived ! Conceived of a virgin wife—of one who had been married as a virgin ; born of a virgin mother—of one distinctively so called to show that she belonged to the class of virgin wives, and had not been either a widow or divorced before her marriage to the father of her child,—what more logical than, under such promptings, to conclude that he was miraculously so conceived and born, without the intervention of a human father ? Though even here differences arose ; some believing in a supernatural conception, while others maintained that the generation of Jesus was human and natural, and that the Christ only descended upon and took possession of the body **that** had been thus **prepared for it, in** the form of a dove at his baptism.

But he had been miraculously recognized **at his** baptism. Had prepared himself for his mission life by a prolonged fast. Had been sorely tried by, and triumphed over, the Tempter. Had proclaimed **the** kingdom **of God.** Had been looked up to as the Word of God. Had called himself the Son of **God.** Had suffered himself to be called the Christ. **Had** been transfigured—when Moses and Elias had appeared to and been seen conversing with him. Had triumphantly entered into Jerusalem, and been publicly hailed as him that was to come in the name of the Lord. Had given his body and blood to his disciples, to be solemnly eaten and drunken of them as a substitute for the body and blood of **the** Paschal sacrifice, whereby they were to celebrate and even commemoratively renew the sacrifice he **was** about to make of himself for them. Had then died upon the cross **to** take away the sins of the world—as his faithful disciples knew, by destroying their **root,** the law, but, as their supplanters were now assured, as the expiatory and atoning sacrifice for all sin.

Could anything be more complete and conclusive **than** the witness here given that Jesus had been, was, the long-expected Christ, who had come to found a spiritual kingdom, but having failed to do this during his lifetime, owing to the dullness and slowness of apprehension of his followers, had come back as the risen Christ to finish his work?

In this way was Jesus—that Jesus who before his death had declared that he had finished his work ; who with his last expiring breath said, " It is finished"—made the Christ of the Scriptures.

In this way was a spiritual sense given to all his natural acts and sayings.

In this way was his wholly natural teaching spiritualized and supernaturalized.

But even while spiritualizing and supernaturalizing the life and teachings of Jesus, it was not possible to obliterate the characteristic features of that life and teaching.

It was impossible to disguise the fact that he passed his time in the open country, avoiding the towns ; and that he appealed to nature for illustrations to his discourses.

It was impossible to hide the fact that he lived on the terms of a most affectionate intimacy with his disciples. That he playfully gave them names of endearment. To Simon that of *Peter*, the "first-born," because he was the first to follow him ; and " the free," because by following him he was freed from the bondage of sacerdotalism. To the sons of Zebedee, *Boanerges*, "sons of thunder," because of their desire to call down the lightnings of heaven upon villages which refused to receive him. That he suffered his followers as playfully to call him their "Word," their "Christ," their "Saviour"— which indeed he was.

But it was possible to make it appear that these names were solemnly given as baptismal names, or with reference to an imparted spiritual and supernatural mission ; and so doing, to change the import of the given name, or even the name itself, as the Hebrew *Peter* into the Chaldee or Syriac *Cepha*, rendered *Cephas*.

It was impossible to veil the fact that he was warmly attached to the family of Lazarus, and that one member of that family had a special attachment to himself.

But it was possible to make it appear that the member in question had so sinned, that his attachment to her could only have rested on compassion.

It was impossible to deny the fact that he took part in marriage-feasts and joined in social gatherings ; that he had been called a gluttonous man and a wine-bibber ; and that he was the friend of publicans and sinners.

But it was possible to show that he frequented

this society because those to whom he was sent were to be found there.

And this was true; for those to whom he addressed his teachings were reputed sinners—that is, breakers of the law; for none others were called sinners in those days save those who did not observe the prescriptions of the law.

But then his teaching was not a recall to the observances of the law, but to the intuitive teachings of nature.

Hence he taught that they were to love all, not merely their own friends; whereas the law required that they should hate their enemies.

Hence he taught that they were to forgive those who had injured them; whereas the law commanded them to exact retribution.

So that to claim Jesus of Nazareth as the predicted and expected Christ, is to admit that the mission of that Christ was not the restoration of a kingdom founded on the Jewish law, but the establishment of a social order to be based on the subversion of that law: which is at once to admit that he was not "the Christ."

There is no Christhood to the child of God. To him the Messianic plane is the plane of nature, in which the spiritual and the animal combine, and find their complement in the human.

The follower of Jesus is, as Suetonius incidentally infers, a *Chréstos,* a user of life ; one who does not enfold the talent given him by God in a napkin and bury it in the earth, but makes a fruitful use of the same in the way intended by his Father ; or, circumstances preventing this, puts it out to interest by promoting the life uses of others.

To such, when Jesus came to be called the *Christos,* he became and was affectionately remembered as the *Chréstos.* And when the followers of the *Christos* were called *Christianoi,* these recognized each other as *Chréstianoi.* But, being the few, in the course of time, through the influences to which they were subjected, they, with their designation and the doctrine it had been used to recall, were absorbed into the Christian body, and lost sight of in an imposed dogmatism and common designation ; just as Jesus was, so to say, absorbed by and lost sight of in the risen Christ, when he was called, what he had never been, Jesus, the Christ, or Jesus Christ. Yet even so every child of God remains in the hands of his Father, and is shown by that Father that his vocation is to be a *Chréstian,* or user of life, and not a *Christian,* or depender upon unction — upon doctrine.

THE SOUL.

A PROBLEM IN BIBLE ONTOLOGY.

What is the soul? We speak indifferently of soul and spirit, as though these terms were synonymous. We use the words as though they expressed one and the same condition of individualized existence. We treat of this as the condition into which the vital principle that passes from the human at the death of man enters. We regard it as the condition in, through and by which the individual, on leaving the human to enter the unknown, is perpetuated.

But are the words soul and spirit synonymous? Do they express one and the same state of future being? And are the soul and the spirit of man representative of different conceptions of this state, of conceptions whose differences arise from varied views and reflect diverse perceptions?

It may be that the indiscriminate use here arises from a confusion of thought. It is possible that man once held the doctrine that the soul state and the spirit state were different conditions of being. It is even probable that this doctrine was widely spread and generally accepted.

Under such a doctrine man would have been taught that he could but pass into one of these states at death—since either would have differed widely from and been opposed to the other.

Under such a doctrine he would have realized that the use he made of his human life necessarily determined whether that life was to be continued in the soul or in the spirit state.

Had such a doctrine been once held by man, its tendency would have been, or the influences to which it became subject would have caused it, to merge into, be absorbed by, and so lost sight of, in the Christian and more recent view of the ultimate destiny of the human. And then the terms soul and spirit would have survived as representatives of a changed form of the idea they had originally conveyed—a form under which different aspects of one and the same state of being were imputed to that which they respectively designated, instead of different conditions of being ; and with this the confusion of thought resulting from indiscriminate use would as necessarily have arisen.

According to the Hebrew sacred Scriptures, the

soul is the self, as opposed to and distinguished from the spirit or "breath of life" which is infused into the body that the soul may be constituted.

Hence the soul and the self are expressed in Hebrew by one and the same word—*Nephesh.*

So intimate is the union between soul and body, according to the Hebrews, that even the dead body is by them called *Nephesh;* and they accordingly drew the distinction between the living soul and the dead self, not merely to distinguish between the animated and the inanimate body of man, between the living human and the dead corpse, as has come to be supposed, but because they held, and to show that their doctrine was, *that the soul might die, the man yet living.*

Was this ancient doctrine, glimpses of which can be caught in the Kabbalah, that man is a being in process of creation?

Did it inculcate that the spirit of man enters his body to be changed in that body during life, and, by the uses of life, into a spiritu-material being, that it may pass out of that body at death, no longer a mere spirit, but a duly organized spiritu-material being—the being under creation in him?

Did it affirm that man failing to make the uses of life necessary to the attainment of the end sought, this change from spirit to soul was not effected, the aim of the life was lost, the soul dying, so to say, during the life of the individual, at whose corporeal death the spirit returns to the state of being from which it had been drawn?

Did the teachers of this ancient doctrine hold, as their view of the immortality of the soul, the immortality of the duly created spiritu-material being under creation in man, on its passage—at the death of its matrix, the human body—to the soul state?

Was this the limit of the immortality they attributed to man? And are traces of the transition from this view to the received teaching still discernible?

The Hebrews called the soul *Nephesh.*

The living soul they designated *Nephesh chaiah.*

This *Nephesh chaiah*, according to them, proceeded from, or was produced by, the infusion of the spirit, or breath of life, into the quickening body of man, and was to supersede and take the place of that spirit in the thus constituted self—so that the spirit passed into, was lost sight of and disappeared in, the living soul.

The Greeks called the soul *Psuché;* the Latins, *Anima.* But whereas the Hebrews had associated the spirit with the wind by giving both the same designation, *Ruach*, and even identified them as the breath of life, the Greeks severed this association, calling the spirit *Pneuma* and the wind *Anémos;* and this dissociation was continued by the Latins in their *Spiritus* and **Ventus.**

The Greek *Psuché* represents the Hebrew *Nephesh chaiah.* So closely, indeed, does it represent the original Hebrew, that there is a suspicion, and per- haps more than a suspicion, that it was derived therefrom and is but a transformation thereof; for when the unpointed Hebrew is treated as a single word, and the formative letters *Nun* and *Jod* are removed therefrom, the simple addition of the letter *u,* and reading of the Hebrew *Hé* as *Héta,* gives the Greek *Psuché.*

Of course this intimate association between the Greek *Psuché* and the Hebrew *Nephesh chaiah* may be a mere coincidence, though even so viewed it cannot but be regarded as a very significant one ; but the way in which it points to the transition in reading the Hebrew letter *Hé,* through the Greek *Héta,* to the Roman H—which is thus shown to have been the *Héta* Latinized—is more than sug- gestive ; and under any view the Greek *Psuché,* like the Hebrew *Nephesh chaiah,* represents that into which the condition of life indicated by the Hebrew *Ruach* passed.

But beyond and yet within this coincidence, if

coincidence **it be, there** is found another—not the less significant, not **the** less suggestive, that it can be held to be of the same character, though in another form ; for what are the relations of the Greek *Anémos* to the Latin *Anima ?*

Whatever these may have been, may be, one thing is certain—that the Greek *Anémos* represents the Hebrew **Ruach, the** designation **of that** from which *Nephesh chaiah,* and with this *Psuché,* proceeded ; so that the Latin *Anima,* in designating **the** same, is associated with that which proceeded from the common parent of its Greek representatives, *Pneuma* and *Anémos*—that is, *Ruach.*

Is it not in such relations as **these** that the traces of transition in doctrine are to **be** sought ?

Do not these relations, thus co-ordinated, suggest that the ancient doctrine in regard to the soul was that it proceeded from the union of spirit and body, and was the resultant of the uses made of its life by the thus constituted self?

While under such a doctrine, would not the human **have** been viewed as a matrix in which the creative **work** was still going on ? Would it not have been held **that** his life, rightly used, was the process by which the living soul is ultimately produced from the animated body of man ?

THE SPIRIT.

A PROBLEM IN BIBLE ESCHATOLOGY.

What is the spirit? Formerly the teaching was received that spirit is a subtle influence, universally diffused, whose presence is only cognizable through its action upon matter.

According to this teaching, the tendency of spirit is to activity, that of matter to the inert condition ; so that under it all active material relations are due to the interaction of spirit and matter, either following the impulse of its own innate tendency.

Spirit and matter, in their primary or diffused states, were in this regard held to be equally incognizable ; but the tendency of spirit caused it to seek, by association with matter, channels through which its activity might find vent.

Under this impulse, the elements of spirit and the elements of matter, mutually combining, brought spirit and matter together in the form of the heavenly bodies ; and owing to this manner of

O

constitution, and the delimitation given to either through the form thus acquired, each heavenly body individualized the elemental spirit whose activity had brought it into being, and became itself the body in, on and through which this thus individualized spirit was enabled to act.

But this thus individualized spirit and matter, these heavenly bodies, so created in constant succession, were functioning organs—the organs of that Being of whose substance the primary diffused spirit and matter had, before disintegration, been constituents.

Hence each of these functioning organs consists of a spirit and a body, either of which was individualized or constituted by the instrumentality of the other. So that the interdependence of either on the other, in the embodied state, is complete and absolute ; each heavenly body being thus a living organ, whose spirit and body, on dissociation, tend to dissolution and ultimate return to their primary elemental state.

The earth, thus viewed, is a living functioning organ, whose spirit guides and controls its functional activity.

The special function of the earth is the production of life and the development of living beings.

Hence the earth is not merely a living and functioning, it is a life-giving organ ; and with its life-giving function—the production and development of living beings—the spirit of the earth is occupied.

These living beings are produced by natural process in such wise that a series of individual spirits—the offspring of the spirit of the earth—passes, each from the germ state through the cell shape (which is an infinitesimal reproduction of the parent form) by cellular interaction, to the organic and animated condition.

In this way each individual spirit is gradually developed by natural process, advancing progressively from a lower to a higher state, by passing in succession through a series of advancing forms until the human is reached, when the spirit is fitted for another order of being.

Hence the spirit of inspiration, the spirit of which revelation has been made to man, is the spirit of the earth, or god of this world—itself subordinate to, and, as a living functioning organ, the unconscious providential agent of the unknown and unknowable Being, the All-Father, whose organ it is ; while the spirit of which man has cognizance in himself is the offspring of the spirit of the earth, an offspring slowly maturing in the human form ; from which, if not transformed during its human life into the living soul, it passes at death, to return, by gradual dissolution, **to the** elemental **state from** which **it** was primarily drawn, and so re-enter the substance of space, which becomes to it the *Nirvana,* **or** *Beatific Vision,* in which all conscious individuality is lost.

THE LIFE.

A PROBLEM IN BIBLE USES.

What is life—the life cognizable of man, viewed as the outcome of the association of spirit with matter?

If the earth is a life-giving organ, producing living beings from the germ state; if these living beings are constituted in a progressively advancing order, whose forms are slowly modified by surrounding influences; if each of these living beings, starting from the germ state, passes by successive lives through a series of advancing forms, and is itself advanced from the germ state to the highest attainable form during and by this passage, so that the being under creation is created by subjection to influences to which, by the circumstances of its successive lives, it is submitted—then is life a use, the natural life-giving process by which creation, the creation of the life to come, is carried on.

While if man is the being in process of creation, so that, at the death of the individual, a created being passes to the state for which it has been created, then is the life of man merely a continuation of the series of creative lives through which the being under creation has to pass; the last of that series, it is true, but still one of the series, and therefore, like its predecessors, a simple, natural use—the complement of the process by which the advancing being is brought to its final state.

To understand how life on earth, the only life knowable of man, as man, is a simple use, it is only necessary to consider nature in its workings.

What man in his ignorance calls nature, which is an active function in the life of the Unknown, has two ends in view in its workings; for it had first to produce advanced forms, and then to use these as matrices for the advancing beings.

The self-seeking impulses of spirit, under which the individual sought and appropriated all that was necessary for its own well-being, or suitable to the gratification of its appetite, irrespective of the consequences to others, was the agent in the production of the advanced forms; and what is called "evil" in the world, that process of natural selection under which the weaker is universally sacrificed to the stronger, is at once the outcome of this impulse, and the method by which the most excellent bodily forms are obtained, preserved and advanced; so

that evil, as it is considered from the human standpoint, is the necessary consequence of the natural
process of creation.

But there was a due compensation here, for two
classes of spirits were formed by this process—the
aggressive, who recklessly appropriated all to their
own uses ; and their victims, who were sacrificed
to this self-seeking. Indeed, there was a double
compensation ; for while the aggressive spirits by
their eager self-indulgence developed the advancing forms, their victims were passed more rapidly
through the advanced forms thus produced by them.
And then in man the balance was restored. For
with man came the knowledge of "good" and "evil,"
and with this the perception of its sole remedy, the
forgetfulness of self through love.

Now the aim of the Unknown, whose functioning
organs were the producers of life, was the creation
of beings whose actuating and controlling impulse
should be love.

Hence, as the fruit of love is self-forgetfulness,
only those capable of self-forgetfulness are capable
of love.

But the victim spirits had been prepared for self-
forgetfulness by their long training in subjection,
and had learnt the value of love by a constant
endurance of indifference ; whereas the aggressive

spirits, through their prolonged practice of self-indulgence and incurable habit of sacrificing all to appetite, could **neither** love others nor forget self.

In this way the victim spirits found their compensation, **as** the loving children **of** the All-love, through love ; and the balance was restored by their passing, at death, through the soul state to the Paradise prepared for them by the All-love ; while the unloving, aggressive spirits then passed to the spirit state, **as the** self-seeking offspring of the spirit of the earth—a state in which ultimate rest is only to be attained through final dissolution.

Now the change from the spirit to the soul state is effected during the human life of the individual spirit without the consciousness of the individua in whom **it is** being produced.

Hence, as only those capable of self-forgetfulness through **love are** susceptible of this change, and as love, the associate of the process by which the being **under creation in man** is created, manifests its presence as an influence which promotes the unselfisi and self-forgetful use of life, and is never dissociate! **from such a use**—**is it** not evident that the life of man is a use, and that **a** loving use of life is essential to the conversion of spirit into soul—a conversion unconsciously effected by unknown natura process during and through that use?

THE SPIRIT PLANE.

A PROBLEM IN BIBLE DOCTRINE.

GOD withholds himself from the knowledge of man.

The spirit of the earth, unconscious of the existence of the Divine Being whose instrument it is, considers itself to be, and reveals itself to man as, God.

The earth is an organ of the Divine Being discharging a function in the divine substance miscalled Space, a function analogous to that fulfilled by the cell in the organic life of the world.

This function is the withdrawal of spirit and matter from space, to which, as spirit and matter, they are extraneous, and their re-conversion from the elemental state to which they have been reduced by the unknown uses of the divine life, to the spiritu-material condition of the divine substance, in which they are once more fitted for the uses of the divine life.

To this function another has accrued—the production of spiritu-material beings fitted to take part in the divine life ; and the production of these beings constitutes the life-giving function of the earth, and makes of it a life-giving organ.

This life-giving function is carried on by natural means, and is a wholly natural process.

Under it, individual spirits are produced, and passed through a succession of advancing forms, and are thus submitted to a series of successive lives until the human is entered, when, during the life of man, the final change is effected by the conversion of the matured spirit into the human soul.

This is the aim of the life-giving or creative and proper function of the earth, as distinguished from its inherent or common function—its combined function being the return of spirit and matter to the divine life, either as spiritu-material beings or spiritu-material substance ; and all spirit and matter acted on functionally by the earth is converted into and passes from it in one or other of these forms.

Creation is a function in the divine life, carried on by the divine organs, and is, therefore, a natural process.

Spirit is essentially self-seeking ; but can only gratify its self-seeking tendency in the individualized and embodied form.

Hence its attraction for and association with

matter, through union with which it is individualized and embodied.

In creation, God uses the self-seeking tendency of spirit to carry on the work; the individualized and embodied spirit of the earth becoming in this way his unconscious agent.

This self-seeking tendency causes the spirit of the earth to seek its own aggrandizement, by founding a kingdom for itself through its offspring.

This same self-seeking tendency causes the advancing spirits, or offspring of the spirit of the earth, each to seek re-embodiment, in its successive lives, through parents of a form of a higher order than that of its previous life; that by living in that form it may further advance, and so prepare itself for a yet higher existence.

This same self-seeking tendency causes the advancing spirits, during the process of re-embodiment, each to build up the bodily form it is assuming in such wise—within the possible limits of its parentage—as will enable it more fully to indulge its appetites during its life in that body; while by its life in that form it will yet further modify the same, and fit it for the parentage of offspring capable of a yet higher existence; so that the bodily forms are advanced by, while themselves advancing, the maturing spirits.

But this self-seeking tendency causes the individualized spirit to sacrifice **all** to its own needs and the gratification of its own appetites—the sacrificed then forming an order of victim spirits, which differ widely from the aggressive spirits by which they have been sacrificed. And the cruelty and indifference of nature, with the so called "evil" resulting therefrom, are due to this method of creation.

The soul state, drawn from the spirit state in the **human form,** differs widely from the spirit state, and is the state of the children of God ; the spirit state being that of the offspring of the spirit of the earth.

The spirit of the earth has no knowledge of the soul state, just as it has no knowledge of God. **It** is ignorant of the existence of the human soul, and believes that the sole function of selective evolution is the creation of the spirits with which it is occupied.

Considering the animal processes by which spirit is matured, and the animal propensities which these processes engender ; and perceiving that the more animalized are the spirits, the more materialized do they become; and that the more materialized spirits are so attracted to the earth that they cannot leave it, but, chained thereto, so to say, are gradually drawn towards its centre, finding in its central fires **the state for which** by their lives they have fitted themselves—the spirit of the earth seeks to de-animalize and spiritualize its offspring in order to detach them from matter, to organic union with which it attributes all the evils of organic and animal life and the propensities engendered thereby.

The spirit of the earth has learnt by experience that material creations are dissolved and disappear.

Its aim is to create a spiritual kingdom that shall be eternal in the heavens, indissoluble—that is, separated from matter.

It does not know that its own individuality is maintained by its material body ; that its power of action depends upon and is sustained by its union with that body.

It is aware that the earth will in due time be dissolved and reduced to the elemental state, and that the bodies of its offspring will share in this dissolution ; and this is why it devotes its energies to the de-materialization, the spiritualization of itself and them—that when the material world passes away, the spirit world may remain.

The aim of the spirit of the earth is the spiritualization of its offspring.

To do this, it reveals itself to man as God ; teaches him that he is in a fallen state ; that the entry of evil into the world was due to the fall, which animalized or brutalized and degraded his nature ; and then seeks to raise by de-animalizing him.

Teaching him that he will be sexless in the heavens, it strives to de-sexualize him on earth, telling him that sex relations are impure and therefore to be shunned.

Desiring to raise his aspirations from earth to heaven, it contemns the natural **and** introduces supernatural methods, which it systematizes as religion ; and knowing that the spirit state is divided into two classes—the earth-bound spirits, and those which have been, more or less, liberated from material ties—it bases religion on obedience to a given **law** and a revealed doctrine, promising the glory of heaven as a reward to those who obey the one and fulfil the other, while threatening the disobedient **with** the pains of hell or central fire of the earth.

But God, speaking to his children through nature —for nature is the only channel through which he reveals himself, its working being his working, a function in his divine life—shows them that they **have** been created to live natural lives on earth, **and that in** proportion as **they** swerve from the **natural** do they vitiate their lives. And, owing to his providential teaching by circumstance, religion after religion becomes distasteful, is protested against and decays by a natural process, to be followed by a revival, a renewed revelation and a modified religion.

Such a religion was Judaism.

Such a religion is Christianity.

Religion always rests on a revealed basis ; is always supernaturally actuated ; always blends the false with the true, that the one may support and commend the other, until it is enabled to interpret the true in its own way, and so convert it into the false—as when it changed the meaning of faith from perfect trust without knowledge, to belief in a doctrinal system revealed as absolutely certain, by which the uncertainty of *faith* was transformed into the certitude of *the faith.*

In Judaism, the spirit of the earth revealed itself as Jehovah, and claimed to be, what it thought itself, the self-existent cause of all.

Then as Jehovah it gave a law, in which it blended the natural precepts not to murder, and the like, with the supernatural commandments to worship, keep the sabbath, and so forth ; and established a Christhood, or order of anointed priests, to administer the law, and offer sacrifice, or serve in the sanctuary, of which the chief, or high-priest, was called "the Christ." And under this law, thus administered, man could only approach the God that gave it through **the** mediation of the Christ or anointed high-priest.

In Christianity, the spirit of the earth appeared as the **risen** Christ to give a revealed basis to Christian doctrine—that by transforming the teaching of Jesus of Nazareth it might supernaturalize and spiritualize **the** same, and so make him appear to have been the founder of a religion.

The mission of Jesus had been a mission of contradiction to Judaism.

He had recalled man from a supposed God-given **law to an** actual God-given nature : for he had enjoined the forgiveness of sins ; had disregarded the sabbath-day ; had taught that man was the son of God, and should therefore **suffer** none to come between him and **his divine** Father ; and had permitted himself, who was no Christ at all, to be called the Christ, **to** show that, through him to his, Christhood had passed away for ever.

And, in so recalling man, there was this marked difference between his way of teaching and that of **Moses** and the prophets—that he spoke simply as **the Son of** God (while calling himself the Son of Man—thus by the one designation interpreting the other) ; never claimed to have intercourse with apparitions, whether of "the Lord," that is Jehovah, **or** other spirits ; never professed to receive instructions, whether *vivâ voce* (through visions or otherwise) from the voice or word of the Lord, or by other spirit channels; and never claimed to have any communication with his Father other than that inner communing and guidance by which that Father directs the lives of all his children; while he emphasized his hostility to spirit teaching by the warfare he carried on with the spirit world, casting out the familiar spirits which sought to use mankind as their mediums; and showed his sense of spirit-derived authority by the contempt with which he spoke of the priesthood. And that the law and the prophets disappeared in Jesus was set forth by the remarkable symbolism of the transfiguration.

Hence with the death of Jesus religion—formal religion—passed from the earth to his followers. With him to his, formal religion then ceased to be; for through his agency man once more stood face to face with his Maker, and so doing abandoned the supernatural for the natural.

But the spirit of the earth, which had revealed itself to the Jew as Jehovah, and was the author of the supernatural and the fosterer of religion, attracted by the career of Jesus, because his teaching was subversive of Judaism, after tempting in many ways and failing to mislead him, brought his life to a premature and ignominious close; and then, the more effectually to undo all that he had done, assumed his **form and** personated him as the risen Christ.

In this way the spirit of the earth, as the risen Christ, in the name and semblance of Jesus and by **his** thus usurped authority, once more founded a religion in which spirit was to be the worker ; and so called man again from the natural to the supernatural, or from nature to what it caused **to be** termed " grace."

Its method was, to interpret the remembered utterances of Jesus in a supernatural sense, and confirm these interpretations by supernatural manifestations.

For this purpose it raised up agents, sometimes by supernatural means as in the conversion of St. Paul, as mediums for the carrying out of its teachings.

To facilitate the accomplishment of this purpose, **it** instigated **or** inspired the writing and manipu**lation of** the New Testament in its received form, **as** it had previously done that of the Old ; and in **these** writings, by a judicious blending of the true with the false, and a skilful interpretation of the one through the other, it gradually caused the false to be read as the true.

Hence, in carrying out this design, it appeared to

the disciples of Jesus on the first day of the week, to transfer to that day the sanctity he had withdrawn from the sabbath.

Hence it solemnly charged the disciples of Jesus to forgive sins—thus at once to give them a spiritual mission and to supernaturalize his natural doctrine.

Hence it interpreted certain passages and teachings of the Old Testament as prophecies of the coming of Jesus as the Christ, to supernaturalize his mission and calling.

Hence it promised to send the spirit, to recall to mind and re-interpret the sayings of Jesus, and sent it miraculously on the day of Pentecost.

Hence it caused to be believed that his casting out of familiar spirits or demons was a casting out of evil spirits or devils only.

In all this the spirit of the earth, with or through its subordinate spirit agents, was the worker.

But even so, man's zeal for religion flags from time to time, and would ultimately die out if left to itself. And so, to maintain the working and the work, the spirit of the earth causes revivals, or raises up new means and agencies, through which great outpourings of spirit are promoted, and marvellous conversions and other results follow.

And yet all of these are simply workings on the spirit plane—manifestations of the power of the spirit of the earth, which assumes that it is God, and acts in the place of, while really acting against, Jesus.

The call of Jesus was from the spiritual to the natural.

His casting out of spirits, artfully interpreted as the casting **out of evil spirits,** was the casting out of all spirits—the rejection of **spirit** teaching.

His recall was and is from the spirit plane, of faith in revelation, **to the soul plane, of a** simple, hopeful, loving trust in God working through nature.

Hence those on the spirit plane are, however unconsciously, under the influence of the spirit of the earth, his instruments and agencies ; while those on **the soul plane are** followers of Jesus, and, like him, **children of God.**

THE SOUL PLANE.

A PROBLEM IN BIBLE TEACHING.

CREATION is a function in the life of God.

Its outcome, in the terrestrial order, is the human soul.

The human soul, or "glorified body" of man, the perpetuated self, is a spiritu-material being capable of the enjoyment of perfect happiness.

This happiness it will attain to in the state prepared for it, to which it passes from the earth.

The basis thereof is love ; its starting-point, the love of God ; its expression, the love of God in man ; its fruition, the love of man in God.

The creation is a creation of love.

Man is created of love for love. And the type of the perfect love for which man is created is that which of two makes one.

Man is united to woman in the divine order, not merely that they may have offspring—which is an accident, so to say, of their union—but that they may become one flesh—one being in two persons.

The unity of these two in the one being is a substantial unity, under which they are moulded of one and the same substance—the substance of the man being transfused into and becoming the substance of the woman.

The spirit of man enters the human frame that it may acquire the power of loving and learn to love.

As man, it meets with objects that arouse its affections, and has the opportunity of recognizing the one to a substantial union with whom the soul aspires.

Man is created for union with one, that his affections may have a centre of attraction.

Hence man united to woman should lovingly devote his life to the cultivation of a mutual love between them—for the growth and development of love is the one object of his being.

The substantial union of man and woman is the basis on which the permanence of the affection between the two has been founded—because unity of aspiration is necessary to the unity of affection ; and unity of aspiration can only be secured by identity of substance. For just as the longings of the flesh are inseparable from the longings of the spirit in the natural human, and combine to produce and maintain the unity of the two, so that where corporeal union ceases, unity of spirit ultimately passes away, and the two that had been momentarily one become permanently divided ; so must the longing of substance be identical with the aspirations of soul in the divine human ; and therefore these must duly re-combine to maintain and perpetuate the unity of the two who, having been temporarily one, are to remain permanently united.

Hence in the soul state the accidents of sex pass away, but the sexual condition and relations remain —because the soul is constituted of one being in two persons, in which the unity of the one with the identity of the two is maintained thereby.

Whereas in the spirit state every function ceases, and a selfish longing for glory takes the place of love ; for the difference between the soul state and the spirit state is this, that the evolved spirit is disembodied and organless, while the soul is the glorified self, and therefore retains all the organs of the natural self, that is of the natural body, in their most perfect state.

The spirit of man, developed and matured in reckless indifference, enters the human form to acquire the power of loving, that it may be transformed into the living soul.

Hence a loving use of his natural life is the duty set before man by his Maker.

This is the duty set before all. No teaching is

needed here; no extraneous guidance necessary. Each one possesses a guide in his own heart, which will never lead him astray if he follows its innate instincts.

A loving use of his present life, with perfect trust in God, as well for the future state for which he is being prepared, as for the actual conditions in which he finds himself, are all that is required of man.

Failing this, he passes into the spirit state, not as a punishment, but because he has failed to acquire the power of loving, and therefore could not be transformed into a living soul. And in the spirit state he enters that order for which by his life his spirit has fitted itself.

The spirit state and the soul state are thus being prepared for coincidently; and the passage of the individual into the one or the other is determined, not by what he believes, or thinks he knows, but by the use he makes of his actual life.

There is a "heaven," and there is a "hell." But these belong to the spirit state, and are administered under the spirit of the earth.

With them the child of God has nothing to do.

To him a teaching from without is wholly unnecessary. Faith—that is, perfect trust—takes its place.

He leaves the future to his divine Father in a

loving confidence, asking for nothing, wishing for nothing, seeking for nothing; knowing that all needful for the loving use of life will be, as heretofore, provided for him as occasion arises.

The limits of the soul plane are determined by these conditions. Hence to be on the soul plane is to enjoy perfect freedom; to be emancipated from all teaching influences ; to be outside doctrinal religion.

Owing to the conditions of life, and especially of civilized life, comparatively few escape the influence of religious teaching. But on those who are being fitted for the soul state, this teaching sits so lightly, and exercises such slight influence on their lives, that they escape its soul-destroying tendencies. These are really emancipated from the toils of religion, though they know it not. They place their trust in God, and are satisfied to leave the future entirely in his hands, actually treating life as a use, and valuing the present as the passing opportunity given them for making a loving use of that life.

To be consciously on the soul plane is to leave all to God, looking for guidance only to the law of love written by his finger on the heart of each one of his children.

Those happily so placed know that inspiration and revelation are not from him, but from the spirit of the earth, and therefore not for them.

They are satisfied that the only religion that comes from him is love ; that the only sacrifice he requires from them is such as he places before them through the circumstances of their lives, all of which, to them, are providentially overruled ; that the only prayer he desires from them is the cry of the heart, lifted up to him in emergency.

To them knowledge—the knowledge of this world —is valueless, as only relating to an order which passes away at death. For temporal experience vanishes with that which it concerns and from which it was drawn, things temporal ; whereas they are being prepared for the uses of a future state, the only preparation for which **is that** training which is acquired through love.

Hence **to be on the** soul plane **is to** be in a state whose sole **aim,** whose beginning and ending and entirety, is love ; that the living soul on passing **to** the soul state may enter into the full enjoyment of the love of God.

THE PLANE OF SALVATION.

A PROBLEM IN BIBLE DOGMATISM.

What saith the Scripture? Believe on the Lord Jesus, and thou shalt be saved.

Understandest thou what thou readest? How can I, except some one shall guide me?

To believe on the Lord Jesus is to believe in him as a teacher; to accept his teaching; to reduce that teaching to practice; to make it the guide of the life.

Every one who so believes is a follower of Jesus and a child of God.

Hence to be a believer in the Lord Jesus is to have a knowledge of his teaching; to reduce the same to practice, and make it the guide of the life. And only those so believing, so living, are followers of Jesus. While to be a child of God is to live as Jesus lived. So that all who so live are children of God, and therefore followers of Jesus, even though they have no knowledge of his teaching or of himself; for all that teaching requires is that man should live the life of a child of God.

Hence the teaching of Jesus was addressed to those not living the life of the children of God, and was a recall to that life. So that the teaching of Jesus must have been a practical exposition of the principles of the way of life intuitively followed by the children of God, and a showing forth of the uses of life by which the divine sonship was alone to be acquired by those desiring the same.

What, then, was the teaching of Jesus?

The first public act of Jesus was to receive the baptism of John.

But the Baptist was a sectarian; and the chief priests and elders of the Jews believed that his baptism was not of God, though they feared to say so openly because of the people.

Why, then, did Jesus receive the baptism of John?

Not to become a follower of the Baptist, certainly; for he straightway forsook him, and declared later that though the Baptist was the greatest of those born of woman, of those whose teaching was not divine—the least of those born of God, of those in the kingdom of heaven, that is of his own followers, was greater than he.

But if Jesus received the baptism of John without becoming his disciple, what motive could he have had for so acting, unless that his first public act should be a solemn protest against Judaism and a formal renunciation of its teachings?

It is obscurely suggested in the song of Simeon that the mission of Jesus was a mission of contradiction.

But if the mission of Jesus was a mission of contradiction, to what was it a mission of contradiction unless to Judaism? While if the mission of Jesus was a mission of contradiction to Judaism, the teaching of Jesus would have been a contradiction to the teaching of Judaism.

Thus a ready means is found for the recovery of the teaching of Jesus; a ready and sure test to the true interpretation thereof.

But if so, then just as the first public act of Jesus was a protest against Judaism, so will his first recorded teaching have been a contradiction of the teaching of Judaism.

To the children of Israel, the law was all in all; the spirit of the law, as the breath of their nostrils; its practice, the fashioner of their lives.

Those rich in the spirit of the law were the interpreters thereof, the teachers of the people and the rulers over Israel—so that theirs was the kingdom of God.

Bearing this in mind, Jesus began his first recorded

instruction with the ever-memorable words, "Blessed are the poor in spirit; for theirs is the kingdom of heaven"—and thus solemnly protested against the spirit of Judaism.

He then told his disciples that they, illiterate men, unlearned in the letter of the law and poor in its spirit, were the salt of the earth and the light of the world. And he told them this because the teachers and interpreters of the law arrogated to themselves these titles. And thereupon he added, by way of explanation, that salt—the self-styled salt of the Jews—which had lost its savour, was good for nothing but to be cast out and trampled under foot; and that light ought not, like the boasted light of the Jewish Rabbis, to be put under the bushel that it might be measured out to those in need thereof, but should be so placed as to directly supply the needs of all; thus significantly condemning the principle with the practice of Judaism, while affirming that the untaught and unillumined of men were open to the teaching and illumination of God.

Under the law was no forgiveness.

The offence once committed, its penalty must be enforced. Retaliation and expiation were its governing principles. Forgiveness under it was impossible. To forgive was to break a law whose provisions once transgressed left atonement as the only remedy, atonement by way of retaliatory expiation.

He charged all to forgive, each his brother's trespasses against himself, and thus set aside the law in its root, retaliatory or expiatory atonement.

Remember the sabbath-day to keep it holy, was the dictum of the law.

A strict observance of the sabbath was the distinctive mark of Judaism. The sabbath was the centre round which Jewish principle and Jewish practice revolved. It was the very essence of Judaism; its observance, the Jew's standard of holiness.

Jesus disregarded the sabbath-day; suffered his followers to disregard it; refused to rebuke them for disregarding it; and in so acting set aside the sabbath-day to his followers. And so complete has this setting aside and abolition been, that the sabbath has ceased to be observed by his followers ever since. And even to the Christian the sabbath has ceased to be; for Sunday, the first day of the week, is not the seventh day or sabbath.

The distinctive sacrifice of Judaism was that of the Passover.

It was celebrated either by a representative or actual sacrifice; and the feast was kept by eating the actual or representative Paschal body at the close of the Paschal meal.

To eat the actual body out of Jerusalem was to break the law.

To eat the representative body in Jerusalem was equally to violate its precepts.

Jesus at his last supper at Jerusalem gave the representative Paschal body to his disciples, and thus caused them to violate the law while breaking it himself; and in and by so doing set aside the law, which enjoined the sacrifice, with the sacrifice it prescribed.

Three distinct teachings of Jesus are thus unveiled.

He taught the forgiveness of sins; and so teaching abrogated the doctrine of atonement.

He disregarded the sabbath-day; and so doing abolished the observance of the sabbath, not merely to his own disciples, but even to the Christian world, which, following his practice, has disregarded it ever since.

He passed over the Paschal sacrifice; and with this Passover all sacrifice ceased to his followers.

These teachings were the outcome and practical expression of his exclusive doctrine that man was the son of God, and in virtue of this divine sonship should permit nothing to come between him and his Father—by it abolishing all mediation, priestly or other.

So far did Jesus carry this doctrine of non-intervention between man and God, that he discouraged united prayer; commanding his disciples, when about to pray, to go each into his closet and shut the door and pray to his Father in secret.

Thus considered, the mission of Jesus was a mission of recall; his gospel, the glad tidings that man should return once more to God, abandoning all that withheld him from direct intercourse with his divine Father; his preaching, a summons from Judaism and every other formal religion to direct communion with God; his church, a calling out from all so called churches or religious organizations to that free intercourse with the Divine which God carries on in the human soul.

The mission of Jesus was a mission of recall.

To what, then, was the mission of Jesus a mission of recall?

To what could it have been a mission of recall but to the plane of salvation?

But if the mission of Jesus was a mission of recall to the plane of salvation, then the teaching of Jesus will show in what to be on the plane of salvation consists.

To be on the plane of salvation in the Christian sense is to believe in, to follow the guidance of Jesus; or, in other words, to believe in him as a Teacher;

to accept his teaching; to reduce that teaching to practice, and make it the guide of life.

Now Jesus abolished the observance of the sabbath, did away with the practice of mediation, and abrogated the doctrine of atonement.

Hence the plane of salvation should, to his followers, be one on which the sabbath is not observed, in which mediation is not practised, and expiation not believed in.

And the reason for this is obvious, when the warfare carried on by Jesus with the spirit world is considered. These doctrines and practices were repudiated by Jesus because they were of spirit origin and were spirit teachings; whereas his single aim was to recall man from spirit teaching and spirit guidance to the inner ruling of his divine Father.

The fall of man was a fall from the inward teaching of God through a natural channel—the conscience—to the outward teaching of spirit through supernatural channels, by revelation.

Hence the recall of man was from the supernatural to the natural; from the spiritual rule of revealed religion to the natural rule of the inner teacher; and, to give full expression to this recall, Jesus even discouraged united prayer.

Thus viewed, the teaching of Jesus was addressed to those not living the loving, trustful life of the children of God, and was a recall to that life. So that the plane of salvation is that state in which man leads the life which should be lived by the children of God—a life whose basis is absolute trust, as well for the future as the present ; a life whose practice is a loving use, a use free from misuse and abuse ; free from misuse or abuse because man is a being in process of creation ; because the process by which he is created is the natural use of his natural life ; and because only from those so living, so using, so trusting, can God produce his children, the human souls.

"THE EVIL ONE."

A PROBLEM IN BIBLE DEMONOLOGY.

THE translations of the Bible leave much to be
desired. Generally motived, always reflecting the
minds of the translators, necessarily limiting the
scope of the original to the aspect at the time attributed thereto, and for the most part used as channels to transmit doctrine at the time predominant,
they can but be, at the best, very imperfect repre-
sentations of the source from which they are drawn.

The original books of the Old and New Testaments
have been long since irrecoverably lost. The extant
copies have passed through many vicissitudes. The
very languages in which they were written, which
no longer survive as living tongues, were, even when
spoken, and while and as used in the composition
of the Scriptures, subjected to idiomatic changes of
a sweeping character, which, in their later aspects,
completely transformed the meaning and value of
the earlier uses of words and phrases, and gave them

a significance in the more recent books, especially
of the Old Testament, which they did not bear at
the commencement of the writings.

Beyond this, and before the documents gained
their present form, they were, as internal evidence
shows, edited and re-edited ; and during the process
the documentary teachings of opposing teachers
were, under misapprehension, combined and interblended; and then the thus agglomerated and amal-
gamated chronicles were expanded and otherwise
modified, according to the impressions and impulses
of the respective editors.

Whatever may have been the source of the original
writings, it is manifest from this that for many ages
the reader of the Bible, even in the so called originals, is only reading that which has passed through
and been moulded in accordance with the minds of
men, and is therefore more or less a reflection of the
impressions produced upon those minds ; for even
in the case of an original inspiration or revelation,
the subject-matter must be adapted to, and will be
modified by, the capacity and intelligence of the
recipient, or medium through whom the communication is made ; just as a picture submitted to many
observers must be adapted to their powers of observation, and even so will be interpreted by each in
his own way, and may not be interpreted by any in

exact accord with the mind of **the artist**; so that whether inspiration and revelation be produced by pictorial impressions on the brain, by suggested idealizations or verbal utterances, the interpretations of these will **be** similarly **and** as necessarily that of the medium.

Besides and beyond this, when the medium **is** merely a scribe or copyist, writing from dictation or otherwise, his copy will naturally be subject to the various errors attendant **on** transcription; and will hardly escape such modifications as flow from preconceived **ideas, doctrinal** or other. And even motived or deliberate and wilful changes are liable to be so introduced, when sufficient reason has been found or imagined to justify **the** same. In translations, such modifications are much more easy, and the temptation to introduce them, as corrections, is very great; and doctrines can be and are in this way, from time to time, grafted on to a **text** which were never contemplated by or included in it.

In these several ways and by these successive processes, the sacred writings of the ancients have been mangled and manacled, so to say.

Typical amongst these mangled and manacled Scriptures are those which **have** reached us through the Hebrews or **Jews**.

These were peculiarly **prone to** such treatment,

owing to the system of writing followed in them, which was vowel-less and essentially oracular—intentionally, so that they might be capable of transmitting more senses than one, of which the vulgar narrative framework was but a symbolical veil for doctrinal and mystical meanings only accessible to those duly initiated therein.

This linguistic framework, if it may be so termed, was very peculiar; for it was so constructed that each reader, according to his degree of initiation, could read from one and the same text, either the vulgar, the doctrinal, or the mystical sense—and this not as an interpretation, but by textually vocalizing the skeleton word-signs, or reading through these the several successive words and sentences which they could individually and consecutively represent; these words and sentences thus and then forming a consistent reading in the sense it then and thus represented.

The Hebrew method of writing is seen, from this point of view, to have been a very remarkable one. It marks and masks the transition from the pictorial to the alphabetic; and is, in another line and order, analogous to the hieroglyphic, and in itself a genuine hieratic system, which must have been carefully devised and skilfully adapted to its purpose.

The Hebrew letters, as originally used, and irrespective of variation in form, were simple ideographs; the so called word-signs constructed of them not primarily verbal in character, but compound ideographs, combined symbols of composite ideas, so that the initiated—those instructed in the system—could read them each in his own tongue ; and hence all could be instructed and even intercommunicate through this system, irrespective of a common language.

Such a system was necessarily a very complex one, and the tendency to progression, which is a tendency to simplicity, gradually developed from it the alphabetic system, through which these hieratic writings came to be read; and then the Hebrew ideographs became, and were finally supposed always to have been, alphabetic letters ; and this is why the Hebrew and cognate tongues were primarily destitute of vowel letters. But this ideographic or oracular character is only attributable to and discoverable in the most ancient portions of these writings, which, with the exception of the Kosmogony, are found as fragments imbedded in other portions of the Book of Genesis and of some of the succeeding books of the Hebrew Scriptures.

Under the transformation just indicated, the ideographic character of the signs was lost; the ideographic symbols were turned into word signs ; and

on to these a verbal sense was grafted, and ultimately crystallized thereon by the vowel points—a
verbal sense itself in part traditional, in part derived
from the supposed verbal significance of the text ;
and thus, step by step, a growing became a cor-
rupting tradition, a tradition falsifying that through
whose artificial re-construction it was itself developed.

When this position of the ancient Hebrew text
has been realized, this view adopted, a very remarkable result follows ; for, as the inquiry is pushed
further and further back, it is found that every
primitive tradition originated in and was the embodiment of a falsification of a yet earlier doctrine.

The historical tradition of the fall of man very
significantly illustrates this position. The earliest
teaching on this subject was, that the first fall was
of spirit. The so called fall of the angels is a
reminiscence of this tradition. According to the
symbolical teaching here, spirit, from being simply
a functioning agent of God, became volitional in its
developed and developing action, and, substituting
its own will for the Divine desire in its regard, so
fell. Hence the kingdom of spirits and spiritual
action, which flow from and are the product of spirit
volition, are outside, and contrasted with and in contradiction to the kingdom of souls and divine action.

The spirit of the earth, with its ministers, agents and spiritual action, having in this way—that is, by self-assertion—established the kingdom of spirits, sought to acquire dominion over man, in order thus to ensure the ultimate passage of the human to the spirit state, and thus recruit itself; and the second fall, the historic fall of Genesis iii., was the falling of man under the influence and dominion of the spirit kingdom and its spirit head—his subjection to the spiritual influences and surroundings brought to bear on him by ministrations originating in and fostered by the agents of that kingdom.

The course of falsification here is an interesting study. In brief—spirit was to man a bodiless, disembodied or deprived and degraded being; and hence was termed by the ideograph *Nachash*, "Deprived."

In the parable by which the fall of man was transmitted, and through which the narrative thereof became historical, such a spirit, ideographically depicted as a *Nachash*, was represented as appearing to and seducing the human race—the man through the woman : this not because of her sex and the sex relation, but because of the peculiar characteristics of her mind, which left her more open to spirit influences.

In the picture form this *Nachash*, this spirit was

represented by a serpent, because, from its desti-
tution of bodily members, the serpent was looked
upon as a deprived and depraved and degraded
creature.

In this way, and owing to this point of similarity,
the spirit and the serpent acquired a common designation ; and then, when the ideographic system had
lost its ideographic character and the original teaching had disappeared, a serpent was held to have
been the seducer of Eve, and the symbolic so turned
into an historical serpent. And with this it came
to be believed that man, as first created, was god-
like in form and constitution, and that the savagery
and brutality into which he is only too prone to
lapse are due to his fallen state. But this is a mistake. When man was created he was human in
constitution, with human affections, human hopes
and human aspirations. From this state he was
seduced. From this state he fell—into the brute
and the savage on the one hand, and under those
influences which have subjected him to a spiritual
teaching on the other—in each instance at the in-
stigation of spirit promptings through self-seeking
aspirations. For this, the earliest view of the fall
of man, was, that it was a fall from the natural into
the supernatural and the animal ; that it was an
accepting of a revealed teaching—a passing under

the control of spirit guides, and becoming finally subject to or even possessed by familiar spirits on the one side, or a falling into subjection to animalizing influences on the other.

After the transformation of the ideographic into the alphabetic system in the Hebrew Scriptures, a struggle grew up between the advocates of traditional and written teaching, indications of which can be traced back to what are practically pre-historic times, in the history of the progressive development of literary methods.

In the course of this struggle, traditional teaching came to be called "the Word."

This Word, as uttered or revealed by the traditionally-instructed teacher to the instruction-seeking neophyte, was regarded as inspired, because in delivering he infused a teaching spirit into the writings with which it was associated by the help of paraphrastic illustrations; whereas in the written or embodied teaching, itself attributed to spirit revelation, these illustrations were wanting, and the inspiration disappeared in a concrete doctrine.

Taking advantage of this, the then accepted view of the natural relations of inspiration to teaching, the paraphrastic teachers (who had received the doctrines they thus embodied and transmitted from a supernatural source through spirit mediation), the more easily to supersede and supplant this natural by a supernatural inspiration (attributed by them to Sophia, the Divine Wisdom), first personified "the Word" as their spirit teacher; and then, at its suggestion regarding thes pirit teacher, thus and for this reason called by them "the Word," as a Divine personage or impersonation, claimed that it was subject to incarnation and re-incarnation—to a succession of re-incarnations; and thus stamped it as the Divine Word, or Wisdom from on high, personified.

In opposition to this view, the advocates of the written teaching, who opposed the assumed to have been revealed verbal letter to the interpreting spirit, called the Scriptures "the Word," and would acknowledge no other. And thus there came to be a natural and a supernatural view of the Word. And, in the struggle between the naturalizers and the supernaturalizers, the advocates on either side sought methods of grafting their respective systems of reading and interpretation on to the letter of the text.

The Masoretes, who represented the literal method, achieved their ends by adding vowel points to the unpointed Hebrew; though antecedent to this their predecessors had endeavoured to give a vowel character to certain of the so called consonants, with which they then interpolated the text. But when

the vowel points were adopted, these added letters
had to be removed.   This removal, however, was
very imperfectly done ; so that, while some letters
were taken away which belonged to the original text,
others were allowed to remain which did not belong
thereto ; and thus corruptions were introduced and
a vitiated text constructed and perpetuated, antecedent corruptions of course still remaining.

While the Masoretes and their predecessors were
thus treating the text, or rather anterior to their so
doing, the paraphrastic teachers or Targumists were
not idle on their part, and the processes which they
used are very instructive.   But what is singular in
this struggle is, that while both sides claimed that
they were clearing up the obscurities of the revealed
Word, and while the one were naturalizers, the other
supernaturalizers, both simultaneously developed as
well natural as supernatural readings by their respective methods.

The method of the Targumists, as has been just
noticed, is very instructive.   It will be most significantly illustrated by showing their attitude towards
the doctrine of " the Word."

The doctrine of a personified divine Word, whether incarnate or to be incarnated, comes from the
East.   No such doctrine was known to the Jews, or
attributed by their expositors to the Jewish Scrip-

tures, anterior to the Babylonian captivity. During that captivity the teachers of the Jews were indoctrinated in the mysticism, as well as in the occultism, and even in the magic, of the East. The supernatural character of this mysticism and its surrounding and associated influences captivated their understandings; and the first-fruits of this indoctrination was the attempt to fasten the teaching they had thus received on to the text of the Scriptures they had inherited—that the authority of the written might be attributed to the unwritten Word, and its sanction thus given thereto.

To do this, the Targums or Chaldee versions of the Hebrew Scriptures, a need for which was beginning to be felt, were devised—though they were primarily written to show the Babylonians that the Hebrew doctrine was not behind theirs in this regard. And through the Targums the doctrine of a personified divine Word was introduced by simply translating the Hebrew for "God" into the Chaldee "Word of God," where God is said in the original to be speaking or acting.

In this way, as in other significant and pertinent passages, they changed "the voice of the Lord God" of Genesis iii. 8, into "the voice of *the Word of* the Lord God," and thus completely transformed the utterance. And yet, any theory of doctrinal development or expansional unveiling to the contrary notwithstanding, this was a direct falsification of the Scriptures. What can be said of a spirit which so inspires its votaries, save that by the practice it suggests it proves itself to be the agent of the father of lies?

This method of falsifying the Scriptures by grafting doctrines on to their representatives which the original text did not contain, was extended to and developed through the Septuagint, where, e.g., "Thou hast pierced my ears" (Ps. xl. 6), was rendered, "A body thou hast prepared for me," as reproduced in Hebrews x. 5; and still further expanded in the New Testament, where, in 1 Tim. iii. 16, "Who (or which) was manifested in the flesh," was altered into "God was manifest in the flesh;" while through the Vulgate special doctrines were similarly introduced, as, in Genesis iii. 15, "She (for he) shall bruise."

The struggle between the naturalizers and the supernaturalizers is still going on. Even in that latest version, the Revised New Testament, it has made itself felt in at least three ways : (1) by endorsing statements which it ought to have rejected ; (2) by leaving undone that which it ought to have done ; (3) by doing that which it ought not to have done.

The Committee of Revisers made it their boast

that they were guided in their decisions by the strict rules of grammar, and they laid special stress upon always having given its due import to the definite article. And so perhaps they have, as far as the presence of that article is concerned. But is it possible to give its due import to the definite article without omitting its force when it is not present? Hardly. Hence, where it is inserted or retained in the translation when not present in the text, it is manifest that there must have been a motive for such insertion or retention—a motive which will usually be found to have been doctrinal in character.

We read in St. Matthew's Gospel (i. 18), "She was found with child of the Holy Ghost." Here the statement is as clear as it is significant; the doctrine embodied in it as precise as it is important. There is no opening for question, no room for doubt. And if the statement is not found in the original Greek, then the motive for inserting and retaining it in the translation must have been a doctrinal one.

But the Greek says, "She was found with child of a holy spirit," for the definite article is wanting.

So again, continuing in i. 20, the Greek says, of that which is conceived in her, not that it is "of the Holy Ghost," but that it is "of a holy spirit."

In St. Luke's account of the incarnation the same

system of interpretation is followed, for at i. 35 it is said, in the angel's address to the Virgin Mary at the annunciation, not "the Holy Ghost," but "a holy spirit shall come upon thee;" so that according to the Greek Gospels the Holy Ghost took no part in the incarnation, whereas according to the translations **it** was operated by that Spirit.

The meaning and motive of the change here speak for themselves; and in all the narrated incidents connected with the conception and birth of Jesus of Nazareth the same system of misrepresentation has been resorted to and retained in the successive versions, not excepting the latest.

The principle here acted on seems to have animated the Revisers more or less throughout their revision; and they seem especially to have lost sight of the influence of the Hebrew mind in the production of the Greek text.

The Hebraisms of the Lord's Prayer give it certain characteristics which stand out in bold relief to the experienced eye, and cause its Hebrew origin **to be** unmistakable. These characteristics ought to **free** its interpretation from all difficulties, and make plain the specialities of its application. And yet there are not wanting those who think that, as Jesus taught this prayer to his disciples, he had in his mind, and reflected in its final petitions, a vision of

what occurred to himself through having been led
of the spirit into the wilderness to be tempted of
the devil ; and these, under this impression, are,
perhaps impulsively, inclined to affirm that he must
have said, " Lead us not into temptation, but deliver
us from the Evil One"—Hebrew idioms to the contrary notwithstanding.

The Hebrew idioms of the Jewish Scriptures
have yet an important part to play in interpreting
some of the obscure passages of the Christian sacred
writings ; for the force and character of the one
have had much to do in determining the scope and
value of the other. This is an obvious conclusion ;
and the more carefully it is considered by competent
inquirers, the more clearly will they see the absolute
truth of this view ; and the time will come when it
will be generally admitted that a complete and
final revision of the New Testament, if attainable,
will only be attained when the true value of its
Hellenistic idioms has been accurately determined
by tracing them back to their Hebrew sources.

But even the misinterpretation and misrepresentation of Hebrew idioms have exercised a very
decided influence in the rendering of the Greek
text ; for cases are occasionally found in which the
evident idiomatic sense of the passage cannot be
recovered even by tracing the Greek words under

examination, through their uses in the Septuagint, back to the Hebrew words which they have been made to represent.

Such an instance is the penultimate petition of the Lord's Prayer—" Lead (or, as the revisers render it, bring) us not into temptation."

Who utters this petition without insensibly and unconsciously interpreting it, " Leave us not in," **or** " Forsake us not under"? But the Greek **verb** *eisphero* does not carry either of these meanings. Neither do the Hebrew verbs it represents through the Septuagint.

And yet the way in which the sense *leave* passed into the meaning *lead*, through misapprehension of the meaning of the original Hebrew of the petition, can be easily traced.

The signification *lead* of *eisphero* is found in two Hebrew roots, *Nuach* and *Nachah*, according to the older lexicographers.

But the sense *leave* is also inherent in these roots, according to the same authorities.

To obviate confusion here, the more recent grammarians and lexicographers limit the meanings *leave* and its derivatives to the former, and *lead*, with its derivatives, to the latter.

But the confusion they thus sought to prevent already existed ; and it was their sense of the diffi-

culties it had created that caused them to draw
this distinction. Under it, the verb *Nachah* was
made to signify to "guide," "lead" or "bring;" and
Nuach, to "leave," "suffer to remain" and "forsake."

But these two triliterals spring from the same biliteral root, or are associated by having the same
persistent stem letters or consonants; and in many
of their inflections, especially in the apocopated and
contracted forms, are, when unpointed, precisely
similar. Hence in these forms, through their power
of being referred to either verb, the meanings *lead*
and *leave*, with their derivatives, are equally attributable to the Greek verbs by which they are severally represented. It is evident, therefore, that the
idioms of the Lord's Prayer in this petition should
be sought through these verbs, when the confusion
of ideas already introduced by earlier interpreters
of the Hebrew Scriptures, and thus derived, would
be at once accounted for.

From this position the way in which the confusion
arose can be very accurately traced; for in the Septuagint the verb *Nuach* is reproduced by (amongst
others) *aphiémi*, and the verb *Nachah* by *ago*. But
to have used the former would have been to have
caused a semblance of confusion by repeating the
verb just previously used in the sense *forgive;* while
the verb *ago* might have seemed to associate the

petition ideally with the temptation **in the** wilderness. Thus the verb *eisphero* may have been chosen
distinctively to represent the word actually used by
Jesus, though to convey the meaning imputed **to**
that word by recent tradition, the source of the
confusion here having been a preconceived idea in
the original translator's mind. At any rate, a careful examination and comparison of the renderings
of these two verbs in the Septuagint will convince
the practised Hebraist that a confusion of ideas,
and with this a confusion of meaning, has arisen **in**
translating the Hebrew verbs *Nuach* and *Nachah*—
a confusion of ideas and of meaning identical with
the verbal confusion unconsciously corrected in the
ordinary use of the Lord's Prayer. The Psalmist
cleared up this confusion by anticipation, for he
sang, " Leave me not to mine oppressors" (Ps. cxix.
cxxi.). Why did not the Revisers follow him here
by translating the final petition, " Leave us **not in**
temptation, but deliver us from evil"? Had they
done so, they would have illustrated the true scope
of revision, and avoided falling into two very grave
errors.

The fact is, that the Revisers of the New Testament approached their work with the spirit of the
pedagogue ; and, judged by their work, they maintained that spirit throughout.

To those so actuated, idiomatic usage is apt to become of less importance than grammatical detail.

That such has been the case here, the Revisers would themselves hardly deny. And yet the idioms of the New Testament are very remarkable, and require very careful treatment. That they should have passed over the very instructive one, " but submitted to him judging rightfully " (1 Pet. ii. 23), in which the rightful authority of Pilate (which is tacitly contrasted with his unrighteous judgment) is set forth, is perhaps not surprising, since the various readings show that this idiom was misunderstood at an early date. It is, however, suggestive that they should have overlooked others which can be supported by the historic testimony of the Old Testament, such as, " for they drank of a spiritual (i.e. symbolical) representative rock " (1 Cor. x. 4), in which the rock is representative as following or representing a pattern or type ; for the rock struck by Moses did *not* follow the children of Israel.

The ties which link the New Testament with the Old are not merely those of reference and quotation. They are so close, that the one may be considered a continuation of the other, certainly in so far as it records the realizations of the predictions and promises of whose fulfilment it claims to give the history. Possibly this is why the Gospels are so full of Hebraisms. But then these Hebraisms point to the presence of Hebrew idioms in their pages.

This Hebrew element in the Gospels, in the three Synoptics at any rate, is so strong, that the first is held by an old tradition to have been originally written in Hebrew ; and some of the various readings seem to show that this was the case. But if this was the case, it is possible that Hebrew idioms have been literally, instead of idiomatically, translated into Greek, at least in that Gospel. Now it is precisely in the first Gospel that the most complete form of the Lord's Prayer has been preserved in the Revised Version ; in it alone that the Revisers have left the last petition of that prayer. Hence it is possible that the Greek copy of the Lord's Prayer may comprise a verbatim translation of Hebrew idioms. Moreover, it is the custom of the Jews to say their prayers in Hebrew to this day. Hence the Lord's Prayer, several of the petitions of which are to be found in Hebrew rituals, would have been originally said in that language—so that the Greek Lord's Prayer must be a translation from the Hebrew. And hence it can be affirmed with reasonable certainty to have such an affinity to the Hebrew, that when critical questions growing out of the niceties of grammatical structure arise, the solution of these should be sought through the Hebrew.

Such a question has been raised in the last petition of that prayer. The tradition of the Catholic
Church has handed down that petition in the form,
" Deliver us from evil." Such a tradition cannot
but carry with it great weight, and should not be
lightly set aside. This tradition has been disregarded by the Revisers, who, because they find the
Greek word for " evil " preceded by the definite
article, have changed the petition into, " Deliver us
from the Evil One."

But the meaning and value of the definite article
should have been sought here, *not through the Greek*,
but through the Hebrew. What, then, says the
Hebrew in this regard? Let that venerable language speak for itself, by way of example. It will
do so without prejudice in the following quotations
from the Old Testament :

" And Manasseh seduced them to do (*eth-ha-ragh*)
more evil than did the nations" (2 Kings xxi. 9).
" So Manasseh made Judah and the inhabitants of
Jerusalem to err, and to do worse (*ragh*) than the
heathen" (2 Chron. xxxiii. 9). " For our fathers
have trespassed and done (*ha-ragh*) that which was
evil in the eyes of the Lord" (2 Chron. xxix. 6).

These are instances of the three several usages,
of which verbatim translations would be, " the very
evil," " evil," and " the evil ;" distinctions which cer-

tainly were not intended to be drawn. The translation of the last of the three is not without suggestiveness. It shows that the translators of the
Authorized Version were thoroughly informed in
this regard.

Then in Genesis iii. 5 we read, "Ye shall be as
gods, knowing good and (*ragh*) evil." And in
2 Sam. xiv. 17, "For as an angel of God, so is my
lord, the king, to discern good and (*ha-ragh*) bad ;"
where the article is wanting in the first example,
but present in the second, without calling forth a
variation in meaning.

These illustrations, which could be greatly extended, are sufficient to show that in the Hebrew
the definite article is used or omitted indifferently,
as far as the sense to be conveyed is concerned,
distinctions in meaning being left to be determined
by the context ; so that the phrases, "from the very
evil," "from the evil," and "from evil," might be
alternatively used, and simply mean, one and all,
"from harm," where no distinctive signification was
otherwise called for ; which is the way this petition
is rendered by the Jews in translations of their
prayer-books.

It is true the phrase *me-ragh*, "from evil," is, as
far as I am aware, the only one of the three that is
to be met with in the Old Testament ; but this is

because the preposition when put before the article absorbs it, and causes it to be dropped (while taking its vowel); so that the phrase, "from evil," in Hebrew includes and may stand indifferently for either. That it can be so used indifferently is best shown by demonstrating that in other words the similar idiom has been so used.

The word *erets*, "earth," offers a suitable example. Thus, in Genesis ii. 6, it is written, "There went up a mist (*min-ha-erets*) from the earth;" but in I Sam. xxviii. 3, "And Saul had put away those that had familiar spirits, and the wizards (*me-ha-erets*) out of the land;" while Genesis xxi. 21 has, "And his mother took him a wife (*me-erets*) out of the land of Egypt;" in which it is seen that the three forms are used indifferently. So again, in Ruth iii. 10, we read, *min-ha-rishon*, "at the beginning," and in Jeremiah xvii. 12, *me-rishon*, "from the beginning," in which the same indiscriminate usage is observed. While that the article can be used and dropped without ostensible reason is learnt from such expressions as, *min-han-nahar v'ad erets*, "from the river even unto the land" (2 Chron. ix. 26).

There can be very little doubt that when the Lord's Prayer was said in the original Hebrew, the article was used in this petition; used with a purpose, to teach the disciples and remind the followers of Jesus that when they so prayed they were not merely to pray to be preserved from evil—that is, from harm in general—but from the then impending evil—the particular evil that, when the prayer was used, seemed imminent.

PROBLEMS IN BIBLE READING.

IN discussing the text of the Greek New Testament, it is necessary to remember that the most ancient MSS. do not date further back than the middle of the fourth century of the present era; and that the earliest versions (which reach only to the middle of the second), owing to their MSS. not being of a high antiquity, cannot be freed from the imputation of having been corrected from the sources of the very recensions whose text they are held to confirm. Nor is this surprising, since correction, which was only too often a corruption of MSS., was the prevailing practice of those days. Beyond this, there is reason to believe that the original sources of at least the Synoptic Gospels have been modified in scope, in form and in character, and greatly expanded; so that these Gospels hardly contain more than fragments or vestiges of the sayings or writings of their reputed authors, embedded in ingeniously adapted extraneous matter, which completely transforms their meaning and teaching value.

Even in this developed and modified form, the text of the New Testament has passed through many vicissitudes.

Written at dictation ; transmitted and re-written from recollection ; quoted and taken down from memory ; submitted to the almost unchecked influences of these and other unsettling processes for more than a century — a century during which teaching was transforming itself into dogma, and doctrinally moulding a floating text — the real wonder is that any traces of the originals should have been preserved. But these have been for the most part preserved with dislocated words ; with sentences whose changed collocation has obscured their idiomatic value ; with substituted words of apparently kindred meaning ; with altered genders, cases and tenses ; with transformed and transposed pronouns and prepositions, and an infinite variety of other slighter variations—not to mention well-known graver errors—all testifying to the fluctuations through which it has passed. Indeed, the looseness of quotation and reproduction was so great during this unsettled term of its existence, that, although it has been said, were the Gospels lost, they could be recovered from the writings of the early Fathers—it has been also pointed out that the Gospel thus recovered would so differ in its language as virtually to constitute another Gospel; and in consequence of this, it has even been suggested that a fifth at one time recognized Gospel existed in those days, from which these derived the passages they cited.

Such are the materials with which inquirers have to deal. Such materials require a careful idiomatic treatment; under which, again, wide differences in rendering are possible. It is to this aspect of the question that I now desire to draw attention.

As Jesus was teaching the people in the temple (Luke xx.), the chief priests and scribes with the elders asked him, " By what authority doest thou these things ?" This question he met with another —" The baptism of John, was it from heaven or of men ?" To which, fearing the people, they answered that " They knew not." Upon this Jesus continued his teaching in the parable of the vineyard ; and at the close thereof, addressing, not the people but his previous questioners, said, " What, therefore, will the lord of the vineyard do unto them ?" Receiving no answer, he continued, " He will come and destroy these husbandmen, and will give the vineyard unto others." Whereupon the chief priests and scribes and elders indignantly exclaimed—are made out by the translators to have exclaimed—"God forbid!"

Now the English idiom "God forbid!" represents the Greek exclamation *me genoito*, which replaces the Hebrew objurgation *Chalilah*—also translated *médamos* and *ileos* in the Septuagint; so that these three idioms in the New Testament thus find a **bond of** union in *Chalilah.*

But *me genoito* says, "Be it not;" while *Chalilah* expresses indignant aversion.

Whether "God forbid!" could be, in any case, the correct rendering of **a** Jewish exclamation, is not the point to be considered now—though if St. Paul was smitten on the mouth by command of the high-priest (Acts xxiii.) for needlessly invoking God, it is clear that even the semblance of taking the name of God **in vain was** forbidden to and avoided by strict Jews. It is sufficient that the designation implicated is not included in the Greek epithet, so **that** its presence is not justifiable in a translation.

Some Hebrew idioms certainly present grave **diffi**culties to the translator. According to the Authorized Version, Job's wife said to her husband, "Curse God and die," which has been softened by the Revisers into, "Renounce God and die" (Job ii. 9). But the Septuagint reproduces her speech as, "Say what is the offence [i.e. confess] to the

Lord and die ;" while the Vulgate renders it, " Bless God and die."

So again, through the same Hebrew verb, Jacob " blessed" Pharaoh, or " bent the knee to" him, by way of rendering him homage, according to the point of view of the reader, at the beginning and end of his audience. That he did one or the other is manifest. That he actually bent the knee, and so humbly rendered homage to the sovereign of Egypt, even as Melchizedek rendered homage to the victor Abraham, is the reasonable view. What is undeniable is, that what Jacob did to Pharaoh, and Melchizedek to Abraham, Job was invited to do unto God, according to the original. So that the Hebrew account, idiomatically rendered, conveys the sense, " Even his wife said unto him, Dost thou still maintain thine integrity ? Humble thyself before God, for thou art dying."

It thus appears that, though some idioms present grave difficulties to translators and revisers, these difficulties have grown out of ignorance, and can be dissipated by adequately instructed inquirers.

But is it not a similar ignorance that has caused *me genoito* to be translated "God forbid!"? And does not such a rendering of such an expression show that the force of idiomatic usage has been so fully recognized by the translators and revisers of the New Testament, that idioms have even been reproduced **and** retained in **its** pages, from which the literal meanings of the words by which they have been transmitted are wholly excluded?

Reduced to its simplest elements, an idiom is a particular usage of a given word or phrase. To decide upon occasion whether *psuché* means "life" or "soul," **is to** determine its then and there idiomatic value. Such also is the effect of the similar decision whether *sózó* means, I "heal" or "save." So, again, only those familiar with the idiom can say whether "unprofitable" or "claimless" servants were the subjects of discourse (Luke xvii. 10). Whether every "idle word" or "reckless charge" was so severely reprehended (Matt. xii. 36). Whether the chief priests and others said he "trusted in" or "presumed upon" God (Matt. xxvii. 43). Whether Jesus **said of the stars** that they shall "fall" or "fade" from heaven (Matt. xxiv. 29 and Mark xiii. 25). Whether the apostles said, "Increase our faith" or "Set faith before us," in the sense, "Explain to us **what** faith is" (Luke xvii. 5). Whether Peter said, "**It is** good for us to be here," **or** "Is it good that we should be here?" (Matt. xvii. 4, Mark ix. 5, Luke ix. 33). Whether St. Paul addressed the Athenians as "superstitious" or as "tolerant of strange deities" (Acts xvii. 22). Whether Jesus said, "The kingdom of heaven suffereth violence," or "is done violence unto," in the sense, "suffereth persecution" (Matt. xi. 12). Whether his teaching was, Whosoever "is angry with his brother," or "provoketh his brother to wrath" (Matt. v. 22). Whether he did not say, "Are ye still sleeping and reposing? It is enough ; the hour hath come. .... Arise : let us go" (Mark xiv. 41) ; and "Sleep ye still, and repose ye? Behold, the hour hath arrived. .... Arise : let us proceed" (Matt. xxvi. 45, 46). It is noteworthy here that St. Luke (xxii. 46) uses the unmistakable interrogative form, "What ! sleep ye ?" In all such cases the context will be a guide to the true value, when this is otherwise obscure.

This is well shown in 2 Thess. ii. 2 ; for although St. Paul uses the word *pneuma* here, he does not signify "a spirit" thereby. He is referring to some bearing false credentials. Hence he warns the Thessalonians against spurious authorizations or "faculties," as they are technically called by Catholic divines—whether by token (for which *pneuma* stands here, through its sense "sign" or "symbol"), word or letter, brought to them as from himself.

But complications sometimes grow out of these simpler forms—complications arising from individual peculiarity in diction, whether of writer or transmitter.

Who that carefully considers the passage will not prefer the reading, "Bear with one another's burthens [i.e. failings], and so fulfil the law of Christ. For if any think there is anything [blameworthy], there being nothing, he deceiveth himself. Yet let each one prove his own work ; and then in his own regard alone will he have approval, and not in regard to another. For each will bear with [i. e. think lightly of] his own burden [i.e failings]" (Gal. vi. 2—5) ; as well as the reading, "Knowing this, that our old man was crucified with [him] that the body might be made inoperative of sin, that we might no longer serve sin. For he that is dead from sin is justified" (Rom. vi. 6, 7). How softened is the tone of the apostle in the words, "But when it pleased God (who excised me from the womb of my mother —i.e. Judaism—and called me through his grace) to unveil his Son in me (that I might preach him among the Gentiles), I was not immediately credited by flesh and blood" (Gal. i. 15, 16). How direct his statement, "For do I now rely upon man or upon God ? Or do I seek to please men, when if I rather pleased men I should certainly not be a servant of Christ ?" (Gal. i. 10). How clear his assurance, "Therefore are ye all sons of God through faith in Christ Jesus. For as many as were baptized into Christ, ye did put on Christ. It is not the Jew

alone, nor the Greek ; it is not the bond alone, nor
the free ; it is not the male alone, and the female :
for ye are all one [i.e. equal] in Christ Jesus" (Gal.
iii. 26—28). How telling his simile, " The which
are allegorical ; for these are the two covenants :
the one indeed made on Mount Sinai, unto bondage
(the which is Hagar) ; for the Mount Sinai in Ara-
bia is Hagar, and she answereth to Jerusalem now,
for she is in bondage with her children : but the
other [higher], *made at* Jerusalem, is free ; which is
mother of us all" (Gal. iv. 24—26).

Then, again, who will doubt, when attention is
directed thereto, that the author of 1 Peter really
wrote, " That also, if any believe not the Word,
through the behaviour of the wives they may be
won without the Word, beholding with reverence
your chaste conduct" (iii. 1, 2) ? As well as, " For
thus also aforetime the holy women who trusted in
God adorned themselves, being subject to their own
husbands (as Sarah, whose children ye were made,
obeyed Abraham, calling him lord) ; doing good
and not fearing [i.e. shrinking from] any abase-
ment" (iii. 5, 6) ? While a remarkable statement is
cleared up in the reading, " It could not be, for God
would be true even [were] every man a liar" (Rom.
iii. 4) ; and another in the further rendering, " It
could not be : for then how shall God judge the

world? For if the truth of God gain prominence through my lie unto his glory, what [then]? Even I am still judged as a sinner" (Rom. iii. 6, 7).

Apart from the question of misread idioms, there is one of overlooked quotations which calls for consideration.

In his First Epistle to the Corinthians (i. 11), St. Paul speaks of a communication he had received under the hands of Chloe. This communication he styles a letter (vii. 1) ; and his Epistle seems to have been called forth by this letter, for he deals with the several subjects treated of therein by referring to them in succession in the words of the writer.

He begins his reproof (i. 12) very significantly with the statement, " Now this I say—because each one of you saith, ' I am of Paul ;' and ' I of Apollos ;' and ' I of Cephas' (But I am of Christ! Is Christ divided ?)—Was Paul crucified for you ? or were ye baptized in the name of Paul ?"

Then a little further on he continues, quoting and answering the quotations one after another :

(*Cor.*) " All things are lawful unto me."

(*Paul.*) But all things are not expedient.

(*Cor.*) " All things are lawful for me."

(*Paul.*) But I will not be brought under the power of any.

(*Cor.*) "The meats for the belly, and the belly for the meats."

(*Paul.*) But God can restrict the use of this and of these. Yea, the body is not for fornication (vi. 12, 13).

(*Cor.*) "Now, concerning the things sacrificed unto idols, we know, because we all have knowledge."

(*Paul.*) Knowledge puffeth up, but love edifieth. Yea, if any one think that he knoweth anything, he knoweth not yet as he ought to know : but if any one love God, this one is made to know [i.e. taught] of [i.e. by] him.

(*Cor.*) "Concerning the eating, therefore, of the things sacrificed unto idols, we know that an idol is nothing in the world; and that none is God but one."

(*Paul.*) And yet indeed there are reputed gods, whether in heaven or on earth : to wit, "There be gods many and lords many."

(*Cor.*) "But to us [there is] one God, the Father, from whom are all things ; and we in him. And one Lord, Jesus Christ, through whom are all things; and we through him."

(*Paul.*) Yet not in all is this knowledge (viii. 1—7).

(*Cor.*) "But meat will not commend us to God ; for whether we eat, whether we eat not, we are neither gainers, nor are we losers."

(*Paul.*) But take ye heed lest this power of yours become a stumbling-block to the weak (viii. 8, 9).

The fact is, that familiarity with classical models and classical methods, and the habit of applying rules drawn from these to the solution of linguistic problems, is not the master-key to the mysteries of the sacred writings. A knowledge of the workings of the human mind, circumstanced as were the minds of the inspired writers, and of the tendency of the impulse imparted by the guiding spirit that actuated them, would be much surer solvents of the difficulties that, in the course of time and through the instability of things human, have obscured their teaching. To learnedly treat the philological structure of the simple but pregnant words of the more or less unlettered authors of Holy Writ as though their language, with its colloquial style and individual peculiarities, embodied a logical and philosophical system moulded into a strictly grammatical composition, rather than that it transmitted a psychological reflection of the untrammelled spirit which had poured itself forth through them, without any regard to the fetters of artistic construction or polished diction, is to fall into a very grave error.

When the whole subject is considered from this point of view, the question unavoidably arises, Is the scholarship of the day adequate to producing a final, or comparatively final, revision, whether of the text or its versions?

When we admit, as we are bound to do, that living language is constantly undergoing dialectic change, and that dialectic change is the agent which transforms one language into another; and when we remember that the Hebrew Scriptures had to be translated for the Jews, and that the Vedas and Avesta are all but unintelligible to those whose sacred writings they are,—we are inevitably driven to the conclusion that finality, which is inseparable from certainty in this case, is unattainable here, at any rate in a translation.

But is finality attainable in the revision of the Greek text? Until the idiomatic value of that text has been fully and accurately determined, this may well be doubted—and idiomatic usage is not to be settled by the rules of grammar; is not to be tested by a conventional standard of the value of the relations of particles, cases and tenses. It is the characteristic expression of individual or class peculiarity of diction; of provincial and dialectic, as contrasted with national and classical, usage, whose untrained energy causes it to break through the restraints of ordinary law.

Some of the idioms of the New Testament are so plain, it is strange they should ever have been misconceived. How did it come to pass that Matt. viii. 19 was rendered, "Master, I will follow thee whithersoever thou goest," instead of, "Master, I will follow thee. Whither goest thou?" The context ought to have been a sufficient guide to the meaning here.

In others, a familiar word appears in an unfamiliar sense. The father of the possessed lad exclaimed, "Forgive my unbelief" (Mark ix. 24), not "Help thou mine unbelief," which would have been very much like saying, Remove my unbelief by healing my son. The idea which underlies the idiom here is recovered by passing from the ordinary meaning of the Greek verb "help," through its less usual sense "heal," to its actual idiomatic significance.

The first of these examples suggests that the transition from a mistaken idiom to a corrupted text is so easy as, under given conditions, to be almost inevitable.

The change of a single letter is at times sufficient; as in Gal. vi. 2—5, already quoted, where the conversion of the neuter into the masculine participle, by the substitution of *Omega* for *Omikron*, was all that was needed.

Sometimes this simple change is associated with the removal of a preposition; as in Gal. iii. 19, "Why, therefore, was the law? It was established because of transgressions, until the seed (concerning whom had been promised) should come, announced by angels, with the hand [i.e. power] of a mediator" —unless this idiomatic force can be given to the text in its received form.

More often one word is changed into another, as in Gal. iv. 24—26, already quoted, where *apo* may have given place to *ano*.

But perhaps most frequently a single word is dropped out of the text. How this has happened is well shown in Mark ix. 23, "What, if thou art able! Art thou able to believe? All things are possible to him that believeth"—in which the repeated verb *dunasai* has been omitted. The various readings here show the successive steps by which a text can be corrupted in good faith and by way of correction.

Dunasai, as used by the father and quoted as from his lips, was changed into *duné*, to distinguish it from the re-duplicate *dunasai*, and obviate the apparent clumsiness of the repetition, *To ei dunasai dunasai pisteusai*, in the unpunctuated text—a clumsiness which, however, at once disappears in the obvious punctuation, *To ei dunasai! Dunasai pisteusai?* But then the older MSS. are for the most part unpunctuated.

Later the re-duplicated *dunasai* was dropped from

the text under the misapprehension that it was superfluous, and therefore an erroneous scribal addition.

And then, finally, *pisteusai* was expunged as irrelevant and meaningless.

But this analysis gives clear evidence that the older documents have handed down and represent the most corrupted text. Indeed, strictly speaking, the received text is idiomatically correct in this instance (*To ei! Dunasai pisteusai?*), since idiomatic usage transmitted by writing does not require the repetition of the verb, whose meaning is implied through and carried by the context.

Such changes as these seem to have been accidental, and, so to say, unavoidable under the circumstances; but a closer criticism of the text shows that deliberate and far-reaching alterations have been made in its structure.

A single instance will suffice here. In 1 Cor. xv. 29, a "hard saying" is found, for which the various readings prove that an enforced harmony has been sought. And yet if St. Paul wrote, "Else what shall they do which are baptized for the sake of the resurrection of the dead," as the context more than implies, then the difficulty disappears in the suggested correction, and it is seen that, notwithstanding all scholarly science and research have done for it, the Greek text still needs revision to regain its idiomatic value.

But the need for such a correction proves beyond this :

(1) That the most ancient MSS. were transcribed from an already corrupted text.

(2) That in the change they introduce—"baptized for them," instead of "baptized for the dead," which has itself replaced "baptized for [or because of] the resurrection of the dead"—they transmit an added corruption to a primarily corrupted text : a corruption, moreover, which endorses and confirms the corrupt teaching its author found already introduced, and therefore, in deliberately endorsing, accepted.

(3) That the received text, because it has the reading "baptized for the dead," is nearer to the genuine, and consequently reproduces a less corrupt text in this instance than the more ancient MSS.

This is manifest, for the change from "baptized for the sake of the resurrection of the dead," to "baptized for the dead," resolves itself into the mere omission of a single word (*anastaseos*) in the Greek, which might have been inadvertently dropped out of the text, as indeed it most probably was ; whereas the change from "for the dead" to "for them," must have been deliberately and wilfully introduced ; and therefore its presence shows that the MSS. in which **it** is found—that is, the more ancient MSS.—have, in their source, passed through the hands of a scribe who **has not** scrupled arbitrarily to alter, and in altering to corrupt, to doctrinarily corrupt, the text he was handing down.

A careful study of the above examples will convince every candid inquirer that a mastery of the idioms of the writers of the New Testament cannot be dispensed with, even in the revision of its Greek text. And then a further consideration of the style and Hebraisms of that text will lead him to the conclusion that a knowledge of the Talmud, and especially of the idioms of the Mishnah, will furnish **him** with **important helps** in the study, and be faithful guides to the meaning, of obscure passages of the New Testament ; and that familiarity with these idioms is the master-key to the solution of many of the more important doctrinal difficulties of the Scriptures.

It is a mistake to suppose that the apostles and evangelists laid stress on the letter of their writings.

So little was this the case, that even in the handing down of solemn spirit utterances, as in the several accounts of the baptism of Jesus—or of the symbolical and figurative records of some of the circumstances of his life and teaching, whether as parables or histories, as in the narratives of the Transfiguration—marked verbal differences occur.

Nor are they more accurate in transmitting written statements—witness the four differing transcriptions of the inscription on the cross.

Beyond this their narrations of facts are sometimes contradictory.

Who was the purchaser of the potter's field? Was it Judas or the chief priests?

What was the manner of Judas' death? Did he hang himself or die through a fall?

Why was the potter's field called the field of blood? Was this because it was purchased with the price of blood, or because of the tragic death of Judas therein?

Moreover, they are sometimes self-contradictory in their narratives.

So little is exactness of detail regarded in the accounts of the conversion of St. Paul, that it is said in one place (Acts ix. 7), "And the men which journeyed with him stood speechless, hearing a voice but seeing no man;" whereas in another (Acts xxii. 9) the statement is made, "And they that were with me saw indeed the light, and were afraid; but they heard not the voice of him that spake to me;" and in yet another (Acts xxvi. 14) it is said, "And when we were all fallen to the earth I heard a voice speaking unto me." Yet, as a mere matter of fact, the men either heard the voice or they did not. They either stood or fell to the ground.

Such disregard of accuracy in narration is not suggestive of careful attention to the niceties of grammatical construction. And yet, even in the present day, it is constantly affirmed that the best grammarian is the best divine.

THE GENESIS OF THE SOUL.

T

THE GENESIS OF THE SOUL.*

PART I.

A NATURAL VIEW OF REGENERATION.

"What is called regeneration is not attitude of mind or
state of feeling, but an organic life, beginning, as all bodily
life begins, from minutest germs ; and proceeding, if unda-
maged or not stifled, to full-grown perfectness."

Mrs. PENNY. *The Spiritualist,* 21st Jan. 1881.

WEIGHTIER words than these of Mrs. Penny
were never written.

Man, only potentially a child of God, is a being
in process of creation.

This being has, in him, gained the highest bodily
form nature is capable of producing.

It gained this form by passing progressively
through advancing stages of existence, in which
the well-being of self was the single aim of each
successive state, self-seeking its actuating impulse.

Owing to this, man—through whom this being

* Revised and reprinted, with additions, from *The Spiritualist.*

T 2

passes to its next state of existence—is naturally self-seeking and selfish.

Hence man is not responsible for the selfishness of his nature, which is due to the process by which his form was developed ; to which process all the evils attendant on the order of nature are also due—for all of these can be traced to some form of self-seeking action.

Man, thus constituted, is perishable ; because to transfer him, with his self-seeking impulses, to an imperishable state, would be to ensure him an eternity of misery.

Now man was created for happiness, as his every aspiration shows.

Hence, since he was created by a process which brought him to his present state as a self-seeking, perishable being, he must have been so created in order that in him a physical bodily form might be gained for the psychical being that was to be transferred, through him, from a perishable to an imperishable state.

This being is the human soul.

It follows from this that man is a matrix duly prepared by nature, that in him the human soul may be generated ; through him the being under process of creation transferred from a perishable to an imperishable state.

But to render the generation of the human soul possible, something is required of man, for he must co-operate in the work.

Hence certain conditions are offered to him— certain conditions of being for which no substitute is available. And, as his is a natural creation, these conditions are offered to him through his nature and natural surroundings.

These conditions are not far to seek; and it is only because, losing sight of the meaning of the working of the natural around and within himself, man has attended to misleading suggestions and yielded to misleading influences, that he fails to grasp them; fails rightly to read the import of that through which they are expressed.

The impulse that has produced the human form is an impulse tending to self; the motive actuating it is self-love, whose expression is self-seeking.

This impulse has produced a being prone to think self its first object.

Now happiness is only for those who seek it out of self; for those who seek, not the happiness of self, but the happiness of that which is outside self, the happiness of others. For is it not more blessed to give than to receive?

Therefore the required conditions must be such as will so change the being under creation as that, from making self its first object, it will seek that object outside self.

Hence, to produce **from** this thus constituted being one not only not prone to make self its first object, but ready to prefer that which is other than self to self, and wholly to disregard self in this preference, an impulse must be given to it whose tendency is from self, whose actuating motive is **the** contrary to self-love, whose expression the contrary to self-seeking.

Only one such impulse can be found.

That impulse is love.

Now love is ˌessentially a selective principle, acting through preference by way of elimination.

Hence love counteracts self-love by substituting the love of another for the love of self; and counteracts self-seeking by overlooking self for the object of its affections.

Charity, that general feeling of benevolence which **should be** extended **to** all, though promoted by, is **not**, although it has been ingeniously substituted for, love ; since by it no selection is made, no preference shown, no elimination effected.

Friendship is the harbinger of love. By it, some are selected from and preferred to the many, and become friends.

Affection **is** its handmaiden. From the chosen

circle of friends it elects a few intimates, for whom a special attachment is formed.

Amongst these, love attracts to one who is preferred to all others, and who is specially preferred to self.

Such a love is rare; such an affection seldom found. But where such a love exists and is mutual, there the natural transmuter, which prepares the human for the action of the divine, is at work.

Such a love gradually roots out every tinge of self-love, and makes meekness, self-forgetfulness and self-denial, habits of the life; and thus so identifies them with the nature that, to those so influenced, their contraries become impossible; and this is why the " Thou shalt not "—given as a commandment for the better ordering of the world—becomes the " Thou canst not " to those so actuated. For these, in whom "love is the fulfilling of the law," would have to break away from and renounce their actuating motive, and yield to its contrary, before they could thus act; and, so doing, would at once destroy the very foundations of the nature their uses of life, under the influence of love, had been building up.

In those who live under the influence of love— and all affection produces these fruits, exercises this influence, each in its degree—this meek, self-forgetting, self-denying nature is slowly built up; and while being built up, and in those in whom it is building up, the generation of the soul takes place.

The generation of the human soul or regeneration of man, viewed as a germinating process, is a passive generation—one of God's still, creative operations ; for the individual in whom it is going on is wholly unconscious thereof. But the process by which it is carried on, though owing to this passivity it is unknown, must be as natural as the previous successive steps in the creation which ended in the production of man, since it is the continuation of a natural operation.

At the same time it is more directly a divine act, because an unrecognized energy, capable of changing the perishable into the imperishable, is operating; and therefore the created soul, whose birth is the death of its human fashioner, is rightly termed the child of God.

The only co-operation of which man is capable in this generation, is that of using his life under the impulse whose motor is love, unselfish love.

The fruits of a life so used are the several qualities known as charity, meekness, self-forgetfulness, self-denial, and so forth, which have been termed virtues.

Hence, in theological and other systems, these virtues have been doctrinally set before man as objects to the attainment of which he should devote all his energies. And hence some have even thought that they are the efficient causes, so to say, of the regeneration of the human.

But this is a mistake. For when charity, meekness, self-forgetfulness and self-denial—self-denial carried even to the extent of self-sacrifice — are practised for the sake of the influence they exercise in the development of self, their motive or motor impulse is centred in self; and this at once disqualifies them as co-operators in the work, because from this work every form of self-seeking is excluded.

Love should be the generator of all virtues, as it is of hope and trust.

When these spring from other sources, and have their root in doctrinal precepts, they cannot fail to nourish self-love, even if that self-love only shows itself in the self-seeking which seeks the generation, or, as it is theologically termed, the salvation, of the soul of the self so seeking its own well-being.

Love is the generator of all virtues because it is of the essence of God—"God is love"—and therefore attracts the divine love to those actuated by it.

It acts by guiding and controlling the natural use of the natural life of man, because he, of whose essence it is, as the Creator of the universe, is the Author of that natural life and its natural surroundings.

This is why nature is the only safe guide ; why all teaching that comes from outside the natural life and its natural surroundings is, necessarily is, untrustworthy.

THE GENESIS OF THE SOUL.

PART II.

A KABBALISTIC VIEW OF CREATION.

THE Kabbalah was a primary embodiment of primitive natural science.

The Kabbalistic view of creation was, that it was the outcome of the functional activity of the life of God.

The Kabbalists* had no conception of space. To them, what has since been called space was the boundless substance of the Infinite, the transparent and impalpable substance of God.

The Kabbalists had a clear conception of the heavenly bodies. To them, these were the organs of God ; some visible, others invisible.

Hence to the Kabbalists the universe was simply

---

* The primitive Kabbalists were not Hebrews. They were the transmitters of a natural science which their Hebrew supplanters misunderstood, misrepresented and misinterpreted.

a manifestation of the activity of the infinite life of God.

It would almost seem as though the Kabbalists were familiar with and understood the meaning of vital circulation ; for they looked upon the heavenly bodies as constituting a celestial circulation in the divine substance ; a circulation not wholly unlike the cellular and corpuscular circulation of the vegetable and animal kingdoms, by which terrestrial life is maintained.

At any rate, they held that the celestial circulation was functional in character, and that it provided for the recruitment and maintenance of the divine substance.

The heavenly bodies, as divine organs, were in their eyes living bodies, though not living beings.

These bodies, they held, were divisible into two classes ; not because the solar were luminous, the planetary non-luminous bodies, but because planets attracted, absorbed and applied to uses those elements of matter which suns kindled, consumed and repelled ; for they were aware that the visible was not the actual sun, but simply a luminous perisphere at its zone of incandescence, caused by the combustion of those elements of matter which, having passed through its far sweeping belt of planets, were thus prevented from reaching itself.

Hence of the constitution of solar and stellar bodies they admitted that they had, nay claimed that they could have, no knowledge.

The satellites they classed with the planetary bodies, as well as the comets ; though sometimes inclined to think that the latter had more special relations with the solar bodies.

Viewing these two classes as living bodies, and considering them through their characteristic differences, they held that the solar were in their essence male—the planetary, female bodies.

Viewing them as organs of the Divine Being, they taught that the function of the planets was to gather up from the divine substance such elements thereof as had, through use, become unfitted for the further purposes of the divine life ; and pass these through certain physical, chemical and physiological or vital changes, in order to fit them for a return to the uses of the divine life, in the divine substance ; and that the function of the solar bodies was to energize planetary action, and take up the work where that action became inadequate, by burning up and consuming all such elements as had resisted or escaped from planetary action (as well as the exhausted bodies of decayed and decaying planets), when these reached the zone of incandescence with which they were surrounded.

The solar bodies, the Kabbalists thought, were produced by a luminous condensation in the divine substance.

They believed them to be imperishable.

The planetary bodies, they held, were created by a radiant energy which, passing from the centre of the universe outwards, kindled and consumed one element in another, so producing water; which, condensing in the vesicular form, accumulated until a watery globe was formed; which, as the nucleus of a planet, slowly absorbed solid and gaseous elements as it took and maintained its place in the general circulation.

These they knew to be perishable.

Their view of the method of this circulation was clear and comprehensive.

The Kabbalists believed in the existence of a central sun, which they taught occupied the vanishing polar point of the north celestial hemisphere, at an unknown and inconceivable distance from the earth.

This central sun was, in their eyes, the head as well as the centre of the universe.

From it, a radiant energy flowed **in every** direction.

To it, a vibrating current was continuously passing.

To this centre they referred the volitional acts of God.

This central sun, whether only relatively or absolutely at rest, was to them the centre of rest; the centre to which all motion was to be ultimately referred.

Round this central sun, they held that, amongst others, a solar body was passing.

This, which was the first of three secondary systemic suns, according to their view of the solar system, revolved round the central sun on a polar plane, a plane parallel to the terrestrial polar axis, and may therefore be called their polar sun.

Round this polar sun the second of these secondary suns was revolving on an equatorial plane; a plane approximately parallel to the terrestrial equator. This may therefore be termed their equatorial sun.

Round this equatorial sun the third of their secondary suns, the actual, visible sun was passing.

These four solar bodies were, in the judgment of the Kabbalists, the organs on whose action what man calls the creation, the evolution of life on the planet, earth, depends.

The channels through which the influence of these bodies was conveyed to the earth they held to be electrical.

The radiant energy flowing from the central sun called the earth into being as a watery globe, in the manner stated.

The tendency of this watery globe, as the nucleus of a planetary body, was to rush to the sun, within the sphere of whose attraction it had been created; but the radiant energy, similarly electrifying both, withheld the one from the other, and so changed motion towards into motion round the centre of attraction, which the revolving planet thus sought to reach.

When this watery globe had absorbed a due proportion of solid and gaseous matter, in the discharge of its functional action in the divine substance, the polar sun made its influence felt, kindling an internal fire; and, by the action of this central fire, fashioning the earth.

So acting, it divided the planet into the three physiological elements, water, air and earth; and, distributing these according to their allotted functions, through their mutual interaction generated the inorganic cell, in which the original watery globe produced offspring after its kind.

In the inorganic cell the equatorial sun found a suitable matrix for its own proper action, producing through it the vegetative action of the vegetable kingdom ; and, through the vegetative action of that kingdom, the organic cell.

In the organic cell the visible sun found its own proper matrix, and produced through this the animal (while maturing the vegetable) kingdom, finally placing man at its head, in whom, through the animating action of that kingdom, it originated the psychic cell.

But the man so placed at the head of the animal kingdom, at the head of the creation, was the animal, the soul-less, the perishable man.

Hence man, so left at the head of creation, al-though apparently its crown, would, by his advent, have marked its close; since creation, culminating in him, would at his death have entered on its decline.

The only escape the Kabbalists saw from this issue was, to hold that man was to the central sun, through the psychic cell, what the organic cell had been to the visible sun, what the inorganic cell to the equatorial sun, and the original watery globe to the polar sun—a matrix prepared for further action.

This further action they therefore believed in, and attributed to the central sun.

Hence the Kabbalists saw in man a matrix pro-duced from the earth by a triple generation, and prepared for submission to a yet further generative process.

U

Hence they attributed this further generative **action to** the central sun, which, as they maintained, acting on man, **on** duly prepared man throughout his life, generated, of and in him, the designed outcome of creation—the human soul.

And hence, because the human soul was, as they held, engendered by the central sun—to which they attributed the centralizing, the direct action of God —they called **the** so generated soul of man the child of God ; and taught that this was the being under **creation at** every stage of the advancing **work.**

Considering the genesis of the soul from this point of view, it is possible to see, not only how it is that the co-operation of man is necessary to the completion of the work to be carried on during his life, but why that co-operation can only be given in **one** way, through the uses he makes of that passing life.

He has been produced from his mother, the earth, by the successive cumulative action of three energies.

These three energies have produced in him a unity, **a** temporary unity, it is true, but still a unity of being.

To preserve this unity, and enable it to be perpetuated, **he must make of it a** harmony during and by the uses he makes of his actual life—*that the relations of his own proper electricity may be harmonious, and so invite, retain and promote the action of the radiant electrical energy of the central sun.*

In this harmony, the union and combined action of these energies—of his own electrical energy and the electrical energy of the central sun—generates, develops and builds up the soul.

Thus the soul is formed, strengthened and matured by the action and continued action of the electrical energy of the central sun.

Hence any diminution in this action causes a proportionate weakening of the soul, damaging or stifling it, so to say ; while on the cessation of this action the death of the soul occurs. And with the death of the soul, the man, though still living, passes out of the order of creation.

But this action is maintained and promoted by the harmonious relations of the proper electricity of the individual in whom it is going on.

While the harmony of these relations depends absolutely upon the uses made of the life, which should be such as to establish and preserve harmony of being.

Granting this—and who will deny that harmony should be the aim of life ?—the reason why man should so live as to maintain the harmonious relations of his own proper electrical condition, *the measure of which is found in the harmony of his life,* becomes at once apparent. And since but one influence, one motive impulse, is capable of producing this result, and can only produce it by acting on and through a natural life, is it not necessary, absolutely necessary, that man should live a natural life, under the guiding and fashioning influence of this impulse ; that death may be, in him, the birth of that child of God, the human soul ; to him, the passage to an Eden of which the imagery of the earthly paradise can give but a faint conception ?

THE GENESIS OF THE SOUL.

Part III.

THE KABBALISTIC THEORY OF EVOLUTION.

THE Kabbalists held that the unknown could only be reached through the known.

They saw in man a being living a two-fold life: the one passive or functional, by which his body was preserved, recruited and maintained in a state of efficiency; the other active and volitional, by which that body was applied to the uses for which it had been created.

Hence, reasoning from the known to the unknown, the Kabbalists believed in a double expression of the life of God.

The Kabbalists knew that the active life of man, which expressed itself through the use of his body, produced a change in the tissues of that body; and that these changed tissues were renewed by the processes of his passive life.

Hence the Kabbalists were assured that the active expression of the life of God produced a change in some of the elements of the divine substance, and that the passive expression of that life was to be found in the several processes by which these changed elements were brought back to their pristine state.

Of the active life of God, the Kabbalists were aware that man had, could have, no knowledge, the unknown here being outside the sphere of the known. But they were inclined to associate its formal expression with the solar bodies, in as well as through which they believed it to be carried on.

The passive life of God they saw unfolded in the creation.

This passive life dealt with elements which had been separated from the divine substance.

These they knew to be elements because they had been constituents of the divine substance. They knew them to be substantial elements because they had been derived from substance. And they knew them to be more substantial than the substance from which they had been derived, through their relations to that substance, and the part they were subsequently called upon to play.

These elements were of two kinds, of which the one was more substantial than the other.

The Kabbalists distinguished them as elemental spirit and elemental matter.

The tendency of elemental spirit was to indefinite expansion ; that of elemental matter to condensation and aggregation.   As elements they had no power of cohesion.

In leaving the unity of the divine substance, the more dense, matter, had drawn the less dense, spirit, with it.

Now the Kabbalists believed that spirit and matter, sent forth from the divine substance by processes of the divine life, carried with them certain inherent impulses.

Hence they saw in the expansion of spirit an instinctive effort to dissociate itself, by repulsion, from matter, and to seek, in attenuation, the transparency proper to the divine substance ; and in the condensation and aggregation of matter, an inherent effort in the latter to retain its hold upon spirit, that both might be renewed together.

The impulses which thus testified in either to a perception of the presence of the other, and the attraction and repulsion which ensued, were, the Kabbalists believed, the elemental roots of appetite and aversion on the one hand, and of affection and love on the other.

Elemental spirit and elemental matter, thus actuated and thus interacting, were destined, by their mutual action and reaction duly controlled, to be agents in creation.

The first creative act combined elemental spirit and elemental matter—a proportion of the hitherto diffused and dispersed elemental spirit and elemental matter—in the form of vesicular vapour.

In this, the vesicular form, which is the normal form of interacting spirit—in this form, which is that of a sphere or cell, spirit was brought under control that it might control.

In this form, by attraction, cohesion, absorption and conversion, once more brought under control that it might control, it originated a planetary body, a primary inorganic cell.

In this form, through the inorganic cell once more brought under control that it might control, it received the power of inducing vegetative action, and of originating incipient vegetative forms ; and then, through the vegetative action so introduced, of transmitting the vitalizing principle committed to it to the organic cell.

In this form, through the organic cell once more brought under control that it might control, it received the power of evolving and developing vegetable and animal forms ; and then, through the animating action so introduced, of transmitting a psychicizing power to, or transmuting the organic into the psychic cell.

These were successive cumulative stages of an advancing work.

At each of these stages spirit was brought under control that it might control—that it might control the building up of the bodily form in which it was about to pass a natural life. And this was spirit's share in the creative work.

But this part of the work completed, with the commencement of its active life spirit was brought under the control of the self, of the created being it had co-operated in producing.

In this being spirit and matter were associated for a common purpose ; which purpose was effected by the uses the created being made of its active individual life.

This purpose was the calling out, the developing and the maturing of the powers, faculties and affections it had been organized to give play to, through the use of the organs by which these were drawn out and expressed.

Now the Kabbalists believed that the germs of these powers, faculties and affections were inherent in spirit and in matter, as already stated ; and that the aim of creation was the specialization of these by attaching their expression to given organs, each

of which arose from the germ state to be progressively advanced and matured **by use.**

Their view was, that the germinating desire was
used to produce the germinal organ through which
the desire was to attain to its fruition, or be realized;
and that this germinal organ, by thus realizing the
desire, increased its own power of realizing that
desire while strengthening the desire itself.

In this way they held that, commencing from
the germ state, advancing spirit by the uses of life
advanced the bodily forms it had co-operated in
producing, and thus created in succession advancing
and advanced types of being, until the human form
was gained.

And further that, while so creating the advancing
bodily forms, these, reacting upon their spirits, developed them, so that at death **the** being under creation left its body, as a spirit, in a higher state than
it had entered therein.

Thus, under their view, action was followed by
reaction in an advancing order, until the necessary
creative matrices were produced.

The progress of this work they held to have been
at first slow ; but when these matrices had been
produced, the progressive passage of spirit, of the
being under creation, through its creative bodily
forms, was greatly accelerated—each spirit passing

through its own series of selected forms, that originality might be gained while individuality was maintained.

Spirit, they affirmed, was led by appetite in this its progressive course—led by appetite and actuated by self-will.

These, they maintained, had their roots in the inherent impulse which originated the interaction of spirit and matter, and were specializing expressions of that impulse.

According to the Kabbalists, they caused it, when disembodied, to desire a body through which to act and to enjoy. They guided it to the parentage for that body best adapted to give effect to its individualized aptitudes. They urged it so to modify the parental influences that the resultant body might furnish it with more perfect channels for the enjoyment sought through it. They caused it, when embodied, to seek for, seize upon and appropriate all that contributed to its own well-being and enjoyment, reckless of the consequences to others; and thus made self-indulgence the incentive to its uses of life, self-seeking the channel through which this self-indulgence gained its ends.

The Kabbalists were aware that such an actuating impulse could but produce selfish beings, beings whose selfishness tended to increase with every step they took in advance ; and that such a channel for giving effect to this actuating impulse could but introduce that competition in self-seeking which lies at the root of, results in and causes, what is known as and called "evil" from the standpoint of the human. But they believed that this motive and this channel were indispensable in the creative order, and were essential to the creative design ; that they were intended to introduce a struggle for existence ; that through this struggle, by a process of selection—of natural selection, in which spirit is the active operating agent—the most fitting, surviving, might originate the most suitable bodily forms, of their respective kinds, for the purposes for which they were adapted ; and that having thus originated, they might, through a continued struggle for existence, preserve, perpetuate and improve these thus selected forms until the highest attainable, the expected, that is the human form, was gained.

The Kabbalistic theory of evolution, reduced to its simplest proportions, is thus seen to have been :

1. That spirit, commencing from the germ state in the cell form, passed through a succession of bodies in an advancing order.

2. That at each transmigration it created the body in which it was about to live.

3. That it selected a parentage for this body

through which it would derive the power of most fully exercising the aptitudes and indulging the appetites it had acquired in the previous stages of the developing process through which it was passing, entering the same by way of generation.

4. That by applying its acquired aptitudes and gratifying its growing appetites in this body, it slowly modified the bodily form it was using, developing the organs thereof by use, while developing its own aptitudes and appetites.

5. That so doing, it was enabled to produce a developed offspring, an offspring with a greater bodily aptitude for indulging similar appetites and a tendency to yet further development.

6. That this double development, produced by the uses of life and directed by those uses—a development in which appetite and organ, desire and the power of gratifying desire, advanced *pari passu* —so worked, that the quality of the being to be produced was determined by the quality of the life producing it.

7. That its working resulted in a struggle for existence, under which the self-seeker most advantageously organized and favourably circumstanced, getting the better of its less favoured competitor, survived to transmit a more favoured offspring.

8. While at death it sent the being under creation

forth from the body in a condition fitting it to enter an advanced bodily form, through which it sought higher powers for the enjoyment of life.

Thus it appears the Kabbalists believed that during life the advancing spirit, while developing its own aptitudes and appetites by the uses of life, developed, in the body it was using, the power of producing offspring better suited for the indulgence of such appetites as it was maturing, and therefore capable of being more easily moulded in the direction the generating spirit might wish the offspring under generation to follow ; and that at death the advanced spirit, released from the body with which it had been temporarily united for the purposes of life, passed into the spirit state in cell form, as a medium for transmitting the advancing being from body to body.

Not that the Kabbalists supposed that all spirits advanced under this process. So far were they from this, that they thought that many retrograded ; while still more, from various causes, passed out of the creative order.

They simply affirmed that regular, progressive, migratory advance was the normal creative action.

They were aware, however, that the spirit so advancing and advanced was a self-seeking spirit ; and that on entering the human it necessarily produced a being whose instinctive impulses were centred in self.

This was why the Kabbalists affirmed that the being under creation in man entered the human form to undergo a change in that form, the aim of which was to direct his impulses, and through these the uses of his life, to that which was outside self.

They believed this change was necessary, that in him the perishable might be transformed into the imperishable, and transferred in a natural condition to a renewed life, a life from which every element of change and instability was eliminated ; and therefore taught that man was a matrix prepared for further creative action ; and that this action, duly carried out, so changed the essence of the spiritual and the material, whose working was through the physical, that the physical was gradually attempered and transformed into the psychical—*interpreted through the Greek as the natural*—because it was a change of state and condition, not of nature and being ; which conversion was regarded by them as a regeneration in the human, and treated as the generation or genesis of the soul.

THE GENESIS OF THE SOUL.

PART IV.

THE KABBALISTIC DOCTRINE OF FUNCTIONAL ACTION.

THE science of the Kabbalah was the science of life.

The basis of this science the Kabbalists placed in functional action.

Reasoning from the known to the unknown, they had learnt that the celestial circulation was associated with life.

Hence they had considered it a vital circulation, analogous in character to the circulation on which the life of organized beings depends.

They did not think it possible to be misled by a false analogy here, because they were aware of the essential difference between vascular circulation, as the necessary accompaniment of organic life—which needs channels and a menstruum through which the circulating globules can flow, be distributed and act—and the non-vascular circulation of the passive life of God, in which such media are wholly dispensed with.

To them, the heavenly bodies were the organs of the divine unorganized Being whose life was the source of all life ; although as units they were the analogues of the organic cells of organized life.

So minute does the knowledge of the Kabbalists appear to have been, that it is hardly possible to doubt they realized the existence of and the differences between the red and white corpuscles of the blood ; and considered the relations of these to finite life were to be likened to the relations of the solar and planetary bodies to the life of the Infinite.

At any rate they treated the cell as the agent of functional action ; and from the study of this, the known, as the agent of organic life, gained their knowledge of the functional relations of the heavenly bodies to the unknown, the inorganic life of the Divine Being.

Now, according to their ideas, the function of the cell, briefly stated, was two-fold.

As a unit, it collected, converted and re-distributed the elements of substance.

In association and combination, it built up organs

and fashioned **bodily forms,** constructing these of cellular elements.

Hence the Kabbalists taught that the **individual cell,** when acting alone, **attracted** to **itself** those elements of substance that **were to** be submitted **to** its special action ; that it absorbed and converted these—this absorption **and** conversion **being its** proper function ; **and that** it **then gave** forth these same elements **in a** changed state **and** modified relations. And they held that the function of the **cell** unit, acting **alone, was** limited to this simple expression.

The Kabbalists therefore believed that **every** isolated cell was surrounded **by an** atmosphere **or aura, a** stream of which **was** constantly passing through it ; **and that this** atmosphere **or aura** consisted of the elements of substance in two states. **That in** one of **these** states the elements tended **to the** cell, **by** which they were attracted. **That** in the other they passed from **the cell,** by which **they had** been converted. **And** that, therefore, **this atmosphere or aura was** constituted of two **currents of** elemental substance, **each in a** different **state, either moving in an** opposite direction **to** the other.

This **was the** Kabbalistic view of the simple function of the single cell.

This they considered to be the common function of all cells.

Hence they attributed it to the highest of the celestial bodies, as to the humblest of the terrestrial cells.

And under this aspect they regarded the heavenly bodies as cells.

In this state the cell was, in their eyes, a simple organ.

Had creation not been superadded to the function thus provided for, the cell would have remained the simple organ it was thus constituted.

But creation required combined action.

For its purposes the single cells must act in association.

Now each cell was primarily, as regards the creation, individualized spirit in a particular state.

This spirit had been created, or individualized, by the close union or combination of elemental spirit substance and elemental matter substance, through the action of the radiant energy flowing from the central sun.

Through this creative action it acquired the powers of attraction, cohesion and combination, without which further creative advance would have been impossible.

A multitude of these thus created spirit cells combining, cohering, and so discharging their common function, or acting in combination, had built up and constituted the planetary body ; had built up and constituted that body by attracting, absorbing, converting, combining and transmitting a further proportion of the more dense elementary matter substance. (For each spirit cell, in performing its share of the creative work, absorbs, digests and appropriates, or uses elementary matter substance ; each spirit cell, or created spirit, thus constructing an elementary body for itself, through which to act.)

The associated spirits that had thus built up and constituted the planetary body, acting through their head, became the individualized spirit of the body they had constructed.

This planetary body, acted upon by the polar sun, produced a multitude of inorganic cells—embodied spirits, elementarily constituted as their parent, but in a developed, a more materialized, an advanced and an advancing state.

These inorganic cells, while constituting the crystalline and mineral kingdom, acted upon by the equatorial sun, combined in or built themselves into vegetative forms, of each of which, acting through their head, the associated units became the individualized spirits. (For, according to the Kabbalists, all forms, as well as all individualized elements, are

associated with or have their individualized spirits
—each its own individualized spirit, constituted of
associated spirit cells, which in combination act
through their head, whose powers of action are
derived from and represent the combination of the
powers transmitted to it by the aggregated cells
acting under it.)

The vegetative action thus introduced and carried
on produced a multitude of organic cells—embodied
spirits, elementarily constituted as their parent, but
in a more developed state, a state in which they
were endowed with an organizing power through
which yet further advance was to be made.

These organic cells, while developing the vegetable kingdom, acted upon by the visible sun, combined in or built themselves into organized, that is
animal forms, passing through these in succession
in a progressively advancing order, of each of which,
acting through their head, the associated units became the individualized spirit.

The animative action thus introduced and carried
on produced a multitude of psychic cells—embodied
spirits, elementarily constituted as their parent, but
in a still more developed state.

This state was the human.

In this state, which was an embodiment in the
highest and noblest of the animal forms, they were

endowed with the power of converting the physical into the psychical, when the conditions were favourable to this specific functional action.

Each **of** these living forms **was** constituted **by** and **was** the embodiment of an advancing spirit **in** process of evolutional creation ; and, to this intent, **brought into a particular state by the** combined action of the associated spirit cells **that had** acted with it to produce, and were acting **with** it to maintain, its then state.

Now the particular **state of an** individualized **or** evolutionally created spirit **or** individual cell, **at a** given time, depended, according **to** the Kabbalists, upon the stage it had reached in **the** line of evolution through which it **was advancing, so** that the stage and the state were reflections each of the other.

From this point **of view** the Kabbalistic conception of functional action in the creative order is not difficult to understand.

An **individualized** spirit cell **in a** particular state, **a** state marking the stage **it has** reached in the evolution of the being under creation through its co-operative agency, selects, **or is** guided to, a parent- **age for the** bodily form it has been fitted to make **use of and desires to enter.**

In the process of generation, through which this bodily **form is to** be constituted **and** constructed, this individualized spirit cell attracts other spirit cells to itself; cells whose particular state fitted them to combine with itself in the work it was commencing; cells whose particular state fitted each for its own special share of that work.

With the help of these, this individualized spirit cell built itself and them into the body of which they, acting through it, were thus constituted the individualized spirit.

The organized body, thus built up by what is called the process of generation, became at birth, from one point of view, a compound organ charged with a common function—a compound organ which, in the discharge of its function, attracted, absorbed, converted, combined, re-distributed and gave off in a changed state, such elements of substance as it was capable of so acting on, each individual organ doing its own special and proper share of the common work. But under another point of view, this same organized body, thus built up, was a living being—a being using, in the processes of its own proper life, the elements it was converting, and carrying on that proper life, or living, by their conversion.

Hence, according to the Kabbalists, every organized being was unconsciously leading a two-fold functional life—a functional life susceptible of a double aspect.

Under one of these **aspects** this functional life consisted in an elemental action ; under the other, in a vital **use.**

But this elemental action and **this vital use** were carried **on** together, **as** different **results of simul-**taneously working processes, **which** were creative, re-creative or conservative, as far as the condition of **the** being was concerned, while they were simply **conversive, and bringing to** a changed state, as regards the elements **acted on.**

Now owing **to this its two-fold** functional life, the Kabbalists held that every organized being, like each simple cell, was surrounded by an atmosphere or aura, which, like **the atmosphere or aura** of the single **cell,** or, again, **like the atmosphere or aura** of the planetary **body, was** constituted **of** those elements of substance on which **it was** functionally to act—by functionally acting on which it was to live —in different states. **And that** of these elements, **those** in the one state being attracted **by were** tend-**ing to it,** to be submitted to its special action, while **those in** the other were passing from **it** after having undergone **the** change produced by that special action, by undergoing **that** change having contri-buted **to its life.**

Hence the Kabbalists **taught :**

1. That **every** organized being had **a stream of**

spirit substance unintermittingly passing through it; this passage being necessary to its continued life.

2. That the organs of the being acted upon this stream of spirit substance and converted its elements, together with those of a similar stream of matter substance which it took in at intervals as food; its life being maintained by the discharge of this function.

3. That the aim of this function, demonstrable from its logical, if not from its observed results, was the due materialization of spirit and spiritualization of matter; that these might be thus brought, as elements, to a renewed state in which they were to be restored, in combination, to the divine substance, from which they had been originally sent forth by the processes of the divine life.

Thus, according to the Kabbalists, every organized being, viewed through its functional life, was to be regarded as a subordinate organ discharging a function in the passive life of God. But this teaching of the Kabbalists concerned the life of the being.

Beyond this, they taught that when the life of the being ceases, and as death takes place, the cell representing the being under creation leaves the body which has been its instrument or organ during life.

It had entered that body in one state ; it left it in another—the change in state having been determined by the uses it made of the intervening life. In this, it followed the course pursued by the elements functionally changed by the organs of the being during its uses of life. And this course was absolute in every case. But here the influence which induced the change was derived from the associated cells, and was the result of the combined action of the entire group.

Now all of these associated spirit cells had been advanced together by the uses made by their head of the life of the being. They had given their head the power of acting ; of using themselves through the life of the being ; of advancing them in the line of evolution itself was following. The uses it made of its life determined the direction that advance should take, and the channels through which it would be pursued. And the death of the being took place when all the associated members of the company were ready to enter on this further advance, each in its own order.

But when the death of the being took place, all did not leave the body together. The head went first—by its departure severing the bond which held them together ; and then the members followed in succession, as the state of the body permitted.

(For the Kabbalists taught that the phenomena connected with and known as the *rigor mortis* pointed to this as the course of dissolution.)

In this dissolution all departed as cells, as spirit cells. There was only one exception here ; but this exception was crucial.

The cell representing the being under creation entered the human form as a psychic cell. In that form it was to be subjected to the fecundating and fostering influence of the central sun, that the organic form it had at length acquired might be so acted on during its then life as to be brought from the physical to the psychic state. For this was the conversion that should take place in man.

Now this, like each of its predecessors, was a functional conversion—a conversion promoted and carried on by the uses made, by the being under creation, of its passing life.

But there was this wide difference between this and the conversions previously effected, that a selection was to be made here of those who by their lives showed themselves to be fit for the psychic state. For only such were to be susceptible of the expected change.

Hence the uses made of the life now not only determined the change, but selected those in whom it could take place.

And hence the Kabbalists taught that man's future state depended absolutely on the uses he made of his present life. And—since the essential difference between the non-psychic and the psychic being was, that whereas the non-psychic being sought the fulfilment of its own will, thus developing self-will and strengthening *will* in itself, the psychic being controlled its will through and subordinated it to *affection*—they affirmed that a life controlled by unselfish love was the life in which the conversion of the non-psychic into the psychic, or the regeneration of the human and genesis of the soul, takes place.

THE Kabbalists looked upon evolution as essentially an elective process.

They saw a selection, a natural selection, taking place at every stage of the creative work, and as, in their eyes, the workings of nature were the workings of God, they considered this natural to be a divine selection, carried on with design and to effect a purpose.

They realized the vastness and far-reaching character of this design from the fact that what is known as "evil," in human parlance, entered into the working, and was a necessary agent in giving effect to the work.

But the realization of this necessity revealed to their acute minds the existence of a further necessity, the necessity that the Designer should control the working of such an agent, to secure the success of the work.

They had seen this control exercised at the very outset, through the radiant energy flowing from the central sun, which, similarly electrifying suns, planets and satellites, restrained the impulse that drew each towards its centre of attraction, and, holding them apart, converted motion towards into motion round the respective centres.

This radiant energy they held to be the channel through which the needed general control was carried on.

That such a control was exercising its influence over evolution seemed to them self-evident. The co-existence of degraded and degrading, of retrograde types of being, with the advancing types through which progressive development was attained, together with the disappearance of intervening and no longer serviceable types, could not but be, in their eyes, a conclusive proof of the fact; and they believed that all man required was a fuller knowledge of the details of natural action, and a more careful comparison of its results, to bring this clearly out.

Close observation had convinced them that degradation of type was associated with decay of intelligence, and marked a general decadence of the being subjected to it; while the conjoint existence of great ferocity, with something like a complete deprivation of the organs of intelligence in some of these types, especially those of the reptile order, constrained them to see through this—the matured fruit of recklessly aggressive self-seeking—the cause that had led to the exclusion of these, individually, collectively, and, as a necessary consequence of this line of reasoning, selectively, from the advancing order of nature.

The Kabbalists knew that the being under creation by process of evolution was, in the disembodied condition, a creative spirit in a particular state and advancing order.

They were aware that this being's advance was carried on in the embodied state by its uses of life in that state.

Observation had shown them that the bodily advance through which the advance of the being was gained, was obtained by natural selection through that struggle for existence in which the fittest survived to transmit an improved, an improving and improvable bodily form.

Observation had further shown them, as already stated, that this progression was accompanied by retrogression; **and** this observation had satisfied them that a selection was going on in the advancing beings ; **a** selection analogous to the selection taking **place in** the advancing bodily forms ; a selection **under which** the fittest survived, or were maintained in the advancing series, all others dropping in succession out of the creative order.

This selective action they attributed to the influence **of the central sun.**

The motive for this selection and **the** principle **on which it was based, they** thought, were not far to seek. And the realization of this motive, and of the principle through which **it is** applied, is the **key to the** comprehension of their scientific system.

The effect **of natural selection on the** advancing beings, they **saw, and were not able to** understand **how any one** could fail to see, must divide the **advancing spirits into two** classes.

This was **a** foregone conclusion **in** their minds. **For the impulse** under which the selection was carried **on was one of reckless** self-seeking, that **sacrificed** others to self.

Under this impulse the self-seeker most favoured **by circumstances,** whether **of** organization or surroundings, promotes its own well-being at the expense **of** less favoured competitors ; and overcomes these in a struggle for existence through which the least favoured were extinguished, in each conflict in succession, by their more favoured opponents.

Such was the law of selective evolution as indicated by the teaching of the Kabbalists.

Under this law the less favoured were sacrificed to the more favoured advancing beings, necessarily so sacrificed.

This course of procedure originated, developed and matured an aggressive disposition in the successful self-seekers ; and, through the action of this disposition, simultaneously applied through the uses to the purposes of life, weakened, subordinated and subdued the self-asserting tendencies of their sacrificed victims—weakened, subordinated and finally subdued these by impeding and preventing their exercise of the power of giving way to the same. And the necessary, the inevitable consequence of this was, that the advancing spirits were divided into two classes, the one of aggressive, the other of victim spirits.

The Kabbalists took a wider survey of creative activity, and formed a higher conception of its meaning and purpose, than have for many ages entered into the minds or been grasped by the understandings of their degenerate successors.

They knew that those who fixed their attention on what was going on around them, and limited the scope of their vision to the narrow range of what they thus learnt (without attempting to reason **beyond** and trying at least to feel their way, though it were but by groping, from the known to the unknown), while so seeking (even though they should succeed in arriving at a wider generalization), could not fail to mislead themselves, and, as would-be teachers, deceive and misguide others.

The observer whose horizon was bounded by the outcome of the phenomena of life, must, they were aware, have his judgment obscured by the ordinary, the persistent, the universal way in which *the evil* overcomes and casts out *the good* in so circumscribed an area of vision, until, overwhelmed by the visible and only too real consequences of what it scanned through the distorting medium of such a narrow conception, he is driven to seek outside nature for the cause of and remedy for that, to the cure of which nature, as he finds himself driven **to** conclude, has proved wholly inadequate.

Such an observer, they had realized, was only too ready to jump at the conclusion, either that nature works automatically and blindly, without definite **aim ; or** that *evil* has its own proper author, who had introduced or intruded it into the world—introduced it by the permission of, or intruded it in opposition to, the original Author of *good.*

This was their trial.

They knew and taught that the impulse which originated what, from man's restricted point of view, appears to be *good* and *evil*, was the pivot on which selective creation turned. But their knowledge had been disregarded, their teaching unheeded.

They had seen the lamentable errors they repudiated not only fallen into, but developed and expanded into doctrinal and dogmatic systems whose acceptance and extension they had been wholly powerless to prevent. And through these they were brought into contact, in its green state, with that which ultimately, in the dry, distorted and absorbed their own teachings, after causing their knowledge to pass away and be forgotten.

And yet the conceptions of the Kabbalists were so grand, so clear, so simple, it seems impossible to reject them when they have been once presented to the mind and fairly grasped.

They held that just as the Creator used a tendency to centralization, to concentration, to individualization, expressing itself through attraction, as the motive impulse of the elemental; so was he using a tendency to self-assertion, to selfish acquisition, possession, use and enjoyment, expressing itself through self-seeking, as the motive impulse of the creative part of his work ; and therefore maintained *that self-seeking was the creative, the designed creative impulse.*

But they held that this creative impulse operated in two ways, and hence they taught :

1. That while self-seeking, by natural selection through evolution, developed in a progressively advancing order, and so created the bodily forms, or matrices, through which the being under creation was to advance to and gain its ultimate condition ;

2. It simultaneously, again by natural selection, marked out and set apart, as a distinct class, the beings from which those who could be brought to that condition were necessarily chosen.

And they taught that this second selection was made in this wise :

They saw that its aim must be the separation of those capable of giving up their self-seeking tendency—of exchanging it for a tendency to the surrender of self—from such as were incapable of so surrendering their own wills, that they might be prepared for transference to that state for which, as children of God, they were designed.

They further saw that, since the advancing being must itself co-operate in and promote this part of the advancing work as it had co-operated in and promoted the previous stages of that work, some motive adequate to take the place of and replace the motive that has hitherto actuated it, must be provided, to furnish it with the necessary impulse.

Seeing this, they further saw only one motive adequate to supply this impulse, and so produce the needed change.

That motive was Love.

And then, seeing this, they yet further saw that love was the only basis on which enduring happiness could be built up.

Now the Kabbalists believed that the aim of the creation was the production of beings capable of uninterrupted, of enduring happiness in a renewed life and higher state; a happiness into which the subordination of self through the surrender of the will must enter, in order that it may be enduring.

Believing this, they were sure that beings whose wills were becoming stronger and more unyielding through a successful struggle for existence, carried on by the indulgence of appetite at the expense of their unsuccessful competitors, could not be made susceptible of a change which would be a subversion of the nature they had derived from their evolutional series of existence.

While at the same time they were assured that

those whose wills **had been** constantly subdued by and sacrificed to **the** more energetic wills of their aggressive **opponents were, for** that very reason, susceptible of **and** capable of undergoing the **re-**quired change.

Hence they could **not avoid** the conclusion, **that the order of beings from** which **those capable of being so transformed must be** selected, **was** the **class of victim spirits whose** evolutional course had been, however involuntarily, one of **the** subjugation **and** sacrifice of their own wills from the beginning. **Indeed, they drew a fundamental** teaching **from this, that** the sacrifice **of self, to be** efficacious **in this** regard, should be called for by circumstances ; **or** imposed, **not** self-imposed.

Under this **view,** they **taught** that, as the aggressive spirits advanced **and increased** in aggressiveness, **as soon** as **the tendency to self-assertion** growing out of this disposition had reached such **a** height as to deprive the beings actuated by it **of** all **chance** of success **in the** second selective struggle— **as** regards **the final aim of** creation—they were excluded from the creative **order by** the controlling influence **of the radiant** energy **of the** central sun, and then **passed into the class of** retrograding spirits, **in some of which** aggressiveness became **ferocity in the** re-embodied state. **And in** this retrograde order they held that there was a gradual subsidence of intelligence, and an ultimate diminution of all powers, until the capability of re-embodiment was lost.

This elimination, they maintained, was taking place at every stage of the advancing work—finding its culmination in man ; in whom, by similar process, the confirmed self-seeker was rejected as the final selection was made.

And in this final selection they saw a wonderful providential compensation. For those who had been the victims, in that struggle for existence by which the bodily forms had been advanced, were precisely those capable of undergoing the final change when the ultimate selection was made.

And these were capable of undergoing this change because, their wills having been habitually contradicted and subdued by those that victimized them without their consent, when an adequate motive presented itself for themselves subduing that which had been throughout brought into subjection and subdued by others, this was not difficult to them.

To the Kabbalists, nothing seemed more reasonable than this view of creation ; nothing more clear than the reason for the change sought in man ; nothing more effectual, potentially, than the means by which man's co-operation in producing the same was to be secured.

Will had been the outcome of the dominant action of the spirit state. Spirits make it their boast that they are all *wills.* Love was to sway the soul.

Hence, according to the Kabbalists, the distinguishing sign of those in whom the genesis of the soul, or regeneration of the human, is going on, is— that in these, *will* is giving way to, and being changed into, or cast out by, *love.*

THE GENESIS OF THE SOUL.

Part VI.

THE KABBALISTIC CONCEPTION OF DUALITY IN CREATION.

SPIRIT and matter, banished, according to the Kabbalists, from the presence of God, instinctively desire to re-enter the divine life.

Sent forth from the divine substance in unstable association to gain more stable relations, they will be restored to the divine unity when and as they regain, or are renewed in, their own original and proper unity.

Now this unity the Kabbalists held could be regained in either of two ways.

The unity sought was the unity of the divine substance, with a view to re-participation in the divine life.

In this unity spirit and matter had participated before they were sent forth from the presence of

God; and so participating, had participated as a unity—a unity in which, through forming one with the divine substance, they had formed one with each other.

Spirit and matter, thus viewed, the Kabbalists considered must have existed in the divine substance as spiritualized matter or materialized spirit, and therefore must re-enter that substance, or regain their substantial condition in that form.

Hence they taught that the spiritualization of matter, which is the materialization of spirit, or substantial union of either with the other, was the aim of the passive and functional life of God.

This spiritu-materializing function they saw was carried on by organs acting functionally to that intent; organs constituted in each instance of a spirit acting through a body.

Of these, the spirit, by process of generation, created the body through which it was to act. (For spirit is the creative agent, and the recognition of this fact caused it to be ideally personified and addressed by the earlier ritualists—as well as by the later, as in the *Veni Creator Spiritus*, and other aspirational invocations—as the Creative Spirit).

Of these, the body, re-acting thereon through the uses of life, developed and matured the therein embodied individualized spirit.

Thus spirit and matter, as a spirit in a body, were acting in association in these thus constituted organs.

Now these organs were at first unorganized, or constituted of inorganic elements.

To this primary class of organs two other classes were, in due time, added—those of organized and animated being. But in each and all of these spirit and matter were acting in association.

Spirit and matter were brought together in these organs that they might act and re-act on each other.

This action and re-action constituted the functional life of the organ ; and by this functional action spirit and matter were constantly given off by the organ in a spiritu-materialized condition, or state of substantial union.

But the exercise of this function gradually exhausted the organ, until at length, unable to continue its specific and proper action, the organic relations between spirit and matter ceasing, the spirit was set free and the material body dissolved ; both spirit and matter, the spirit and the matter whose association had constituted the organ, gradually resuming their elemental state, to be again similarly re-associated, and act and re-act in a similar manner.

This applied to and constituted the inorganic relations in functioning organs.

Had what is called the creation not been super-added to the work, this function would have been discharged solely by inorganic organs, in the way described.

But creation was superadded, and this simple was thus made a compound function. And it was the creative character imparted to the work that gave the creative impulse to spirit, and caused it to develop organized and animated organs, thus making it "the Creative Spirit."

In this creation spirit and matter were simple agents.

In it the end sought was still the same—the spiritu-materialization or substantial union of spirit and matter, that both might thus be restored to the unity of the divine life.

But this substantial union could now be gained in either of two ways:

1. Functionally, through a process whereby ele-mental substance was produced by organic action.

2. Vitally, when a living being was created through organic use.

Now the aim of creation was two-fold:

1. To give stability to the association of spirit and matter, or cause the temporary union between

them to become substantial, that they may be constituted as or included in a substantial unity, which was the functional end sought.

2. To individualize this spiritu-material substance in organized and animated forms, or create personal beings ; beings whose substantial condition would give stability to their vital relations and cause these to be enduring.

The peculiarity of this creation was, that while the functioning organs or agents were perishable, their products acquired the stability of which the producers, as producers, were not susceptible.

The effect of this was, that man, viewed as the outcome of this creative activity, was an organ in which the two agents, spirit and matter, were in unstable association. And to this his subjection to death was due. For man, as the Kabbalists maintained, was perishable, because in him spirit and matter were merely acting in association, and had not been brought into the state of substantial union.

Now, as an organ, the two-fold aim of creation was being carried out by him as his generic function.

Spiritu-materialized substance was constantly given forth by him during life.

A spiritu-materialized being was to pass from him at death :

While the two agents, spirit and matter, which

by their unstable association had been used in co-
operation to produce this double result, the residual
spirit and matter, dissociated by death, passed into
a condition of slow dissolution, whose outcome was
a return to the elemental state.

Such was the Kabbalistic view.

But, according to the Kabbalists, **in man a process of selective** elimination **was** going on — an
elimination which followed and was determined by
the uses he made of his passing life.

The effect of this eliminative action was, as they
affirmed, that when and as the being under creation
in him fitted itself by its life to pass from the perish-
able to the imperishable state, **it was** gradually
changed **by** the processes of life, under the guiding
and controlling influence **of the** central sun, or
brought into a spiritu-materialized condition, in
which its vital organs and organic constitution and
relations were so **acted on** and attempered that at
death a living soul—a being created of spiritu-
materialized substance—passed from the body it
had hitherto animated to enter into the divine life ;
this passage to the divine **life** being thus gained
through, and the fruition of, **the natural** life of which
it was the fulness and completion.

This **living soul was thus, as** they maintained,
not spiritual by nature—a mere spirit.

Still less was it material—a simple body.

It was a spiritu-materialized being; a being constituted of the one substance which, by its characteristic unity, they at once recognized as the divine substance.

This being, in virtue of its constitution, at once passed to the divine life, to enter which it had been created; therein to take the active part for which it had been designed.

Only such a being, they believed, could be admitted to the divine life.

All others, they maintained, owing to the unstable relations of their constitution, necessarily passed, through an ultimate dissolution, back to the elemental state from which they had been derived, to re-enter the order of functional life, until that substantial unity was regained through which alone the passage to the divine could be re-opened to them.

But in man a selection was going on.

Hence only in some men did this change take place.

Only from those who had fitted themselves by their lives for the expected change did the living soul pass from the human to the divine life.

This living soul was, such was the Kabbalistic teaching, a spiritu-materialized being, and not a spirit.

It had entered the human form as a spirit in order that during its human life it might be changed, transformed into a living soul, or brought from the spirit to the soul state as a spiritu-materialized being.

This change could only take place in man.

The being under creation had, in all its antecedent embodiments, entered the body as an advancing, and passed from it as an advanced, spirit—had always passed from the body as a spirit.

But as a spirit it could not enter the divine life, according to the Kabbalists.

All it could do as spirit, as advancing spirit, was, create bodies in which to pass temporary lives in unstable relations; create these by process of generation, as long as the power of so creating was permitted it.

Hence, if during its human life it so lived as not to gain the soul state, it passed from this, its final embodiment, at death as a spirit, a spirit that had failed to fulfil its mission.

But, so passing, it passed out of, and therefore was and remained outside, the creative order.

While, because so passing and remaining, the faculty of creating natural bodies simultaneously passed from it.

But as a spirit its relations were, necessarily were, as the Kabbalists believed, unstable; so that the

only course now before it—a course which it could
not avoid, though circumstances might prolong the
process—was that of dissolution and return to the
elemental state, from which once more to seek, or
be passed through functional action to the substantial unity it has so far failed to acquire.

The Kabbalistic doctrine of the duality of creation is thus seen to have been :

1. That spirit and matter were, by the creative
processes, recalled to the divine life.

2. That they could be brought back to or re-enter
that life in one of two ways, either in substantial
union as elemental substance, or in created unity,
as individualized, organized and animated personal
being.

As a consequence of this, they held that the
spirit state or spirit world was only an incident of
creation, which, after having done its work, would
be ultimately dissolved, with the planet with which
it had been associated, to pass in the elemental state
through another cycle of functional action, and so
on ; this being the only way in which substantial
unity could be regained.

The living soul was, in the eyes of the Kabbalists,
the designed outcome of creation ; the imperishable
human, the being sought by the divine Creator.

Man, in his substantial and imperishable organic

and organized state, was to be, from the Kabbalistic point of view, the vesture sought through the human for the divine.

Hence the Kabbalists held that, just as he had been used in his perishable life as an individualized organ **in** the passive or functional life of God, so was he in his imperishable state to be a personal organ of the active divine life.

That is to say, the Kabbalists believed and affirmed that the human soul was called into being that the divine life might be incarnated therein, and the divine human thus constituted.

The Kabbalists further believed that the divine was to be constituted, like the human, of one being in two persons.

They had seen the sex principle asserting itself, from the very outset of the work and throughout the same, as the active basis on which the whole was to rest.

They had satisfied themselves that the powers, faculties and affections, which were brought to maturity in man, had their roots in the instinctive **aspirations** of spirit and of matter—those aspirations which elemental spirit and elemental matter had brought with them as inherent properties when they passed out of the divine life.

They had seen that these powers, faculties and

affections tended, of themselves and when left to themselves, to the dissociation of personalities and their resolution into selfish individualities; that love was the only influence that opposed an effectual barrier to this tendency; and that love only gained its completeness in the dual unity, marriage.

In this dual unity in its perfect state, where the unity is absolute, they saw that the aspirations of both members of this unity became identical.

They were aware that generation was a condition of the present relations of life, and would cease in the divine human.

But they knew that, even in the divine human, *identity of substance must be maintained, that unity of aspiration may be preserved.*

Hence they considered that the union of the sexes had, in the human, a higher purpose than simple generation, though that purpose was only too seldom realized.

That its intent in man was to bring the two beings thus united, when the conditions of their lives permitted, into one substance, or make them one flesh, that they might be two in one—this, *that the aspirations of both might be identical.*

They looked through and beyond this perishable condition to that imperishable state to which the human was but the passage.

Thus looking on these relations, they saw that the two beings so united were made one, *that they might pass into the divine life as one being in two persons.*

Thus looking on these relations, they further saw that all whose unity of being did not commence in the human would gain it in the divine human, when the full meaning of the tie which should, but seldom does, commence on earth, would be brought out, *as the means by which integral unity of being was gained, that, through a perpetuated identity of substance, unity of aspiration might be maintained.*

Hence the Kabbalists held that, in the divine human, man and woman—the man and the woman who constituted or we're to constitute, in each instance, the individual members of the divine life—were the two persons of a single created being in whom the divine was now incarnated, that it might be completely identified with the natural, from and through which it was derived.

And they taught that in and through this dual unity of being—which, as a dual personality, was intended to preserve that identity of substance necessary to a true unity of aspiration—the relations of man and woman will find their specific purpose, and full and mature expression in the divine order.

THE GENESIS OF THE SOUL.

PART VII.

THE KABBALISTIC VIEW OF THE SPIRIT STATE.

THE Kabbalists held that man could have intellectual cognizance of that which was beyond the reach of his unaided natural senses, remembering always that the unknown can only be reached through the known.

They had seen that the relations between spirit and matter, as functional and creative agents, were unstable ; but they at the same time saw that the tie which bound the spiritual to the material in the natural was so close, that these, viewed as separate states or worlds, became integral parts of an organic whole, and would therefore be inseparable until the planet in and through which they were associated was, with all its constituents, finally dissolved and reduced to the ultimate elements from which it had been originally derived.

The basis of the spirit world, from their point of view, was the spirit atmosphere or aura which enveloped the earth.

This aura, which permeated the planet to its very centre, and was held to include the moon as the satellite of the planetary body, was the agent through which the spirit of the earth acted, and maintained its headship and control over the several members working under it.

The Kabbalists taught that spirit and matter were diverse forms of one substance, which differed *inter se*, and were to be distinguished from each other through formal differences in density.

They taught, moreover, that, while spirit and matter were of different densities, there was a wide difference between the density of spirit as spirit, and that of matter as matter. But in teaching this, they did not imply that the scale of these respective differences was such, that the more dense spirit substance toned into the less dense matter substance. On the contrary, they maintained that they formed parallel scales of affinity, in which the more dense spirit tended to and was attracted by the more dense matter substance ; and so on throughout the scale. Indeed, to distinguish these more clearly, they defined the differing densities of spirit as different degrees of opacity. But these differences were only cognizable under certain circumstances, and were chiefly recognized through their results.

These distinctions the Kabbalists regarded as important ; so important, that they made them the basis on which their views of the spirit world, as an organic whole, rested.

They held that, functionally, spirit and matter of corresponding opacity and density tended to coalesce ; and that the resultant created spirits, in the disembodied state, were constituted on a scale in which the differing opacities and transparencies of elemental or uncreated spirit were reproduced. And that these spirits in the embodied state attracted, appropriated, digested and assimilated elemental spirit and elemental matter whose condition was conformed to their own.

They therefore taught that there was a wide difference in the condition of created spirits ; and that in the intimate association between the spirit world and the world of matter, the more opaque spirits in the disembodied state were drawn towards the more dense parts of the material world, and therefore tended towards the centre of the earth, where they found the conditions most suited to their state ; while the more transparent spirits passed into the surrounding aura of the planet, the most rarefied finding their home in its satellite.

The operation of the same law of affinity, the Kabbalists maintained, produced a double manifestation of the spirit of the earth, equal to a double individualization thereof, in which a dual unity of spirit is shadowed; a simulated dual unity, whose divergent methods tend to promote a single **aim**.

Under this double manifestation, acting from the centre of the planet through its centralizing spirits, the spirit of the earth was a materialized and materializing or opaque spirit; while acting from its transparent atmosphere, or even from the moon—as the ruler of spirit—through the rarefied spirits, **it** was the transparent, spiritualized and spiritualizing head which administered the whole.

This double manifestation of the spirit of the earth was essentially a functional division, that, controlling the whole functional action of the planet, it might separate the spirits into whose constitution a preponderance of matter had entered, from those in which the material constituents had been minimized; for each of these required a different functional treatment, carried on under the control of the head.

The aura of the earth was thus constituted of elemental spirit passing towards and from the centre **of the** planet **in** different states, on and through

which the spirit of the earth acted ; and was filled
with created disembodied spirits in different conditions, elemental, advancing, matured and retrograde;
of which the elemental and advancing spirits formed
the class through which creative energy was working, the matured and retrograde spirits having passed
out of the creative order.

Of these, the first class need not be further noticed.
Their course has been already fully stated, and they
are too much occupied with their allotted share of
the work in hand to concern themselves with the
occupations of other spirits.

The matured and retrograde spirits form the spirit
order, properly so called.

Of these, the retrograde spirits were classed by
the Kabbalists as malicious and malignant elemen-
taries ; though spirits that are simply tricky, as
well as others whose agency was at times bene-
ficent, were of this class, which included fairies,
elves, mineral spirits, and the like.

All of these were passing through gradual degradation and decay to ultimate dissolution, their ranks
being replenished by constant recruitment.

In these, the material elements preponderated ;
and they, like the matured opaque spirits, of which
they formed a subordinate order, could only make
their presence known to and communicate with

embodied spirits in human form through matter, and only with facility in the dark.

The matured spirits were those which had failed to fulfil their mission in human embodiment.

They were divided into two classes, which, commencing with the most materialized, dense and **opaque** spirits, whose condition bound them to the earth, and whose inclinations led them towards its centre, passed, in a graduated scale, to the most spiritualized, transparent and ethereal, whose repulsion for matter was so strong, that when for any reason they were brought into relations with it, they were filled with horror and aversion.

But although these spirits formed a single, graduated scale of being, their starting-point was not from the most to the least dense, from the opaque to the transparent.

Their starting-point was from the surface of the earth, from man ; from which and from whom they passed upwards or downwards, as the case might be. And the life of the individual determined which series of spirits the departing spirit was to join at death ; each entering at once, according to the constitution it had acquired during life, the transparent or the opaque class.

Thus, according to the Kabbalists, the spirit world was divided into two classes or kingdoms.

Now the several spirits carried with them into these kingdoms the aptitudes and appetites they had acquired during their successive embodiments.

Their principal aptitude was to progressive evolution, through an ever-advancing series of bodies.

This they had applied in the creative order, by creating bodies in which to live, and through which to advance.

But now, outside the creative order, they had lost this power.

They could, however, simulate it ; and, according to the Kabbalists, did so by organizing themselves into companies, in which spirits in a similar state, with similar appetites and inclinations, combined under a head for a common purpose, and to do a common work.

Hence each of the two spirit kingdoms was divided into many companies or bodies, which were called spheres, because the constituent members, as far as they had any form proper to themselves, had the form of the sphere ; so that each company or body was a compound sphere, with its centre or head, under which the members acted.

Now spirit organization and progression were carried on in both of the spirit kingdoms in this wise.

The spheres were graduated in an advancing

order, commencing with the lowest class of spirits and ending with the highest; of which the head represented, and was in the closest union with, the spirit of the earth.

Each of these spheres had a head or centre, whose state was in advance of that of its members.

To each sphere a particular work was committed by its head, a work conformed to the aptitudes and appetites of its members.

This work the head carried on through its members; their incentive thereto being their own inclination, each doing its own share of the work in its own way. But the work was the work of the head, and done in its name; and the members, while doing it, bore the name of their head, whose work it was.

This name was the name of the sphere, which was a relatively permanent organization whose head and members were successively changing.

Under this system, the members of each sphere by doing their work contributed to the advance of their head, and at the same time prepared themselves for further advance. And as each, whether head or member, was fitted for advance, it passed to the sphere it was qualified to enter.

The line of progression was thus from sphere to sphere, ever onward.

But in this progression the work of the members was primarily and principally for the benefit of their head, which gained its power of advancing through them.

Hence this power was a cumulative power, accumulating in the heads ; so that the heads carried a cumulative and accumulating accession of power from sphere to sphere, until at length the whole accumulated power was absorbed by and concentrated in the spirit of the earth, which was held, like Saturn, to live by devouring its offspring.

For all this seeming progression was simulated, and merely marked successive stages of spirit dissolution, in which the many were, one after another, slowly dissolving and passing away, through their force being absorbed by their heads, which carried or transmitted it upwards and onwards to the final absorber of all spirit force, the spirit of the earth.

Progression in this wise was the order of advance in the spirit world : progression with a purpose.

But just as the two spirit worlds were the opposites each of the other in character and characteristics, so was the order of their quasi-progression ; for while the starting-point of both was from the human, the tendency in the one was upwards, to spiritualization—a spiritualization which culminated in that highest degree of spirit attenuation, dissolution ; whereas the tendency in the other was downwards, to materialization—a materialization whose culmination bound the so materialized spirits to the earth until the dissolution thereof.

But each of the spheres in either of the kingdoms laboured to advance its members by its work. For each believed it had a work to do. And this work was in regard to their starting-point, man, to whom their attention was constantly directed.

The spiritualizing spirits sought to spiritualize him, that he might be fitted to enter, and be applied to the uses of their kingdom, and so gradually dissolved and absorbed.

The materializing spirits sought to materialize by animalizing him, that he might be captured for and adapted to the uses of their kingdom, where, by progressive materialization, he would add to the functional power of their head.

In this way the two kingdoms, the one of transparent, the other of opaque spirits, came to be respectively classed as the kingdoms of bright and dark, and thence of good and evil, of blessed and unblessed spirits, because the one sought to spiritualize, or, as was supposed, to raise man from a fallen state ; while the other devoted its efforts to animalizing and degrading him, and so reducing him to a yet lower condition.

And these kingdoms, the heaven and hell of theologians, were associated with light and darkness, because the members of the one could act in the light—more easily by moonlight; whereas the members of the other could only act with facility in the dark.

And yet both of these kingdoms, while working according to their respective natures and conformably to their inclinations, were acting functionally under one and the same head, and to the same intent—to procure the due spiritualization of matter and materialization of spirit; which in either was obtained, as a resultant mean, by counteracting and reversing the process of the other.

And this was why the head of this one kingdom in two branches was in the one a spirit of darkness, and in the other a spirit of light; while in reality and in itself it was the spirit of the earth.

These spirit kingdoms, the Kabbalists held, were simulated kingdoms; an ephemeral and fantastic phantasmagoria in which dissolution was made to resemble or feign progressive life. And hence they called all spirits "simulators" or "personators."

They likened the action of spirit in these kingdoms to the uncontrolled action of the human spirit in sleep, and looked upon it as the dream side of creation, considering it an uncontrolled action or dream in the life of God.

THE GENESIS OF THE SOUL.

PART VIII.

A NATURAL CONCEPTION OF THE SOUL STATE.

God, through Nature, the aim of Creation.

THE observation of nature led to the conception of God.

No idea of the divine, apart from nature, is innate in man. Reflection bids him realize the necessity for divine action, to draw good out of the evil which everywhere invades his surroundings and seeks the possession of himself. And since the aim attributed to this so much needed action is to draw good out of evil, and evil everywhere prevails, it becomes evident that this assumed action, to be efficient, must be everywhere present, everywhere operating in some unperceived way. And then this necessary action is associated with a cause, which must itself be everywhere present, everywhere initiating action, everywhere carrying on the incepted action.

This cause became to man, when thus apprehended, what is now known as God.

The existence of God is thus revealed to man as a primary necessity of the nature of which his own life is the outcome. And the method of this revelation impresses him with a sense of the unity and individuality of this divine Source of good ; but at the same time abstracts the idea of personality from his conception of the Divine Being, since personality is inseparable from the limitations of form, and thus contrary to that faith in the universal presence and action of a divine influence which is the necessary foundation of the thus grounded belief.

Not that this primary conception of God was as an abstraction. On the contrary, man felt that in him he lived, and moved, and had his being ; that he was everywhere present, as is the space of the universe.

Still less was it grounded on the perception that good prevailed over evil in the workings of nature, though great good was associated with and the outcome of those workings ; for experience ran counter to any such conception.

Man's belief in God had its roots in the faith that good would ultimately prevail over evil in nature ; but that it could only so prevail through the influence of some unknown, some unobserved, controlling guidance.

Thus the perception of a necessity for a divine **control in** nature was the foundation of man's belief in the existence of God.

But the perception of this necessity required, as a necessary corollary of the conditions under which it was exercised, that the divine control thus predicated should be functionally applied through the workings of nature ; which, again, led to the perception that the workings of nature were functional processes of the life through which the needed divine control was to be applied ; and this to the recognition of the fact that a knowledge of the existence of God is revealed to man by the workings of nature.

But if God thus manifests himself to man through the workings of nature, then is it evident that the progressive evolution of nature is the outcome of functional action in the life of God, through which the divine is gradually unfolding and manifesting itself in the natural ; and thence that the divine life is a functional life, carried on by natural organs, as **is the** derived life evolved therefrom : for only under such a view can **it be** maintained that God is the Creator and Sustainer of the natural ; that he manifests his divine presence and action in nature ; and that he will ultimately cause good to prevail over **evil in the** workings thereof.

The One thus seeking to draw good out of evil could, according to man's view, only do this out of love.

Hence man's primary conception of divine action was that of an influence actuated by and urging to love.

And hence, as a consequence of this conception, where there was an intense yearning for affection, there the divine impulse was held to be actuating.

From this starting-point a natural conception of the universe was possible.

Viewed as a whole, it is the outcome of the functional activity of the passive life of God, and the means by which the functioning action of that life is carried on; so that *the processes of nature are functions in the life of God.*

And then, regarding the outward manifestation of divine action as a yearning after affection, the meaning of creation becomes apparent. It is a gradual unfolding of the divine in the natural, with a view to the ultimate manifestation of God in nature.

The functional Character of Creation.

Creation is a function in the life of God.

In it, the yearning of God seeks to express itself.

Through it, the love of God would obtain a reciprocal love.

By it, the desire of God gains appeasement.

This unfolding of God in nature is essentially a functional, a natural process.

Spirit, interacting with matter under control, evolves bodily forms as matrices for the advancement of life ; and, through the life uses of these, individualizes and progressively advances the spirit seeking evolution thereby.

Thus each living body is the matrix or fashioning vesture of an advancing spirit.

But each advancing spirit contains and is the vesture of a latent spark of the divine essence, which, accompanying it through a progressive series of evolutional matrices, by the successive life uses of which it has gradually fashioned the same, enters the human form to develop therein the process by which it has hitherto advanced, and complete the work it had initiated.

Now the initiating spark of this interacting evolutional process was a spark of the divine essence, and therefore contained a germ of the divine love. This spark, latent in that through which it was evolving, was slowly developing the necessary organs and form through which to manifest and mature itself in the human.

The Meaning of Creation.

Thus the meaning of creation is this, that through it God seeks objects of affection and organs of love. And since love always raises the objects of its affection to its own level, and ennobles the organs through which it gains the power of expressing itself; and since nothing lower than God could be raised to the divine level and so ennobled,—he seeks these through the evolution of his own essence. While further, since love to be reciprocal must be mutual and spontaneous, the divine essence in process of evolution becomes latent in the several successive matrices in and through which its evolution is to be accomplished, that its nursing mothers may have complete freedom of choice and liberty of affection.

Hence the divine, while passing through spirit and matter into nature, and then by natural process through the inorganic, the organic and the animated, into the human, loses sight of its own divinity; so loses sight thereof that it may re-pass from the create to the increate, should the instruments through association with which it has sought evolution ultimately fail to fit themselves for the final transition for which it had sought to prepare them.

Immortality, conditional in Man.

Man is only potentially immortal.

The processes by which he was evolutionally created required this; for self-seeking was the impulse which, in the individual, led to a gradual advance in form till the human was gained; a self-seeking which, through the advantages it gave to some over others, introduced a process of natural selection which ultimately produced the result sought.

But then this self-seeking impulse developed a selfish animal nature, a nature wholly unfitted for affection.

Hence the task set before man in his uses of life was to change his inherited self-seeking impulses into self-forgetting tendencies. And it was because many would fail in so doing that the divine remained latent even in man.

And this task was set before man because the Divine Unity, the one impersonal God, is seeking through the human, in a multiplied personality, the means of giving expression to his love, and so manifesting himself in the flesh.

But just as in the evolution of bodily forms a selective process was necessary, that the needed advance might be secured, so in the evolution of human souls an elective process is required, that the ultimate end may be gained, and the divine at length shine forth in the divine human. And the divine is latent in the mere human that it may finally quit that which is incapable of ultimate divinization.

The two Impulses latent in Man.

Man is the lamp of life, a lamp whose flame burns internally, that the light thereof may shine through the life.

In the fashioning of this lamp, appetite, elemental in spirit and in matter, through the instrumentality of these under divine impulse and control, gradually evolved aptitudes and faculties, with duly adaptable organs for the usage of the same ; aptitudes and faculties which expressed themselves, through their acquired organs, in the successive lives of the advancing being, by the uses made of the succeeding lives; and which, by so expressing themselves, gained an increasing power and an improved means of self-expression.

Thus appetite, elemental in spirit and matter, is seen to have been from the first fashioning the lamp of life, as it were for itself, for the manifestation and indulgence of its own propensities.

Hence the process of fashioning this lamp was

from the beginning a process by which the elemental was specialized, the latent was manifested and became apparent, apparent in the life.

This lamp, thus fashioned, was kindled — rekindled, so to say—by a spark of the divine essence. But, in the act of kindling, the divine remained latent with the flame it had produced, the lamp only showing the light thereof through the life.

Thus the process of using this lamp as a lamp was, like the process of fashioning and kindling the same, a process by which from the very first the elemental was to be individualized, the latent to be manifested and become apparent, apparent in the life.

But the process of kindling imparted a fresh impulse to the lamp, so that it is now actuated by two incentives, one of which gaining the ascendancy will determine the course of the life.

Now every kindled lamp can be extinguished; can burn itself out; must burn itself out if the combustible material be consumed, or the supporter of combustion withdrawn therefrom.

Hence man, as such a lamp, is only potentially immortal, the governing impulse of his life determining his ultimate relations to the infinite.

The Conditions under which Immortality is attainable.

The conditions under which this potential is convertible into an actual immortality are those which permit the evolution and ultimate manifestation of the divine, latent in man.

What those conditions are, is to be, can be, learnt from the study of nature in its workings around and in man.

By observation, man learns to distinguish between good and evil; sees that evil is the result of uncontrolled appetite, of appetite indulged for the gratification of self; that good is the outcome of appetite under control, of appetite indulged for the gratification of that which is not self.

In this way he realizes that appetite, as a fashioning instrument, is convertible by the uses of life into a self-asserting will or a self-suppressing desire.

But this self-suppressing desire is akin to, is the root and fruit of, love.

It is, moreover, a divine impulse; for self-suppression is the one cognizable attribute of God, who is unknowable or latent in the universe.

Hence, that the enkindled lamp of life may continuously burn in man, and his potential be converted into an actual immortality, it is necessary, absolutely necessary, that the uses of his **life shall be** such as will induce to the conversion of **self-**asserting **will** into self-suppressing affection ; **such** as will lead to the suppression of self, that it **may** be transformed through love. For the divine can only be developed in, through and as love ; since **only that** which is loving and lovable can pass from the human to the divine life.

The functional **Life** *of the Soul State.*

Now the active divine life is the life of the soul **state ; so that** the passage from the human to the divine is a passage to the soul state ; to a state of which the conditions of the life therein are unknown and apparently unknowable.

But are the conditions of the life therein actually unknowable ?

The conditions of life in the soul state appear to be unknowable until it is recognized that this state constitutes and is the active divine life ; for then, **calling** to mind that, though the unknown can only be reached through the known, yet that it can be so reached, the inquirer once more turns to the known for information and guidance.

Now the known here is the natural.

This natural, working throughout nature as in himself, is **a** functional action ; an action whose function is based upon use, and is carried on with a view to further use. And to this use there is no apparent end as long as the functional action is uninterrupted.

This discharge of function is associated with life ; is necessary thereto : so necessary, that where function is not, there life is known not to be.

This association of function with life is a natural association. It is not only a natural association ; it constitutes and is the natural, is nature.

In the individual being, this association causes the life to be two-fold, passive and active.

Of these, the passive is the life of maintenance ; the active that of use.

The life of maintenance is carried on by circulating organs, without the consciousness or conscious intervention of the individual.

The life of action, by active members under control of the conscious will.

But space is full of circulating organs, which, with it, constitute the universe.

This circulation of the universe is a natural circulation, for it takes place in nature.

It is, therefore, a functional, and consequently a passive circulation. And, as in nature a passive circulation forms part of, constitutes, promotes and is inseparable from an individual life, a life formed

for use and action ; so the passive life of the functioning whole of the thus individualized universe
must be held to be associated with an active life,
just as the functioning life of the individual is associated with and forms the basis of the active life of
man.

Now a wide difference exists in the method of
the basic circulation of the universe as compared
with that of the subordinated circulation of individualized super-planetary life ; for the one is infinite,
the other finite, in its relations ; the one constituted,
so to say, of independent organs, the other depending
on a duly fashioned circulating organ and system,
though even here the central organ of the universe
appears to combine the functions of the heart and
brain.

Thus, while in the individualized life of man
existence is maintained and carried on in a fashioned
body, of which the duly combined organs and members constitute the individual being, in the individualized life of the universe the limitations of form
being necessarily and absolutely excluded, unity in
the whole is combined with individuality in the
parts or organs of its passive existence, and therefore will be similarly combined in its active being—
that is, in the active divine life.

But man is a potential organ of the divine life—

the organ through which the love of God is to gain
the fulness of its expression.

Hence man, on passing into the soul state, or
entering the divine life, does so as an organ—rather
as a member of God; the active divine life in his
regard being the life he is called to in that state.

But every step leading to that state has been gained
by natural process, and is the outcome of nature.

Hence the soul state, as the outcome and product
of nature, is essentially a natural state—a continuation in an advanced, a higher order, of the state
through which it has been gained.

The necessary Continuity of functional Action.

It has been seen that the divine life, as manifested
through the circulation of the universe, is provided
with natural organs whose functional action is
directed to maintain the integrity thereof; or, in
other words, that organic functional action is inseparable from the life of God as revealed to the
understanding of man through nature.

But if organic action is inseparable from the
passive life of God, and is necessary to the active
as well as to the passive life of that image of God,
man, then will it be as inseparable from the active
divine life carried on in the soul state, or form an
integral part of the life of man in that state.

Now function in the physical and physiological **is the** foundation of action in the moral and **mental,** and therefore in the psychological and psychical order. Either rests absolutely on the other; so absolutely, that without the one the other could not be.

It is through the physical and the physiological that God has fashioned man, manifests himself to him, develops the divine in him, fits him for and transfers him to the soul state.

Without physical and physiological action, none of these can be; without physical and physiological action, none of these can continue to be. Is it reasonable, then, to suppose that without physical and physiological action man could continue to be in the soul state?

To secure immortality therein and thereto, some provision must be made for the supply of the combustible material and the supporter of combustion to the lamp of life; some way provided for the re-creating or recruiting of that which the uses of life exhaust, and remove from the still natural, though glorified, body of man.

The Need of functional **Use in the Soul State.**

There is no use in nature without consumption; consumption of that through which the power of use **is gained, of that on which** the power of use depends.

Life is a use ; a use with regard to further use ;
a use by which a usable, a use-power giving material
is consumed ; and therefore, if the use is to be
continued, a use under which the usable, the use-
power giving material is renewed.

This faculty of renewing consumable material is
the maintaining power of life.

Remove it, and when the store of usable material
is consumed, death ensues.

In this renewing, in this restorative power, the
persistency, the oneness of nature consists.

But the persistency, the oneness of nature is a
reflection, a manifestation of the persistency, the
unity of God ; and therefore of the methods and
processes by which the unity and continuity of the
divine life is provided for.

Hence action in the life of God, as in the life of
man, is use—a use which, as in the life of man,
consumes that on which the power of use depends ;
and the circulating heavenly bodies are the organs
by which the usable material and power of use in
the divine life are continuously and constantly
renewed, their functioning processes the means by
which this renewing is accomplished.

Now use is the outcome of desire, and develops
affection—affection for the outcome of the use.

But affection to be maintained needs that that

through which it is maintained should be constantly renewed.

It demands reciprocity on **the part of** its object ; **and that** reciprocity, once gained, can only be preserved, that is, continuously renewed and so maintained, by unity of aspiration.

But unity in aspiration is the outcome of unity of being, and therefore demands a substantial unity, or unity **and** identity **of** substance ; a renewable, a constantly renewing, substantial unity in those between **whom** unity of aspiration is to be maintained. **And the** provision for this renewable, this renewing, **this** constantly to be renewed substantial unity, for this maintenance of identity of substance, is found, is only **found, in the** sexual **relation.**

Hence, **since affection is** the basis of the soul **state, and since unity in** aspiration is the basis of enduring affection—while unity in aspiration to be continuously maintained must flow from a persistent unity and identity of substance, which is only gained and perpetuated by, and therefore depends upon, **the** sexual relation—is it not evident that that relation will pass with the divine human to and be **continued** in the soul state ?

The **soul** state is the outcome of nature.

Hence **the** basis of nature is the basis of the soul state.

But the sexual relation is the basis of nature.

All of the higher as well as of the lower qualities of man rest upon this basis.

Its aim in man is the constituting of two in one, by making of two one flesh—that the divine may become and be incarnated in this one being in two persons, and so constitute a divine trinity.

But the manifestation of this trinity is reserved for the soul state, in which the natural is, by divine actuation, transformed into the personalized vesture of God.

God in Nature, the Aim of the Soul State.

The circulating heavenly bodies are the organs of God—renewing and renewable organs, by the functional action of which the continuity of the divine life is provided for.

The matured human souls are the divinized members of God—the members through which the divine love expresses itself.

To give immortality to these members, and so provide for the undying character of the divine love, the power of renewing the combustible material and the supporter of combustion in the lamp of life is needed, on the one hand, and the power of renewing the substantial unity of the associated members, on the other.

Hence these powers will be found in the soul state, from which physical conditions and physiological relations are thus found to be inseparable ; so that, whatever the circumstances of the soul state may be, it will comprise these conditions and relations. And the great mistake into which so many of the teachers of men have been betrayed, is that of assuming an antagonism between God and nature, and supposing and asserting that the spiritual must supplant the natural, and that this supplanting should be the aim of life.

With the ·admission of this mistake, which will sooner or later be recognized, its grave character will be realized, and man will then acknowledge that he is only potentially immortal ; that functional processes will be as necessary to his renewed as to his passing life ; and that the sex principle, which is the basis of the natural, will never be eliminated from nature, but will assume its due proportions and true relations to the divine in the soul state ; this because the whole aim of creation is, *by natural process to merge the animal and the spiritual with the divine through the natural in the human, that God, thus incarnated in nature, may be all in all.*

THE GENESIS OF THE SOUL.

CONCLUSION.

THE regeneration of the human by the genesis of the soul is a natural process.

It is by this process that immortality is imparted to man; individual men and women being thereby selected and fitted for the life for which they have been prepared.

It is by this process that the natural mortal gains a natural immortality.

It is by this process that the human is made into and becomes the divine human.

It is by this process that the animal and the spiritual gain their true value in the natural as the divine.

It is by this process that spirit and matter gain their formative and formal unity in God.

It is by this process that the divine trinity (of the One incarnated in two that are made one) is gained, and infinite unity becomes unity in multiplicity, in bi-personal triune multiplicity ; or is transmuted into an infinity in number combined with limitation or finality in form, in which all again merge in the infinite unity of the active divine life.

For there are three fundamental principles in creation :

1. Man is only potentially immortal.

2. The regeneration of the human and the maintenance of the divine human in the soul state is a natural process.

3. The sexual relation, as the basis of the natural, is the basis of the soul state.

The basic character of these principles will be ultimately admitted, and man will then once more recognize and realize his true position in nature ; but until this position is gained, the teachers of men will be blind leaders of the blind, misguiding and deluding all who follow them.

EPILOGUE.

EPILOGUE.

MAN, A CONSCIOUS BEING.

MAN comes into the world as a conscious being, with an aptitude for acquiring knowledge.

His consciousness is an attribute of life; its source as inscrutable as the cause of life; so that to demonstrate the origin of the one would be to unveil the beginning of the other.

Hence the source of the consciousness of man is as great a mystery as is the source of his reason, if it be not identical therewith.

This consciousness man shares with the animated kingdoms of nature; and, if there be any truth in the doctrine of selective evolution, derives it through these kingdoms.

But, indeed, a rudimentary consciousness is found in the vegetable kingdom, in those sensitive plants which shrink from the touch.

Hence consciousness would appear to spring from the primary germ of nascent being, whatever that may be, and to increase in intensity with advance in organization, until in man it gains its culmination.

The awakening consciousness of man is a consciousness of self, of his own existence, of his own needs, of his dependent state.

This consciousness, showing itself as instinct, causes him to search outside himself for that which will supply his needs.

This conscious instinct makes the infant man aware of the presence and person of his mother, and causes him to seek from her all that he requires.

Not always with her, he becomes conscious of the presence of other beings, of beings like unto and yet not his mother.

The presence of these beings awakens and stimulates his perceptions, until, guided by these apart from his conscious instinct, he learns to distinguish his mother from them.

Then he becomes conscious that some of the beings like unto and yet not his mother, take notice of himself; while others only slightly regard or even disregard him.

This leads him to distinguish between them, and his likings and dislikings thus commence.

In the mean time, through the instinctive use of his awakening organs of sense, he becomes conscious of and begins to take interest in his ordinary surroundings, and the changes which take place in them, and learns to distinguish those objects which specially attract his attention ; and, noticing their differences, is guided by these to the recognition of either, amongst the others.

Then, as he is moved from place to place, he is conscious that his surroundings are changed, and that fresh objects are brought under his notice.

In this way he gradually learns to compare person with person, object with object, and place with place ; to distinguish one from another ; to have preferences for one over another ; and so to form primary simple judgments. But this advance is by slow degrees, this progress step by step ; the life uses of his germinating faculties, and the accumulating experience acquired through these, being the agencies on which the onward course depends ; and it is not until he attains to the use of speech that his intelligence begins to unfold itself and his intellectual expansion commences.

Under this process of training, of development, his innate consciousness gradually becomes more distinct as he becomes more practised in the use of his sense organs ; while these on their part simultaneously keep his consciousness constantly on the alert, and so sharpen its precision.

The increasing precision thus gained, through the

training of nature and the experience of use, widens
the scope of the applied consciousness and extends
the field of its operations; and, by expanding his
intelligence and maturing his judgment, leads him
through tentative and fluctuating speculations to
sound and accurate conclusions.

But the bases of these ever-advancing intellectual
operations and reasoned conclusions are solidly laid
in the teachings of nature, from which his consciousness draws its primary inspirations.

To nature, man owes the calling forth of his
imagination; the power of recalling to mind and
drawing mental images of objects he has seen, and
speculating on them; of forming ideas and reflecting on them, and so making them the subjects of
intellectual investigation.

And these images so recalled, these ideas so
derived from a ripening experience, when passed
through the analytical and synthetical processes of
a practised intellect, take the form of knowledge.
And then, as knowledge, they become terms from
which he develops fundamental principles, by the
use of which he facilitates the exercise of his reasoning powers, promotes his own intellectual advance,
and prepares the way for the further advance of his
successors.

For man has no *a priori* knowledge; is gifted

with no innate ideas, unless vague and fleeting reminiscences of some possible previous existence may be so called ; though these, rare as they are, can only suggest such a possibility to him.

Himself a product of nature, all that he produces, all that he seems to originate, is suggested to him by nature, and springs from an increasing precision in the use of, from a more exact and careful attention to the fruits of, the consciousness with which nature has endowed him.

What takes the form of *a priori* knowledge in him, or rather has been assumed to do so, is due to a quickened consciousness, which produces a livelier imagination, a more vivid idealization, and a more acute apprehension. And these, again, by a developing use, gradually evoke, advance and mature the intelligence, the intellect and the reasoning powers, and so build up the understanding ; for the aroused consciousness of nascent life passes through instinctive to intelligent perception, from which, by a developing use, the full powers of the matured mind are derived.

Hence, what has been held to be *a priori* knowledge is in reality a derived aptitude for grasping first principles ; an aptitude due to heredity, to an hereditary self-teaching which simulates intuition, and which may therefore be classed as an inherited

faculty. While the first principles so deduced, which
have been embodied in such aphorisms as, " Everything that happens, every effect must **have a cause**,"
are based on the experience that every observed
effect has an intelligible cause (just as water flows
from its mountain source to the level of the ocean
to which it tends, not merely through its fluidity
but because of its gravity), and represent the results
of the accumulated observations and experience of
successive generations **of** thoughtful men, thrown
into a concise form for more easy transmission **to**
their successors, and so facilitate the education of
mankind. But all of these first principles or primary and basic ideas spring from a quickened **con-**
sciousness, a consciousness **practised in** the interpretation of **what reaches it** through the organs of
sense, and in drawing conclusions from the observation of nature in its manifold and ever-varying
forms and expression.

Man likes to think himself only a little lower
than the angels, a little less than God ; persuades
himself that he has been formed in the image and
fashioned after the likeness of his Maker ; flatters
himself that he represents the Divine on earth ;
prides himself on his reasoning powers, which place
him, in his own estimation, **so** far above the level of
the brutes (as it pleases him to call the animal co-

denizens of the planet on which he dwells); and,
assuming that he has been specially endowed with
the gift of reason to mark his divine origin, indignantly disclaims kinship with or possible descent
from even the highest of the lowlier forms of animated life.

When he realizes that though, for the purposes
of the present life, he is a created being, he is none
the less a being in process of creation in regard to
any future state to which he may be hereafter called;
—when he perceives that the creation of conscious
life involves as deep a mystery as does the creation
of the reasoning powers, which depend thereon and
are inseparable therefrom, and that both are included in the mystery of the origin of life;—when
he reflects that abstract ideas are derived by analogy, one through another, from a primary idealization or mental image, itself suggested by, drawn
from and based upon a natural source;—when he
sees that they are so derived with a view, from a
more extended comparison, to more accurate conclusions and sounder judgments on the subjects to
which they relate; and that this evolution of ideas
—by the imagination for the exercise of the reason
and development of the intelligence, the intellect,
the understanding—is a natural operation;—he will
perhaps be led to acknowledge that a process by

which the reasoning powers **are, so** to say, fed, or
furnished with materials by exercise on which they
are developed and matured, may simply be a continuation, under another form, of the process through
which they originated ; and that he has no right to
suppose that he has been specially endowed in this
regard, or gifted with innate ideas and provided
with an *a priori* knowledge, of which, indeed, it can
be so easily shown, not only that he has no need,
but that its possession would go far to neutralize
the specific aim of his being.

Man's ideas, however abstract, however intimately
associated with his own being, and apparently dissociated from the nature of his surroundings, are all,
directly or indirectly, derived from natural sources.
His seemingly **implanted** knowledge, however
closely it may assume the semblance of an *a priori*
character, is but the manifestation of an inherited,
a quickened aptitude to grasp the concentrated
results of the accumulated observation and experience of ages.

The idea of *existence* he draws from his consciousness of his own existence.

The idea of *necessity*, from his own needs.

The idea of *space*, from his **own** necessity for a
place wherein to subsist, and use the functions and
exercise the prerogatives of life.

The idea of *necessary existence*, from the necessary existence of space.

The idea of *being*, from the objective being of nature.

The idea of *possible being*, from the existence of beings on all parts of the earth which he has explored in succession, which suggests the possible existence of beings in those parts which have not yet come under his notice.

The idea of *universal being* and *universality*, from the universality of space.

The idea of *infinite existence* (or *being*) and *infinity*, from his inability to imagine limits to space.

The idea of *eternal existence* (or *being*) and *eternity*, from his powerlessness to conceive a period when space was not needed, when no first cause existed.

The idea of *causation*, carrying with it the idea of *God*, from the conclusion that, since every observed event has an intelligible cause, everything that happens must have a cause, however inscrutable that cause may be, which involves the necessity of a first cause—a cause which can have had no antecedents and is the most inscrutable, the most incognizable of all; and which, as the first, the infinite, the eternal cause or author and source of everything that is, must occupy and fill all space.

The idea of *God*, as the Author and Sustainer of

life or **Father of all,** from the relations of a father
to his offspring.

The idea of *spirit,* from the incognizable nature
of God **in space, with whom it thus became** ideally
associated.

The idea of *substance,* from the necessary exist-
ence and extension of space, with the impossibility
of conceiving the existence and extension of nothingness.

The idea of *matter,* **or** solid and tangible, **as contrasted with intangible substance, from the manifold**
objects of the natural world, which, as he conceives
them, and by whatever process formed, must, **as
real** objects, have been made of something. **And**
from **these he** also **derives the idea of** *form,* of
individuality, **of** *unity*—though the type of *absolute
unity* and *immutability* he finds in space.

The idea of *motion,* from all the movements of
nature, apparent and actual.

The idea of *time,* **as** limited **duration, from the**
finite **character of things temporal.**

The idea of the ***division*** (or measurement) *of time,*
as interrupted succession without breach of conti-
nuity, or successive periods of limited duration,
from the alternate succession of day and night.

The idea of *force,* from **the action of the** wind,
with which spirit has been analogically associated,

and by which substance has been, so to say, suggestively brought into contact with man; for the atmosphere, the movement of which constitutes wind, is, to the ordinary tactile sense, intangible when at rest, but in motion acquires a force which causes it to be felt, and at times even makes its pressure irresistible. And it may be observed here that the investigation of the atmospheric relations of the earth and the discovery that the movements of the air are attributable to variations in its density, due to recognized physical influences, have probably done more to illustrate the nature of so called occult causes than any other branch of study, and have made their relations to nature more intelligible to the ordinary mind.

Then as to the more abstract ideas, upon the development and application of which the exact sciences are based, the starting-points of these are invariably found in nature.

The *science of numbers* is simply an implied expression of the possible—the possible enumeration of possible units; for it is only possible to number that of which the existence is possible, non-existence being beyond the scope of computation.

Now *the possible unit is only a possibility as an actuality of nature—as an individual of any kind.*

But every individual natural object is capable of

division, and **by** division loses its unity, or ceases **to be** a unit.

A divided apple is no longer an apple, and therefore is no longer **a** unit of the species apple. Its unity has disappeared in its separated parts.

In the same way, the abstract, **the** ideal unit is capable of division and subdivision—the science of decimal arithmetic is grounded on this truth ; and it is as impossible to conceive an ideal unit, that is, a unit incapable of infinite division, as it is to find the ultimate atom.

The human mind cannot conceive an indivisible unit, short of the annihilation of the idea, with its subject—the natural object or unit which the idea is, **even if unconsciously,** supposed to represent ; so that the science of numbers originates **in** an idea derived from the observation of nature, and is merely **an** illustration of the way in which the reasoning **powers of man, similarly** derived, by whatever process, from nature, attain to their higher developments ; and shows that they do this through the application of principles, deduced from the teachings of the natural order, to the investigation of the workings of nature.

So again the mathematical sciences, in all their evolutions, depend for their exactness absolutely on the accurate determination of the value of their

several units of departure, which are the natural
basis on which the whole carefully constructed super-
structure rests, as on a solid foundation.

The same may be said of geometry, derived from
thoughtful observation of the heavens, and of the
relations of the stars to each other ; which led to
the defining of their mutual relations by imagining
and devising geometrical figures ; as well as to the
depicting of the same, as in the signs of the Zodiac
and the other signs of the celestial sphere.

The triangle will have been amongst the earliest
devised of geometrical figures. It is commonly
called three-sided, as in the equilateral triangle.
But this is an evident misnomer ; for a solid equilateral triangular body—one whose base as well
as each of its sides form equal triangles—must have
four co-equal sides or surfaces, while a triangular
plane will as necessarily possess five ; whereas an
ideal triangle, depicted by mathematical, that is,
imaginary lines, can have no sides at all, being
simply a phantom of the mind, to which, if sides
be imputed, these must be the sides of the object
it constructively represents. Hence an ideal triangle,
as the abstract idea of a triangular body and therefore as the type of an abstract idea, can only be
correctly defined as an imaginary figure constructed
of three mathematical lines enclosing a mathema-

tical space—which is equal to nothing enclosing nothing.

An accurate description of an ideal triangle would define it, on mathematical principles, as the linear way of showing the mutual relations of three determinate points in space, when these are not on a right line. But this is a digression.

Beyond this, just as the bases of the exact sciences are found in nature, while the principles deduced from them are devised by the reason and intellect of man, so are the bases of the applied sciences, with the principles flowing from them, similarly derived.

The architect gazing with wondering eyes on the vaulted heavens, draws from them the idea of the dome of a St. Peter's; or walking pensively down an avenue of stately trees whose meeting branches shade him from the sun, seizes therefrom the idea of an arched and columned aisle; and then from a leafy foliage growing round the fragment of a broken plinth, that of a foliated capital with which to crown his graceful columns.

To follow the origin of the ideas which underlie all the several sciences in succession—to show from whence the sculptor, the artist, and even the engineer draw their several inspirations—would but be to lead to similar, to analogous results, and demonstrate that they are all derived from nature; and that the sciences, which flow from their development and application to practical purposes, are but the natural outcome of its teachings after they have passed through and been operated upon by the developed mind of man.

But, indeed, the crowning proof of this fundamental truth is found in the symbolism by which objects not ordinarily observable in the natural order—spiritual or spectral phenomena, to wit—are depicted ; for to symbolize that which is outside nature, man is obliged to have recourse to nature for his symbols; as any one familiar with the symbolism of the Scriptures will be aware. Hence he depicts the Divine Creator as a venerable man ; and the Spirit, so called, of God, in the form of a dove.

The senses of man are to his consciousness what his bodily organs are to his animated being, agencies through which the conscious self is brought into relations with that which is outside, which is not self.

By the use of these, the innate consciousness of the conscious being is cultivated, so to say ; and then this cultivated, this developed consciousness re-acts on the agencies and organs through the use of which its development is gained, and, by applying them to more delicate uses, increases their sensitiveness and makes them more acute, so as to enable them, and through them the conscious self, to perceive qualities and properties, semblances and resemblances, the existence and presence of which they, and it, were at the outset incapable of distinguishing and denoting.

In this way, that is by the sustained uses of life acting on the inherited results of those uses thus perpetuated, the sensitiveness of the sense organs can be rendered so active, so subtle, so acute, that, in succeeding generations, individuals are produced who seem to have special senses, or a sense use, of which those differently endowed by evolutional cultivation can form no conception, whose methods are beyond their comprehension, and whose expression they therefore, perhaps contemptuously, ignore.

The so called spiritual senses are of this class. But these are not special senses. They are simply the outcome and result of the sustained cultivation of consciousness in a particular direction—in a direction which prepares and fits the conscious being, through whom these find their expression, to become an adaptable instrument in the hands of spiritualizing teachers, whether personating spirits or their adopted human agents. And then the deputed agents in this use look upon the results produced under their guidance as an irrefragable testimony to the divine origin, and therefore to the truth, of the teaching they would thus sustain and perpetuate.

The spiritual cultivation of the consciousness of man is the aim of all religious teaching. Through it his teachers seek to bring him into sensible relations, and then into communication with spirit, that he may, in the end, become subject thereto.

But even when the highest attainable results have been gained in this direction, the outcome is simply a consciousness cultivated in its spiritual tendencies, and so rendered susceptible of the controlling influence of spirit.

The intended result of this cultivation is the withdrawing of man from the developing uses of nature, that he may become subject to influences which seek his advance through an action from without thereof—this under the impression that the natural is a fallen state, in which the spirit instincts and senses of man are overmastered by their grosser animal supplanters.

The root of the desire, on the human side, for the spiritual cultivation of the consciousness of man, that is for his spiritual evolution, is the idea that his was a special creation, a creation of a higher order than the creation at the head of which he now finds himself; that, as originally created, he had special spirit senses, of the use of which he was deprived by his fall; and that the germs or traces of these senses still survive in favoured individuals, and are to be developed by proper cultivation.

And yet the lesson to be learnt by the ever-varying outcome thereof, when rightly viewed, is that a
selective evolution is going on through the consciousness of man, analogous to the selective evolution by which his bodily form and organization
were gained ; and that the all-important consideration here is, the choice of the direction in which the
cultivation of his consciousness should be carried on
by the individual man, that it may be rightly developed. But such a view cannot be expected to
satisfy the spiritually-minded, who seek in spiritual
evolution the appeasement of their desires.

As long as man clings to the idea that his was a
special creation, a creation effected apart from that
of the created world with its animated and inanimate objects, on which he passes his life ; as long
as he accepts the narrative of the fall of man under
its traditional guise ; so long will he need a belief
in something more than an innate consciousness as
the source of his intelligence and intellect.

The belief in the fall of man, as traditionally
understood, implies a certainty that he received a
divine afflatus on coming forth from the hands of
his Maker—an afflatus which carried with it a measure of divine light ; and that having degraded his
spirit, and deprived himself of the divine light by
his fall, the remnant of that divine light—his intellect

and his reasoning powers—stands in need of a divine guidance from without. And this entails the further belief that he needs a re-integration of his spiritual nature, that he may have a restoration of the divine light; and that he can only attain to the same by seeking it in a prescribed way. And this, again, demands a belief in doctrines and a submission to a devotional training which tend to and assure the attainment of the end sought. For *without the absolute acceptance of such a teaching as an inspired revelation, of such a belief as a necessity of his being, he can have no grounds for the certitude of that on which he has learnt to rest his hopes of a future existence in the kingdom of God.*

And yet, notwithstanding all his intellectual strivings, his reason has, so far, failed to furnish him with a solid and assured, an incontrovertible basis for the doctrines on which he relies; far less has it given him an absolute certainty of their truth—witness the divided teachings on this subject which distract his mind.

When it dawns upon him, as perhaps some day it may do, that he is a natural, not a spiritual being; when he awakens to the fact that he exists as the outcome of a gradually evolved and evolving natural process; when he recognizes that his completed organism, with its perfected faculties, is a product of the maturing influences of the life uses of successive advancing existences, through which, though now no longer conscious thereof, he has already passed,—he will realize that all that is necessary for the full development of his being is the continued experience of the same influences ; and then he will come to understand that his ignorance concerning the working on and in himself of the processes which have done and are doing so much for him has a meaning in it—a meaning which involves no less than the meaning of his own life.

The meaning of that life must often have perplexed him. Something seems to tell him that there is a spiritual side to his being ; to suggest to him that he should seek to develop this spiritual side. But then the natural side of his being resists any and every such attempt ; and he thus finds himself the battle-field of two sets of impulses which are struggling for the mastery of his conscious self.

In this struggle he cannot help being impressed by the common belief that spirit agencies are seeking to act upon him ; cannot help seeing that they have largely influenced the world by revelations or otherwise—as he learns from profane as well as from sacred literature and the common voice of mankind.

With this he feels that God must be working in nature, if he is the Creator of all and therefore its

Author—the source and spring of its life. And then he begins to wonder whether the antagonism of which he is conscious in himself, and which reveals itself as an opposition of spirit to nature, of the spiritual to the natural, is not in reality an antagonism between the workings of spirit and the workings of God ; and whether the aims of spirit do not run counter to the aims of God in the development of man.

Searching for the meaning of this, is it strange that he should come to the conclusion that while spirit working *in* nature as a naturalizing agent, that is, in evolving and maintaining the natural order, is the organ of the providence of God, it is, when working *on* nature as a spiritualizing agent, that is, in evolving and maintaining the spiritual order, none the less the antagonist of God and the enemy of man ?

Is it strange that from this point of view he should be led to perceive the significance of his ignorance of the meaning of his own life, *in the impossibility he finds of discovering outside himself an absolutely trustworthy teaching authority and an assured doctrinal system, whose certainty is beyond question, whose truth undeniable ?*

Is it surprising that in this impossibility of gaining certain knowledge, certitude, on those points concerning his welfare, present and future, in which he is most deeply interested, he should see design in his own regard ; *that he should recognize in it the intent to teach him to place full and absolute trust in the inscrutable Author and Source of that nature of which he is the fruition ?*

When his eyes are at length opened to these, the only certainties of his position, he will learn to distrust his spiritual aspirations, and will finally perceive that they are due to an influence working on him from without, and acting outside and against nature. And then it will dawn upon him that this influence has beguiled him into accepting specious doctrines, and betrayed him into becoming the tool and plaything of personating spirits, which have led him astray from the true aim and end of his being, and blinded him to the transparent fact that his Creator, as the Author of nature, can only be understood, approached and followed through its workings and in its works ; for the workings of nature are the workings of God, and the final recognition of this great, this fundamental truth will be the ultimate outcome of the fully matured reason of man.

C. Green & Son, Printers, 178, Strand.

www.ingramcontent.com/pod-product-compliance
Lightning Source LLC
Chambersburg PA
CBHW030945110726
47900CB00004B/1130